VOLUME ONE

Trying to Fly with One Wing

The INNER City CONCRETE JUNGLE

MOE LOVE

THE INNER CITY CONCRETE JUNGLE
TRYING TO FLY WITH ONE WING

iUniverse books may be ordered through booksellers or by contacting:

iUniverse
1663 Liberty Drive
Bloomington, IN 47403
www.iuniverse.com
1-800-Authors (1-800-288-4677)

ISBN: 978-1-5320-3910-2 (sc)
ISBN: 978-1-5320-3909-6 (e)

Library of Congress Control Number: 2017918913

Print information available on the last page.

iUniverse rev. date: 12/16/2017

Trying to Fly with One Wing, Volume One
The Inner City Concrete Jungle
Moe Love

CHAPTER 1

To understand how this man, who you're about to learn about, became the man he is today, you must first be made aware of his beginnings. He's, in the twilight of his life, and was recently released, after serving a year on a two-year sentence for attempting to sell two pounds of marijuana to a confidential informant. It was not his first time being confined in a state's prison facility. He's served more than twenty years of his adult life as a convict, and it's my hopes and prayers that his experiences may prove to be the wakeup call necessary to prevent someone else from making the same mistakes. This is his story, as told by him.

When my mother was a young woman she married the man of her dreams. She had never loved anyone the way she loved her new husband, but her bliss turned into horror at a family reunion. While there, she discovered she had married her first cousin. Hurt and humiliated, she left her southern state and sought refuge with her eldest brother Clarence, who had settled in the northern city of Newport.

Clarence had done as so many young black men had to do to escape the Jim Crow laws, and sharecropping traps of the south. He'd migrated to the north seeking gainful employment in one of the many factories. Clarence was a tall, good looking man with a gorgeous wife named Elizabeth. He had found a joy that wasn't possible in the south, because of its laws designed to make a black man feel less than human. Up north, he was a man with a future, and what he believed was true happiness and security.

His wife also worked in a factory, and they were trying to raise four children. They needed help, and my mother was willing, ready, and able to offer that help. She grew up the second eldest in a large family, so she always had plenty of chores and responsibilities. She had years of experience cooking, cleaning, and caring for the needs of others. So, it was a golden opportunity, as far as she was concerned. She had been raised by sharecroppers, and she believed there was much more to life and the world than she had been exposed to. She was determined to claim her share.

She had met her brother's brother-in-law and found him to be quite attractive. All the flirting between them lead to continual sexual encounters, and eventually she became pregnant. My father was already married, and had a little girl. He thought he was just enjoying a little sex on the side, but it proved to be much more than that.

His wife refused to forgive the betrayal, and divorced him. She got full custody of their daughter. She knew that the family members had known about the affair, and done nothing. The way she saw things, she had been betrayed by the entire family, so she cut her ties with all of them.

From the very moment I entered unto this world, I was viewed upon by my father as a symbol of his painful mistake. I became the object of his rage and the sight of me filled him with regret instead of love. My mother tried everything she could to find acceptance in the bosom of my father's family, but she was unable to do. She was viewed as a home wrecker by my father's sisters. It proved to be a sin beyond their grace, therefore, they never fully embraced her. My father's brothers all loved and accepted my mother. Even all my cousin loved her dearly, but my father's sisters served as the family's monarchs, and their stance kept the atmosphere stressful, and my mother at arm's length. It was a painful burden for her to carry about, but she bore it with her head held high until she

I had a cousin nick named Buffy. She was much older than I, and served the role as my nanny. I was too young to go to the restroom alone, so she would assist me. She began molesting me, and I enjoyed it so much I wanted to do it again. Buffy explained to me that we could only do it again if I continued to remain silent about our encounters. I understood if I ever told anyone, she would never do it again. Needless for me to say, I never told a single soul until I was a grown man. I only told a few women, and that was only to explain to them how I became such a sex addict with a foot fetish. Buffy enjoyed molesting me for many years.

My parents had six more children after my birth. First came my three brothers, Albert, Anderson, and Sonny. My Sisters followed. There was Pandora, whom we called Babysister, Rudine, and Marilyn, the youngest of us all.

My childhood was everything except normal. I grew up on the east side in a neighborhood filled with gifted athletes. We called our neighborhood's recreational park, the playground. There were so many gifted athletes in my age group at our playground that they were forced to field two separate softball teams. Both teams competed in the City's Parks and Recreations athletic league. For three straight years, we played against each other for the city championship. The team I was on lost every year to the other team in tightly contested games. We also dominated track and field.

Members of our track and field teams routinely finished first, second, and third in every single event. We were by far the best in the city. I lived on Fisherman street, and we would have foot races every night. The fattest boy on our street was the fastest. He won every single race he competed in. Nobody could beat Matthew. His brother was the second fastest, and I was always third.

Every year our city would send the top two competitors in each event, from each district to New York to compete in a national track meet. Every year Matthew and his brother Adam would finish first and second place. If I had been from another district I would have made it to the city finals, and the national meet in New York.

Our coach, Mr. Wiggins used to console me all the time by telling me I would have easily taken third if I had been in the race, because no one ever came close to beating the Henderson brothers, except me. I was extremely happy, as well as proud, of them both, however, it was very difficult for me as a child, to watch them leave for New York every year and return as heroes dressed in ribbons.

My father began cheating on my mother so much, it became painfully obvious to us all, that he was the one reason for her tears. She tried everything she could think of to please him enough, so he would want to stay home, but nothing worked until she began telling him that I was too bad for her to handle alone.

She insisted that he stay home to help keep me under

control. That's when the many horrible beatings I received from my father began. He began beating me with extension cords. I knew that my mother condoned the abuse, because she initiated it. I began to hate her, and since she claimed I was so bad that she couldn't handle me, I decided to try to live up to it. One day my mother was beating me, and the true reason I was receiving the beating was because my father wouldn't stay home. As she beat me I stared at her with a facial expression that revealed the depth of the hatred that resided within my heart, and I refused to shed a single tear or whimper a sound. No matter how hard she struck me with the extension cord, I held back my tears. It was extremely difficult not to respond and painful, but my point was made when I sensed a fear in my mother that I had never sensed before.

When my father returned home, she explained to him exactly what had happened in detail. She made sure that he truly understood why she had panicked, and also why there was reason for great concern. My father roughly grabbed me by my neck, and guided me to the basement after retrieving a couple of extension cords. He stripped me naked, and tied my hands together around a pole with one of the extension cords, and proceeded to beat me with the other.

I gave him the same facial expression that I had given my mother, and once again I refused to cry. My father was a huge man. He was six feet three, and he weighed well over two hundred and sixty pounds. He struck me with all his might without success in forcing me to cry. I passed out from the pain, but I was proud of the fact I had not shed a single tear.

That was the last time I allowed my father to beat me

without fighting back. My brothers untied me as I dug deeply within myself to find the strength to force a smile. I did my best to convince them that I was fine, tough, and unhurt. After receiving the desired assurance, they went back upstairs to continue playing. I took a seat on one of the steps and reflected upon the events of the day.

While beating me, my father had said, "Oh, you're not gonna cry huh? You'll cry, or I'll beat you to death!" His tone was extremely harsh, bitter, and filled with hatred. At that very moment, It became painfully obvious to me that my father actually hated me. Even though I had just received the worst beating of my life, without sheading a tear, the thought of my mother and father not loving me was more than I could bare in silence. I could no longer find the strength necessary to withhold my emotions nor my tears, and I wept uncontrollably.

Weeks later my mother informed me that her cousin had been released from prison, and was going to move in. He coincidentally, had the same name as her brother Clarence. I was eleven years old upon his arrival, and the very first thing I noticed about him, was his walk and cool demeanor. It was my first clear example of what cool was. After he had gotten settled in, he began telling me all about himself. Immediately he began teaching me things that would remain with me for the rest of my life.

He taught me to keep my hands out of my pockets, and to always be prepared to defend myself. After sizing me up, he asked me if I knew how to fight. My favorite book in the school library was entitled, How to Box. My response was quick and sure. "Of course, I know how to fight!" I answered proudly. He ordered me to put up my dukes, and I had no idea what it was he was asking me to do. He understood exactly what was behind the puzzled look on my face, and explained, "That's just a cool way asking a fella to put his fist in the fighting position." I smiled and without any further instructions, or hesitations, I put my dukes up. He smiled back at me and stated, "You have an excellent stance." He immediately proceeded to show me what was necessary to improve it.

I asked him how he knew so much about boxing. He had a faraway look in his eyes as he reviled to me that he used to be a fighter. He told me he had been a champion in prison. The only reason he quit was because someone whipped him who wasn't supposed to. From that day forward, I was in my cousin Clarence's face, trying my best to soak up all he was willing to teach me.

He taught me how to jab, throw right crosses, and left hooks. He also taught me how to throw several different punching combinations. He taught me how to shine my shoes so well that you could see your reflection in the shine. He taught me how to iron clothes, and how to make creases in my shirts, and pants. He taught me how to pick out acceptable choices in fashion. I mimicked everything about him, including his facial expressions and his walk. I was observing him so closely, I learned all the so called cool words, and phrases. More importantly, he introduced me to jazz. The first jazz tune I fell in love with was Cannonball Adderly's tune entitled Mercy Mercy Mercy.

I started calling my cousin Clarence, Uncle Houston, because everybody that was close to him called him Houston. He was old enough to be my uncle, and was so proud of me that he would often show me off to his friends, and some of our family members who came to the house. He would have me give brief demonstrations on the art of throwing different punching combinations. Uncle Houston would call out the combinations, and I would demonstrate the different combinations by shadow boxing with precise accuracy. I threw one perfect combination after another.

The elementary school I attended was located one block away from our home on Barns and Lambert. That was truly a blessing, because my shoes were always so old that they had holes in the soles of each of them. I would place cardboard inside my shoes to cover up the holes, however, the snow would always soak through the cardboard. By the time I would arrive at school, every wet winter's day, my feet would be soaking wet and freezing cold. Eventually there were holes in every pair of socks I owned too.

Pope was the name of the school I attended, and the place I first laid eyes on Samantha. She was so different from the rest of us. Her father was black, but her mother was white. She was the very first mulatto I had ever seen, or met, and she became my very first serious crush. She lived quite a distance from the school, but I walked her home every single school day. I was constantly in trouble for coming home late from school. I joined an organization sponsored by the Triple A Corporation called the Safety Patrol. It consisted of boys with responsibilities that included, helping children cross the streets safely, and to report bullying. That eliminated the trouble I got into for coming home late from school, and allowed me the opportunity to spend time walking Samantha home from school.

I never told Samantha how I felt about her. I never felt like I was handsome enough to be her boyfriend. My mother was always telling me that I was an ugly child. She was only kidding, however, after hearing it so often, I began to believe her.

One day after I had walked Samantha home, I was running a little late, so I decided to take all the short cuts I knew on my way home. As I Walked through the alley which lead to the rear entrance of our backyard, I ran into Terrell, and his younger brother Gregory. They were the new kids in the neighborhood, and I had no idea they lived so close by. Terrell dressed exactly like my Uncle Houston had taught me to dress. He and his brother wore their hair chemically straighten in the many different styles that were possible. We called the straighten hair conk back in those days. He and his little brother were the only kids in the entire school who wore the expensive hair style.

Terrell had an older brother by the name of Gene Dawson who had a hit record out, and appeared on a local television dance show. He always had Terrell with him. Terrell would dance as his brother performed. Terrell's popularity and reputation sored, as a result of the television appearances. He became well known, far beyond the mere boundaries of our school. He was the most popular kid in the entire neighborhood.

There was a teenage boy with them, and he was the one who approached me. "What's happening my man?" he asked as he walked towards me and offered me his hand. "My name is Houston, and these guys here are my little cousins, Terrell and Gregory." He acknowledged them with a simple nod of his head in their direction, and continued talking. Houston was tall, light skinned kid, and he was truly filled with confidence just like. He wore his hair in

9

a conked style, and everything about his appearance was perfect. He looked like he would be a celebrity. He appeared to be the type of fella who had never considered rejection to be a possibility. "Do you know how to slap box?" he asked. He went on to explain to me that slap boxing was exactly what it was named. It consisted of boxing opened handed by slapping, instead of punching with your closed fist. After I assured him that I understood the concept, he asked me if I would slap box with Terrell. "Okay." I answered as I put my dukes up, and got into a fighting stance. I was excited by the opportunity to try all the things Uncle Houston had taught me.

Terrell was pretty good, but my jab was just too much for him to overcome. He wasn't an easy target, and he did something that the shadows I had been boxing couldn't do. He hit me back almost every time left myself open. We were really going at it before Houston stepped between us, and ended the session. "That was great!" he yelled with excitement. "Ya'll both did great. Ya'll should run together and rule the neighborhood." he added as his huge smile displayed his approval,

Uncle Houston began working at Stanley's Chinese restaurant, and we weren't spending as much time together as we once did. I couldn't wait to tell him all about my encounter with Terrell, Gregory, and the teenaged boy with the name the same as his own. I knew he wasn't working that day, so I ran home. Upon entering the house, I asked my brother Albert if he had seen Uncle Houston. He informed me that Uncle Houston had gone to the garage. "He goes to the garage everyday about this time of day" he added.

I turned the door knob and opened the garage door. I

was puzzled by what I saw. He stood in the shadows, and held a spoon in one hand, while holding a burning match under a spoon with the other. He held the match's flames to the bottom of the spoon. There was a bubbling brown liquid in the spoon, and I could not figure out what it was he was doing.

"What's that Uncle Houston?" I asked. He calmly explained to me that there was a hole in the spoon, and he was fixing the hole. Uncle Houston had never lied to me, so I had no reason to question his explanation of the activities. He ordered me to go away, and give him the privacy necessary to concentrate on fixing the spoon. I had never disobeyed him, so I complied with his order.

A few days later my mother and father told uncle Houston that it was time for him to find a place of his own to live. They never gave us an explanation about the abrupt announcement, but years later I realized Uncle Houston was a heroin addict. He moved a few weeks later, and I never saw him again.

December rolled around, and I graduated from elementary school. The school I would be attending was Georgia Jr. high school. At that particular school, a boy had recently been stabbed to death. I felt a little apprehensive about attending such a dangerous school. However, I was thrilled by the thought of being associated with teenagers. I was at that awkward age where you're too old to play with the little kids, but too young to hang out with the teenaged kids. You only fit in with other children your own age.

On the last day of class, before the day of graduation, I walked Samantha home. She was suddenly approached by a group of boys in our class. They informed her that they all wanted to take her out to lunch after the graduation, so they insisted she choose one of them.

Okay" she said, "… but whoever I choose, will also be my boyfriend." They all gave signs of agreement, and waited to see whom she would choose. To everyone's surprise, including my own, she said, "I choose Marvin." Everybody called me by my nickname, which was Tone, except Samantha. I could not believe I had just heard her call out my name. The girl whom I had secretly loved, and believed I wasn't good looking enough to be her boyfriend, had just chosen me to be her boyfriend. My heart pounded so loudly I was sure everyone could hear it beating. The image of that moment, which held Samantha's smiling face, was seared into my memory.

The next day we had a fantastic time on our date, after the graduation. My mother gave me enough money to pay for hamburgers and french-fries for the both of us. She also explained to me that the boy was supposed to pay for everything on a date with his girl. "This girl your girlfriend, right?" my mother asked. I blushed, and admitted to her that Samantha was indeed my girlfriend. After we ate, Samantha broke the news to me that her family was moving. As soon as my dream was realized, it was shattered.

CHAPTER 2

Georgia Jr. High was all that I had hoped it would be. I was clicked up with the cool kids. Everyone suggested I have a serious talk with my parents about my school clothes. I wasn't even on the radar to compete fashionably. The most important part about being cool wasn't as simple as knowing what style of clothes to wear. You had to wear the fashions as well as create and set trends.

I skipped school a lot during those days. All the teasing I had received about my clothes was getting to me. I found sanctuary skipping school at Terrell's house and every time we skipped school, Terrell's cousin Houston, would have sex with a different beautiful girl. We always had a blast, learning all the words to the latest recordings by manually manipulating the arm of the turntable on the stereo.

Terrell taught me how to do all the latest dances, and as a result of the lessons, I became a very confident dancer. We always made all the pancakes we could eat from pancake mix. It proved to be more than just a break from the teasing I'd been experiencing at school. I dressed like an elementary school kid, and everyone else was trying to dress like adults.

Georgia Jr. High school was approximately a mile walk from my home. Usually I hid inside a stall in the boy's restroom to remove what remained of the torn-up cardboard from the inside of my shoes, but I became too comfortable. After a while I believed no one ever would come into the restroom during that particular time, so I made the mistake of removing the debris from my shoes right out in the open.

A kid was hiding inside one of the stalls, smoking a cigarette. While peering through the space between the stall's door and the wall, he was able to witness my entire ritual. I never realized he was there until the word of my daily ritual had spread throughout the entire school. I was no longer considered one of the cool kids, but Terrell remained a loyal, true friend, regardless of what the other kids were saying about me, and it did get pretty ugly.

There was rumor that I was gay, because I wore such tight fitting clothes. No one knew my father simply refused to purchase clothes for me, and I was growing at an alarming rate. All my pants were too short, and too tight. When Terrell broke the news to me, about all the ugly rumors, I was devastated. No matter what was said about me behind my back, Terrell remained a loyal and unwavering friend, but I still felt I was all alone in this world

The summer came, and my grades were awful. I had skipped school so much I was held back for a half of a grade. My parents were so through with me by this point, they didn't even care. I truly was alone in this world, and didn't have a clue as to how I ended up that way. I truly had no one I could turn to in time of need, other than Terrell, but he was only a child himself5.

My birthday was coming up, and I was sure no one cared. I wanted to do something special for myself, but I had no idea what I could do. I discovered the Salvation Army sold adult clothes cheaply. You could actually purchase a pair of pants for twenty-five cents, or a shirt for ten cents. I began cashing in soda pop bottles to buy clothes. I would iron the clothes the way Uncle Houston had taught me. They weren't the best of the latest fashions, but at least they weren't children's clothing.

I found a box which contained ten pairs of old shoes inside our garage. The thought of selling the shoes to the Salvation Army to get some money to celebrate my birthday, seemed like a great idea. If I could sell the shoes to the store for fifty cents a pair, I would have five dollars to spend on my twelfth birthday. I took the box of shoes to the store to sell. I could barely contain my excitement as I talked to the manager of the store. She explained to me that they never brought any of the things that were sold at the store. "Everything is donated." She informed me. The devastating news took my breath away.

As I was leaving the store, a tall, fat, black man about my parents age, very politely approached me. He informed me that he knew where I could sell the shoes. I leaped at the opportunity to renew my plans. "It's my twelfth birthday, and I truly would be thankful if you could help me get the money sir." I added. When he instructed me to get in his car, I hesitated. "What's wrong?" he asked. I knew better, but I got in anyway.

We rode quite a distance from the Salvation Army's store located on Main and Maxwell. I used to ride my bike all over the east side, so I was very familiar with the area. To my surprise, he pulled into an alley on Barns near Kercheval, and produced a hand gun. I believed he was about to rob me of the shoes, until he reached across me, and locked the car door. My heart raced, and I had difficulty breathing as my chest tightened. I became frozen in fear. I had no idea what to expect.

He was a big man with huge slobbery lips, and reeked with the smell of alcohol. I knew he was about to seriously hurt me, so at that time I began to cry. He ordered me not to cry in a very harsh, threatening, and intimidating tone, but that only made things worse. I began to cry louder, and more uncontrollably. No matter how hard I tried, I could not stop crying. I couldn't do anything, other than tremble with fear, which only enhanced his frustration, and his anger. He became impatient with the whole ordeal, once he realized I was gripped with fear.

When he was finished using me, he dropped me off on Barns and Main. As I stood outside of the car, he rolled down his window, and handed me a five dollar bill. "Happy birthday!" he said as he pulled the big car away from the curb. I tried my best to see his license plate number, but I was near sighted without glasses, so I was unable to recognize the letters and numbers. He drove off leaving another damaged, shattered soul in his wake. It was obvious I wasn't his first, nor would I be his last.

I told no one. Who could I tell? I couldn't tell my parents, and Uncle Houston was gone. The black community had no faith in the local police, because they were all mean white men, and it seemed like locking black people up, was their only true agenda. There had been plenty of incidents whereas some black person in the community had called the police for help, only to end up getting arrested themselves.

I was overwhelmed with shame, and I wished that I had never gotten in that car. I wished that I had never been born.

I hated myself for not being able to stop the assault. I hated the whole world. I wished I could kill everyone who had ever tried to hurt me. I went home, went to the basement, and laid down on a large pile of dirty clothes on the cement floor.

I prayed that I would go to sleep and never awaken, but I did. I prayed it all was just a horrible nightmare that I would awaken from, but it wasn't. My day ended with my assailant being the only one to wish me a happy birthday. I had to go on. I did so, but with a promise to myself to get better prepared, so I could better defend myself. I promised myself nothing like this would ever happen to me again. I didn't realize it at that time, but a seed had been planted inside the very essence of me, and it would grow to become the roots of a ruthless, cold blooded killer.

For the rest of the summer I was a very sad and lonely boy. I was curtain that no one in the world cared for me at all. I often would spend my time riding my bike through the neighborhood, searching for fruit trees to climb and eat from. I would sit in the trees and enjoy eating the apples, pears, peaches, cherries, or grapes. I would sit in the tree and eat until I couldn't eat another bite, and cry. I did a lot of crying that summer. I felt absolutely horrible, worthless, and filthy. I felt as though the world had literally chewed me up, and spit me out.

I did my best to avoid everyone, because I was afraid that someone would be able to look into my eyes, and read the truth about what had happened to me. I guarded my secret like it was a priceless jewel. I had been taught to never talk to strangers, and I definitely knew better than to get into the car with one. I didn't realize it at the time, but I was extremely fortunate to be alive after having a close encounter with a pedophile. So many children are abducted every day, and are never seen alive again. I was a fool to risk my life for a few dollars. I blamed myself, even though that monster had taken advantage of a defenseless child. I blamed myself. I knew better, but there's a desire inside of me to have material things so great, I'm willing to roll the dice with my life on the line. I still have my moments when I wonder if I will ever quit being so risky, in hopes of material gain..

I had a friend named Thomas who was a loner. He had dreams of becoming a high school basketball star someday. He played basketball all day every day, and most of the time he played alone. That summer I would play basketball with Thomas whenever I found him playing alone. We would play one on one, or fight twenty-one until enough guys showed up to joined us in a game of half-court basketball. When enough guys joined us to play four on four, we would add a player to each team. Eventually enough guys would show up for us to play five on five, and that's when the fun began, because we were able to play full court.

I found peace on the basketball court. While playing basketball, I wasn't thinking about the world beyond the court. All I thought about was the task at hand. I was playing like any other normal child. I even began experiencing moments of joy, because I was getting better. The victories were beginning to mount.

There was a horse shoe pit, with a fence built around it, next to the basketball court. A new kid wanted to play horse shoes, but he needed a partner in order to participate in a doubles match. He pointed a finger at me, and asked me if I would be his partner. I tried to inform him that I wasn't that good, but he insisted that it was okay. "I'm good enough to beat these chumps by myself. I just need a partner." I agreed to be his partner. There was no way for me to realize just how much my life was about to change, and never be the same.

I lied about not being very good at playing horse shoes. I was good, and I played well, but the new kid was much better. We took on all comers and destroyed every opponent we faced. We won most of the games by a shutout, and held down the horseshoe pit until the playground closed!

The new school year was starting the next day. The basketball games I had won, and dominating the horse shoe pit had helped to get the dreaded day off my mind for a while. My parents had taken all my brothers and sisters and I to Big Time Discount Department store, to purchase our school clothes for the upcoming school year. When it was my turn to pick out my clothes, my father picked out a bunch of children clothes. I asked my father could I get some that were more like the clothed adults wore, and he responded, "Sure." He proceeded to return every piece of clothing to the shelf he had picked out. We went through the checkout line, and he paid for all the remaining clothes.

Once we arrived home, I asked my father when we were going to buy my school clothes, and he said, "You told me that you didn't want any school clothes. I tried to explain to him that there must have been some sort of misunderstanding. "I didn't mean that I didn't want any school clothes at all! I just wanted some big boy clothes sense I was gonna be going to Jr. high school." We stared at each other for a moment before he broke the silence by saying, "Well I'm not gonna get yo ass shit. Now go play and get out my face before I beat yo ass!"

I went to the basement full of regret and fear. I knew I was sure to be the butt of every single joke. I was going to be teased for sure, if I showed up for the first day of school dressed in old, too little, tattered clothing. The first day of school was like a fashion show, and that was something I wasn't looking forward to. I still had holes in the soles of my shoes.

When it was time to turn the horse shoes in, we hadn't lost a single game. The new boy told me that his name was Chance. I told him my name was Tone, and asked him where he lived. He informed me that he had just moved on Fisherman that very day. I told him I also lived on Fisherman. He couldn't quite explain exactly where on the street the house he had moved in was located, so we walked to his house, so I would know where he lived. The house turned out to be just three doors down from our house.

He introduced me to his mother. She was a beautiful, tall, thick, light skinned woman with long thick black hair, which fell midway down her back. He introduced me to his older sister Margo. She was a high school student. I remember looking at her body and noticing that she had a body like a ful grown woman. She had big breast, a small waist, and a big buttocks, with huge shapely legs. Lastly, he introduced me to his younger brother Alfonse.

He told me he didn't know how to get to Georgia Jr. high. I promised him that I would show him. I explained to him how I was going to skip school, but I would show him where the school was first. He asked me why I didn't want to go to school. He couldn't understand why anyone wouldn't want to go to school on the first day. That was the day that everyone got dressed, and showed off their new clothes.

Everyone went to school on that particular day, even if they only showed up for that purpose, like some people only go to church on Easter.

I told him about my father, and I could see how sorry he felt for me. He said, "That's alright man. I've got plenty of clothes, and you're welcomed to wear anything I got." He told his mother my story, and she said I should pick out an outfit to take home to wear to school the next day.

Chance's closet was amazing. It was like looking through a fashion model's closet. Every one of the latest fashions was in his closet. He had the popular walking suits in many different colors, silk pants, silk and wool pants, gabardine pants and shirts, knit shirts, and shirts of all colors with the high low collars. You name it, he had it. I had never seen such an extensive wardrobe. I picked out a green walking suit, and some green lizard shoes. I thanked him and his mother, and headed home.

When I got home, my father stopped me and asked where I had gotten the garments. I told him all about Chance and his wardrobe. I explained how his mother had insisted that it was alright for me to wear the clothes. To my surprise my father ordered me to return the clothes right then, and added, "If I ever catch you wearing somebody else's clothes, I'm gonna beat yo ass!"

Broken hearted, confused and totally disappointed, I headed out the door to return the clothes. Chance's mother met me at the door, and wanted to know why I was returning the outfit. She listened to me closely and she gave me her undivided attention. It made me feel like I mattered. I told her about my encounters with my father. I told her everything about our relationship. I told her the whole story about how he had refused to buy me any school clothes, and about his threats.

She was unable to hold back her tears. I could see she was trying extremely hard. She asked me if I were hungry, and I answered, "All the time." with a chuckle. She took me into her arms, and gave me the most powerful and loving embrace I had ever received. I was so emotionly moved, I became overwhlemed, began to cry uncontrollably. She and I cried together. When I raised my head from her bosom, I noticed that Margo, Alfonse and Chance also had tears rolling down their faces.

"What can we do Mom?" he asked. His mother told me to call her Aunt Pearl from now on, and she had a plan. "Leave your house in the mornings, like you're going to school. Come down here, change your clothes, and leave here going to school. When you get out of school, come here first. Then just change your clothes before you go home." She cupped my chin in the palm of her hand, and looked me right in my eyes as she told me, "You can eat anything that's in my kitchen." I had never experienced that type of access to food before.

The next morning, I got dressed knowing that I wasn't putting on the clothes I would be wearing to school. I made sure that everyone believed that I had no problem with going to school dressed in my old clothes. I had pressed my clothes with care, making sure the creases were perfect. They were clothes that I had purchased from the Salvation Army. After spending an ample amount of time in front of the mirror, no one was the wiser. I left out the front door as though I were walking to school. I went to Aunt Pearl's house, just as she had instructed. When I arrived, she told me to fix myself a bowl of cereal, and to hurry up so we wouldn't be late for school. I enjoyed a huge bowl of Frosted Flakes as I listened to a new singing group called, The Intruders, singing a song entitled, A Love That's Real, on the radio.

After I was dressed, I stopped to admire my image in the mirror. I had never been dressed like that before. For the first time, in what seemed like years to me, I experienced a semblance of joy, as well as a sense of self-worth. I was amazed at how powerful being dressed up had made me feel. I was excited about going to school, and thrilled by the possibilities life offered. I stood there, frozen in time, admiring myself for the very first time in my life. I couldn't wait for all the kids, who always teased me, to get load of me!

Aunt Pearl's plan had been working perfectly for weeks. A girl named Ruth sat next to me in the afternoon math class. She was an amazingly beautiful girl. She was tall, and although she was slim, her body was quite curvy. She had long legs as well as long, thick, black wavy hair, which she wore in a ponytail. She was always staring at me. It was obvious that she was impressed by the way I dressed. One day I decided to try a line on her that Chance had taught me.

"How are my chances?" I asked. She smiled and lowered her gaze before asking, "Your chances for what?" "My chances of being your man, before this class is over?" I added. This time she blushed before asking me if I was serious. "I'm more serious than a heart attack!" I responded. "Your chances are great, if you're serious." After a long conversation, accentuated with in depth explanations of why I wanted to be her man, Ruth became my girlfriend that afternoon.

Chance turned out to be quite a fighter. He easily

whipped the worst bully in the school. He grabbed him with his hands and raised him above his head before slamming him on his back. He landed upon a log, strategically placed on the ground in the parking lot. After that fight, our popularity escalated. I no longer had to try to hang out with the cool kids. We were the most popular and the best dressed kids in the entire school. We were the cool kids now, and you had to be in our circle to be considered one of the cool kids. Everything was going well for me. I couldn't remember when I had been happier. We were walking home from school one day when Chance suddenly snatched a white woman's purse, and shouted, "Run!" before he broke out running as fast as he could. He had a huge head start on me, but I was fast enough to easily catch up to him. We made it back to our street, and hid out in his garage as we went through the contents of the purse.

There was one hundred and sixty dollars. "Now we got some cheese!" Chance said, as he handed me eighty dollars. He suggested that we catch a bus to the barber shop to get our hair done into a conk hair style, by a professional barber. Most guys got their hair done by friends, in basements and bathrooms. The majority of the time, it truly could not compare with a fresh hairdo from a professional shop.

After getting our hair done, we went shopping for clothes, and headed home. I tried to go to the Salvation Army store, but Chance insisted that we went to a department store, and brought brand new clothes. I was a little nervous because I had to march before my parents, and spring a new hairdo on them that I hadn't gotten permission to get. I knew that anything short of getting a bald head would not change the condition or texture of my hair. There was nothing they could do about it.

I was more concerned about what my father's reactions would be once he saw I had shopping bags full of new clothes. He was giving a poker party that night, and I believed that because there would be guest in the home, it would be the perfect time to find out if he had any objections towards the idea of me purchasing my own clothing. My father surprised me. He was actually happy that I brought myself some clothing, and there wasn't a confrontation. "You better keep your hair up, or I'm gonna make you get it cut." was all he had to say about my hair.

Snatching purses became almost a daily activity for us, so we had money enough to travel to other parts of the city whenever we wanted. We spent a lot of time in the projects. The projects were supposed to be apartments you could rent, based upon your income. It was after a few months of waiting on buses to ride to the west side and back that Chance was ready to try other means of transportation. He declared he knew how to drive, and steal cars. I didn't believe him, so off we went. He felt a need to prove to me that he wasn't just talking, and he really could drive, and steal cars.

We walked to a street named Mack. There were several factories on Mack, and if you stole a factory worker's car, they wouldn't even realize that it was missing until their shift was over. If you timed it right, you could have a car for hours before it was reported stolen. True to his word, Chance stole a 1966 Electra 225. At that time, the car was the most popular model of Buick's. Hustlers called it, a Duce and a Quarter. Chance drove amazingly well. He taught me how to drive and steal cars over the following weeks, and I became very good at it. As a matter of fact, I believed I had gotten better at both, driving and stealing cars.

Chance and I hung out every day, and he taught me quite a few things. He woke something up deep within me. He said that I had larceny in my heart. He taught me how to take care of myself, and insisted that I learned to depend on no one. He used to tell me all the time that if you depend on someone other than yourself, you are setting yourself up for a guaranteed disappointment.

The battles between my father and I intensified. I was determined to never allow my father to hit me again, without fighting back. I was as equally determined to ever allow anyone to touch me again, without trying my best to send them to the cemetery. After wearing a pair of his orange suede shoes without permission, an altercation with him lead to my father putting me out. The cold streets of Newport became my home, and I officially joined the numbers of homeless throw away kids.

Life became extremely difficult for me. I had survived a brutal winter, by sleeping in abandoned buildings, and unlocked cars. Aunt Peral had no idea I had been put out, so I continued to wear Chance's clothes, and eat food there, as though everything were normal. I began brushing my teeth and bathing there as well. I continued to go to school to keep up appearances, but my grades suffered.

Easter was upon us, and Chance wanted me to accompany him to an Easter party. The problem was simple. We needed cash. It seemed like a great idea to rob a hardware store that we knew of. The store seemed to be a relatively easy job. Chance took the largest hammer from a rack of hammers of various sizes, and viciously hit the old man, who was attending the store alone, upside his head. I watch as the old man's head gave way to the impact of the hammer, and split open up like it were a melon. As he landed on the floor, I heard a gunshot fired. I ducked and looked around the store. I tried to locate the direction the shot came from, and there was no more gunfire, nor was there anyone else in the store. I turned my attention to Chance when I was unable detect the source, and was horrified by the small hole in the temple of his head, with blood oozing from it.

I knew I had to leave him alone, to go get him some help. If the bullet wound had been on any part of his body, other than his head, I would have gotten him out of there. He crumbled to the floor, before I was able to reach him. I looked into his eyes, and promised to return with help, and got out of there like a bat outta hell. I knew exactly where I had to go.

It just so happened I had been talking on the phone romantically to a girl who lived around the corner from the store. I was very serious about Linda, and had told her all about Chance, so when I showed up at her home, desperate to use her telephone because Chance had been shot, she understood the gravity of the situation. I told Aunt Pearl Chance had been shot, but there was no way I could tell her he had been shot in the head over the phone.

Before I could return to the store, the police had already arrived. Chance was being lead to the back seat of a station wagon, in handcuffs. I could not believe what I was seeing. How could a sixteen year old boy be forced to walk, with a bullet in his head? Chance made eye contact with me, and he had a faraway, apologetic look in his eyes. It was as if he was apologizing for letting me down. I was shocked! Nothing could have been further from the truth. He taught me the most important lesson of all. He taught me that I mattered, and I was worthy of love. He'd also taught me quite a few things about getting money to take care of myself.

After conducting an extensive investigation, it was discovered the old man had a twenty-five, automatic pistol in one of his pant pockets, and once he was knocked to the floor, by the blow from the hammer, the gun in his pocket discharged, and shot Chance in the head. He died three days later, and I lost the best friend I'd ever had.

There was an older guy by the name of Vincent, but everyone called him Preacher. He was only twenty one years old, but he seemed so much older than me. He lived in his grandmother's basement. I was cold at nights, because I had no shelter. I was also depressed all the time. Chance died because he was trying to help me, so I believed I was responsible for his death.

One day, Preacher convinced me to try injecting heroin. He didn't tell me it was heroin, so I had no idea what it was I was doing. Preacher promised me the drugs would prevent me from feeling any pain or the cold from the elements. I agreed to give it a try, and it worked. I was so high, I was numb. I mean truly physically and emotionally numb.

Most people say I had a death wish following Chance's passing. The truth of the matter was, I did have a death wish. I missed Chance horribly, and would've welcomed any opportunity to be reunited with him. I wasn't willing to simply lay my life down, but I took on all comers. If someone started a conflict with me, I would delight in the opportunity to indulge in violence. I was six foot one, and weighed one hundred and seventy-five pounds, but I was only a teenager. I had a serious attitude, and I was eager to demonstrate that I was more than capable of using excessive force, whenever it proved to be necessary. A lot of men mistakenly took me for an adult, and thought I would be an easy victory for them in a fight, but I was eager to fight them just to prove them wrong. Chance was gone, and I hoped and prayed that I would join him soon.

I adored my Aunt Elizabeth's eldest son Roderick. He was everything that I'd hope to be someday. He had a solid reputation on the streets, and was well known and respected. One day he got into an altercation with a man about bullying a friend of his. My cousin was eighteen years old, short, and very muscular. He leaped into the air, and sliced the man across his eyes with a hook knife. The man grabbed his face in agony, as he pulled out a twenty-two pistol. Recognizing the danger, Roderick turned and ran down a narrow hall, in hopes of escaping. With one of his hands over his eyes, the man fired his pistol blindly, and aimlessly, in the direction of the retreating footsteps. A bullet found the back of Roderick's head.

I was very impressed by the way his friends presented themselves. I met them at his funeral. They were clearly gangsters. I wanted to prove that I belonged among them, even though I was much younger than they were. They all hung out over Aunt Elizabeth's house while she was away at work. My aunt and uncle were now divorced.

I had a new girlfriend named Darla, who lived down the street from my Aunt. She thought I was older than I really was, and I never told her anything differently. The west side became my new home, the more I hung out with her and my cousins.

Darla was a tall beautiful high school girl. Her hair was long and always well done, with not so much as a single hair out of place. She attended Clark High School located on Clark St. near West Vernon. She was always in the running for the title of best dressed every year. I met her while attending a cabaret where my cousin Renee, and Uncle Dale were performing.

Renee was Aunt Elizabeth' second eldest daughter. Renee was a beautiful red bone with natural blond hair, which was considered red in the black community. She also attended Clark High School, and had a beautiful voice. She was a member of a female singing group called the Sweet Inspirations, and they recorded a hit song entitled, Just Because You've Gone and Left Me. They were on the same television show that Terrell's brother used to perform on, as well as the radio all the time. They performed at cabaret halls, and all the top notched clubs throughout the city.

I was her favorite cousin, and we used to lie across the bed talking, laughing, and smoking cigarettes all night long. Roderick was her older brother. Many considered him to have been one of the baddest dudes on the west side, even though he got killed at the tender age of eighteen. Renee used to tell me that out of everyone in our family, I was the one most like Roderick. "One day you're gonna be one bad mothafucka!" she used to tell me.

Being the late Roderick and Renee's cousin, as well as being Darla's new boyfriend, did wonders for my popularity. My name was ringing as my popularity grew, however, Newport was a hard core, city. No matter how solid your reputation was, you were tested. You had to live up to your reputation. I was excited by the challenge and looked forward to the opportunity to prove myself.

I had become addicted to heroin, and continued to inject heroin daily. Preacher helped to keep me supplied with the drug, as I ran back and forth, from the west side to the east side, and back to the west side again, every single day in stolen cars. Eventually it became too much for me. I had to find myself a supply on the west side. I found a penny cap house that sold capsules of heroin for one dollar. All I needed was a half of a capsule to get high. Preacher taught me how to inject myself, so I was able to keep my habit up without assistance.

Aunt Elizabeth told me my father was complaining about my staying with her. She explained that she could no longer stay in the middle of the feud between my father and I, so I had to leave. I became a homeless heroin addict, but to my surprise Darla never stopped loving me. Even though she found out I was only fifteen, homeless, had dropped out of school, had become a heroin addict, and I became physically abusive, she still never stopped being my girl.

I was openly accepted by all of Roderick's partners, and we would hang out over my Aunt's house while she was at work. Renee, Rodger, Otis, and Steven were still living with Aunt Elizabeth. Renee loved to drink, and would out drink us all every day. Rodger was Aunt Elizabeth's second son. He was a year older than me, but we were exactly the same size. I wore his clothes a lot. Otis was a couple of years younger than me, and Steve was in elementary school.

Through the day, I hung out over Aunt Elizabeth's house while she was at work. In the black community, there were plenty of households whereas the parents or a single parent had to leave teenagers in charge while they went to work. Those homes became teen hangouts.

CHAPTER 3

Everyone talked constantly about a pimp named Slim. Chance had once given me a book written by Robert Beck entitled, Pimp the Story of My Life by Iceberg Slim. I studied the book as though it was a required curriculum, but I had never met a pimp. I wanted to meet Slim, and learn all that I could from him. According to all the stories I'd been told, I learned he taught skills that were life altering. I believed he could teach me how to improve my current conditions by teaching me how to pimp hoes. I knew that someday he would come through, and I would receive the opportunity to convince him to teach me the ways of a pimp, but during the meantime I had to sleep in abandoned houses, cars and garages, so it was a must that I concentrated on surviving.

The book actually gave me a whole new perception of women, and how they were to be treated. Besides the women in my family, I began treating all women like they were hoes. I referred to them as bitches in all my conversations, or discussions. The more I read the book, and the more I embraced the philosophies expressed in the book, the more I wanted to learn about pimping.

At some point in our young lives, most black boys, in the urban communities, are exposed to the pomp and glitter of pimps. Pimps perform daily rituals on stages all across America. They drove the most expensive cars, set the trends for fashions, wore diamond studded watches as well as large diamond rings, had several of the most beautiful women in the city selling their bodies and giving them all the proceeds. They also carried around ridiculous amounts of money in their pockets. Everywhere these men went, they were very well received and respected. They were the celebrities of the ghetto, and almost every boy exposed to them, and their lifestyle, conjured up dreams of being a pimp someday.

Things had gotten progressively worse for me, but the fellas still treated me well. It was tough, but we shared everything we had. Just when it seemed that things couldn't get any worse, Bernard ran through the door excitingly informing us that Slim was walking up the steps to the house. As he walked through the door, I understood immediately what all the fuss was about. He had an air of confidence, and a shine I had never witnessed. There was a calmness about him that helped me to truly understand the meaning behind the word, "cool". He was so nonchalant it appeared quite obvious this man didn't have a single issue to be concerned about.

He was dressed in all white. His white Stetson hat was worn cocked to the side of his head, making the straightness of his black conked hair visible. His shirt and pants were made of white gabardine. His double breasted, cashmere coat, with its' belt tied in the front, was so white it reflected the light, and gave the illusion of illuminating the entire room. He wore white alligator shoes, to complete his impressive all white outfit.

Whenever the light hit his diamond studded watch, or

any of the many diamond rings he wore on his fingers with the long, manicured fingernails, the room would explode with brilliant colored lights. What was even more impressive to me was how well dressed, and beautiful the women who accompanied him were. One of the women had on a white fur coat and stood by his side clutching tightly to his arm. I heard someone near me whisper, "The woman holding his arm is his wife, and the dude with them is her brother. He's the AAU's and the Golden Glove's heavyweight champion."

There also were three other women with them. They were all beautiful women as well, and were also dressed in all white. They looked like they were angles, but they were his hoes. Slim announced that they were headed to attend the Players Convention. Curtis Mayfield and the Impressions were singing their latest hit entitled, Moving on Up, on the radio, and I wondered was the song a sign of things to come.

He finally asked about me, and was informed by Rodger that I was his little cousin, Tone. It seemed to me that he had barely noticed me, but I was wrong. While laughing, he stated, "He don't look little to me." He asked me if I had heart like Roderick. I responded with a nod of my head, because I was so star struck, I couldn't speak. "I know you have heart. Your name is ringing! Everyone is talking about this kid. They say you're a beast, just like your cousin Roderick was. Listen up youngster, I'll be back to get you one day soon, so be ready. There's a lot I have to teach you."

It seemed as though his soul purpose for stopping by, was to meet with me. I had been waiting and hoping that someday I could convince this man to be my mentor. "Be ready." were his final words, and he left just as suddenly as he had appeared. I realized that I'd just had a life altering encounter, and the spirit of his presence lingered with me, long after he had left.

After he left, the fellas exploded with joy. They talked about his clothes, his wife, his hoes, and about his interest in me. I spent the evening listening to them exchange stories about Slim. The man was a living street legend, and I marveled at every story I was told. They told me that Roderick taught them everything they knew about the streets, and Slim taught Roderick. There was no envy at all among them, and they were genuinely happy that I had been chosen by Slim to become his latest apprentice.

A few weeks later, on a mild spring afternoon, I was hanging out in front of my aunt's house, when Slim unexpectedly showed up walking. He had on a pair of black lizard skin shoes, along with some grey, shadow striped pants. His shirt was a thin, grey knit, which he wore underneath a black and grey square neck sweater. The final layer of clothing was a fashionable, waist length, black leather jacket. His hairdo was so neat and fresh, he appeared as though he had just stepped out of some barber's chair.

He instructed me to walk with him. "We're going to walk through the neighborhood, and I'm going to introduce you to everybody as my baby brother. Everybody thought me and Roderick were cousins anyway, so they'll believe me." He reached behind his back, and pulled out a nickel plated, thirty-eight, snub nosed revolver, with a white pearl handle. He handed the pistol to me, and instructed me to place it in the waist band of my pants at the small of my back. I did as I was instructed, and it was a perfect fit.

The way Slim explained it to me, it was because I was only fifteen, I wouldn't be sent to prison if I got caught with a pistol. "As a matter of fact, you could rob a bank or kill somebody, and it would still be possible for you to only get a slap on the wrist, because of your age. I'm only schooling you about this, so you'll know I'm not really putting you on front street." We began walking before he suddenly stopped and added, "Let's get this understood right now. For now, if we run into any static, just hand me the pistol, and let me handle it. Okay?" I smiled, and answered, "Okay." as we continued on our walk.

In the short time since I had last seen him, I'd grown, and I could no longer fit Rodgers clothes. I was dressed like a bum, and Slim realized why I appeared uncomfortable. "Don't worry about your clothes. The next time anybody sees you, you'll be cleaner than the Board of Health." A car rode by us with the radio playing Jerry Butler's latest hit entitled, Never Gonna Give You Up, with the volume turned up. I thought of Darla as I song along. It was her favorite song.

We had been walking through the neighborhood, and everybody we ran into, that he knew, he would stop and talk to them. During their conversation he would introduce me as his younger brother. Our last stop was over Preston's weed house. He was also a street legend. Whereas Slim was well known as a pimp, Preston was known as a drug dealer, and a killer. He was not a large man. He was dark skinned, and a very sharp dresser. He always looked deeply into your eyes whenever he spoke to you. It was as though he could read your thoughts.

I liked Preston and it was obvious that he liked me also. He called out to his woman, who was in the back of the house, and asked her to drop whatever she was doing, and come to him. He introduced me to his her. Her name was Sharon. She was a light skinned, strikingly beautiful, full figured woman, with an amazing smile. He told her I was his young new friend, and to give me a trey pack. A trey pack was a three, dollar package of marijuana. He also sold duce packs for two dollars, and joints for fifty cents. He instructed her to give me a trey pack whenever I came by, even if my money was short. She asked him should she give me a trey pack even if I had no money, and he instructed her to give it to me on credit. "As long as he doesn't want anything more than a trey, give him whatever he's asking for." I told him what a pleasure it was to meet him, and thanked him for everything as we were leaving his house.

We stopped at the store to get some cigarette papers before returning to my aunt's house. During those days, the only cigarette papers that were sold at the neighborhood stores were Tops. We would use a couple of sheets to roll our joints, because the paper burned faster than the marijuana. Years later, I would discover the thin sheets of papers were made to be used to roll tobacco cigarettes.

I enjoyed the potent marijuana I was smoking, as I sat in the overstuffed chair in the living room listening to the radio. The Dells were singing a song entitled, Stay in My Corner. During those times, Newport had three black radio stations that played R&B music. The stations were 1440 W.C. H, B., and 1400 W.J.L.B. on the AM dial, and 107.9 W.G.P.R., on the FM dial. Music sounds so much better when you're under the influence of intoxicants. Marijuana and music went quite well together, and I found myself drifting into a blissful state of euphoria.

"You can't chill yet youngster." Slim added, snapping

me back to the realities of the real world. "We still have a lot to do. He explained to me that since I was on my own, I had to make my own money. He suggested that I teamed up with Bernard and rob neighborhood stores. It didn't take long for me to make the decision to do as he had suggested. The decision was forced upon me, by my circumstances, and deplorable living situation.

Slim was a mastermind when it came to planning robberies. He took Bernard and I to the side, away from everyone, and explained to us how to plan robberies, and why planning was so important. Just when I thought we were through, Slim asked, "What's the most important part of a robbery?" Bernard quickly responded, "It's got to be making sure the guns used are in good working condition." "Wrong.", Slim responded. "That's important, but not the most important."

I said, "Making sure you get all the money." "Wrong again. Although those are both serious and important details, along with planning. Making sure you stay in control of the situation, is so important, I can't emphasize it enough, but even so it's not the most important thing. The most important thing is, getting away. Never forget that."

Neither one of us had ever robbed a store before, so we both were very nervous. Slim had laid the plan out for us. He also made us sit back, close our eyes, and picture ourselves going through every single step of the plan in our minds. He explained that meditation was a very important aspect of preparation, because you must be able to visualize completing a task in your mind, before you actually bring about its' manifestation.

My job was to choose the precise moment to pull my

weapon out, announce the robbery, and control everyone while Bernard emptied the contents of the cash register. After that was completed, Bernard would search the owner of the store for any cash or valuables he may have in his possession. Bernard would follow me as I literally would escort him to safety.

Slim explained how I would have the element of surprise on my side. Everyone present will be in a temporary state of shock, and will give me their undivided attention. "From that point on, you will have control of the situation. If you do like I tell you to do, you won't lose it. Keep a calm serious expression on your face at all times. Demand that everyone looks at the floor, and not in your direction as they lay face down on the floor. Everyone must understand that you mean business." He went into further detail explaining how to make the announcement. I understood why he was trying his best to put emphasis on the fact that my demeanor and the tone of my voice were all very important tools at my disposal.

On our way to the store I felt butterflies in my stomach. Every nerve in my body was tingling by the time we arrived. When I felt the time was right, I pulled the pistol, and ordered everyone to the floor, in a loud, stern voice. I didn't have to fake a serious facial expression. Everyone quickly complied with my order except an old man sitting in a chair. I slapped him across the bridge of his nose with the barrel of the pistol. Using my free hand, I snatched him from the chair by his collar, and slung him to the floor. The chair rolled forward, and at that moment, I realized it was a wheelchair. I refused to show any remorse for what I had done to the old man. When the people on the floor began to complain about my treatment of the old man I responded, "Shut the fuck up!" They did as I ordered, and I felt a surge of power that was almost as intoxicating as any drug I had ever taken.

The getaway was by foot, and before we knew it we were in the comforts of my Aunt's living room, counting the money we had taken. We had taken seventeen hundred dollars, and we split it in three equal parts. We got five hundred and sixty dollars apiece, and spent the remaining twenty dollars on weed, wine, cigarettes, and heroin. Slim and I both needed a full cap to ourselves. We were the only two at that time who injected heroin. The rest of the fellas, including my two cousins Rodger and Otis, snorted the drugs up their noses. It wouldn't be long before we all were injecting the drug.

I had more money than I had ever had in my life, and I was higher than a witch doctor! The fellas enjoyed getting high without having to spend any money. The only Jazz station in Newport during those days was 105.9 W.C.H.D. We smoked weed, drank wine, snorted heroin and listened to Jazz. We enjoyed the sounds of Eddie Harris, Lou Rawls singing, and John Coltrane, as Bernard told the story about the robbery over, and over again. He continuously expressed how cold it was to bust the old man in his face, and sling him from his wheelchair to the floor. I never let on that it wasn't intentional, or that I felt awful about doing it.

There was one more thing Slim wanted to do for me. He took me to meet a very close friend of his named Jerome. Jerome was a tall, slim, very handsome, dark skinned young man. He was a popular drug dealer who drove a brand new, red, 1969 convertible Cadillac Deville. He owned a penny cap spot, two blocks from my Aunt's house, on the Boulevard near Magnolia.

Slim insisted that he and I walk to the spot alone. "A crowd of young black dudes would attract the attention of the cops, and we don't need that." he added. When we arrived, we saw Jerome's car sitting in front of the spot. We walked to the rear of the house, and climbed the stairs that led to a enclosed back porch and the door. I could smell the strong stench of mildew and musk in the air. After Slim knocked we heard a rustling sound coming from behind the door before we heard what sounded like wooden boards knocking against one another and eventually the door swung open.

A young man, lead us to the front of the house where we found Jerome sitting on an old dirty couch watching television. He stood once we entered the room upon recognizing Slim. "My man, what's happening?" Jerome asked as he stretched out his hand. Slim took his hand in his own, and shook it vigorously while offering a pleasant greeting in return. "This is my younger brother Tone." he said as he nodded in my direction. "Tone this is Jerome." he added as he nodded towards Jerome.

"I remember seeing you at the funeral. Roderick was my man." he added as he shook his head. Slim told Jerome that I needed a job, and a place to stay. Jerome was happy to let us know that it wasn't a problem as long as I didn't mind living there at the spot.

The spot was a one bedroom flat, but the couch let out into a bed. There was a closet in the hall, and Jerome informed me I could keep my clothes in there. "I'll pay you one hundred dollars a week to answer the door, eight hours a day, six days a week." Beer by the can, and Wild Irish Rose wine by the cup, were also sold for fifty cents apiece. Jerome explained how to run the bar, after informing me the bar would be my responsibility. Considering how I had been living, this was an ideal situation for me.

"Now I have to go to my real job." Slim announced before hugging me. He considered pimping a job, and all the responsibilities were simply duties to be performed by who ever held the position. Checking on his whores was a major responsibility. He instructed me to meet him over my aunt's house the next day, and left.

As time passed, I became more acquainted with my new surroundings. The floor in the living room was wooden and painted red. It appeared as though the floor had never been mopped. The floor in the room the bar was located was painted grey. It was a small room which probably had once served as a small child's bedroom, at some point in the past. Behind the bar, a radio sat on a wall shelf, and a refrigerator, which also served purpose of a barricade, to block one end. Customers weren't allowed to venture behind the bar at any time for any reason.

I had been reminded on numerous occasions that the sofa lets out into a bed, but I never tried to find out. I didn't know how the bed looked, nor was I certain I wanted to see. I always spread my bedding across the sofa, and slept on top of it. I would lie down on the sofa, and watch a small black and white television set until all the channels signed off the air for the night.

There was a bathroom with a functioning toilet. I used it only when I had to urinate. For any other reason that I had to use the restroom, I always waited until 3:00 p.m. when

I knew my Aunt had left for work, and used her bathroom. I don't believe the bathroom had ever been clean. Addicts would use the room to privately inject their drugs, but I refused to get high in that filth. I injected my drugs in the bar, in front of anyone who happened to be in the room.

In the room that served as the entrance to the dwelling, there was a block of wood cut from a two by four, about twelve inches long, nailed to the floor. There was another block of wood of equal size, nailed to the door. Two long two by four, inch boards were inserted between the two blocks of wood, and that was the designed that secured the premises. Even law enforcement agencies had trouble using force to breach this particular system. There were also conventional locks used, but the makeshift lock offered me the most comfort. A playing card was nailed to the center of the door about five feet from the floor. It covered a bullet hole that was used for a peek hole. There was neither paint nor varnish on the floor. The naked unkempt floor was so dirty it appeared to be the same color grey as dirt.

There was also a master bedroom. It contained a real bed with clean sheets. The closet was pretty small, but most closets were small back in the day. A dresser, some folded chairs, and a folded card table sat in the corner. These luxuries belonged to the man in charge of the house. His name was Pierre, but most called him Sleepy.

Sleepy was hiding out from the police because there was a warrant for his arrest for bank robbery, and first degree murder. He was twenty-one years old, and about the same size as me. Sleepy was a very sharp dresser. His left eye was hidden behind a patch, and his right eye drooped. Parts of his face weren't concealed by the patch, and showed scaring, which was obviously caused by severe trauma. He was light skinned, with hair conked to perfection. He believed he was a lady's man, but I never seen any evidence of it. Every one of the ladies he approached rejected his advances, even though he held on to a sack of drugs, and all the house money was in his pockets.

Jerome had a partner named Powell. They weren't related. Powell's nickname was Beast, and that's what close friends and family called him. He was Roderick's best friend at the time of his passing. Quite a few people claimed to be his best friend, but I had heard of Beast years before I had been officially introduced to him. Beast was only nineteen, but was a true heavyweight. He stood about six feet two, and weighed two hundred and fifty pounds of pure young muscles. I remember once Uncle Clarence was talking to my father about Beast. He said Beast stated there was no man on the planet that could whip him. My Uncle flashed a sly smile, and chuckled before adding, "You know what...? I believed him."

Beast and his woman lived downstairs. He and Jerome came by the place daily, and spent time in the bedroom diluting the drugs with a couple of different substances. They also would patiently stuff the drugs inside individual capsules, by using a special technique. They very seldom hung out for long. They would linger for an hour or two before drifting off into the night.

One morning, a couple of regular customers stopped by. They were trying to sell some twenty-two pistols. Sleepy insisted on trying the pistols out to make sure they worked, before he made a purchase. He gathered a few empty cans, and lined them up on top of the door frame. He loaded one of the pistols, and began shooting at the cans. They began taking turns shooting at the cans, and became deeply engrossed in the amusement they found in competing against one another to see who was the better shot. For a moment, the shooting gallery became a shooting range.

When I was certain they were out of ammunition, I pulled out the nine, millimeter pistol I was given to answer the door with, and got the drop on Sleepy and the two guys. I took all the weapons, including the thirty-eight, caliber pistol Sleepy carried. I felt like a seasoned stick-up man, as I gave them one complied order after another. I took all the money and all the drugs as well.

"You won't get away with this!" he protested. I smiled, and sat down without responding, to their surprise. I wasn't leaving as they had thought. Whenever anyone knocked at the door, I would peek out the window to see if I saw Jerome's car. If I didn't see his car, I would not answer the door. I wasn't about to allow these idiots to be out my sight for one second. The way I figured things, if they were brazen enough to conduct target practice in the spot, there was no telling what length they'd be willing to go in order to regain the upper hand.

It wasn't long before Jerome arrived. Only a couple of people had knocked on the door before he showed up, so we hadn't missed much business. Our clientele consisted of mostly factory workers, so most of our business was conducted during the changing of the shifts. The only exception was on Fridays. Both shifts would show up after cashing their checks about the same time. Some were looking to score a hit instead of eating lunch. This was early in the afternoon on a Thursday. I made all three men place their hands on their heads, and walk with me to the door to let Jerome in. I ordered them to turn around, and not to look back at me while I opened the door. Jerome asked what was going on once he was inside, and noticed the men with their backs turned, and their hands placed on top of their heads.

I explained the entire incident to Jerome. I gave him a detail account of everything that happened, including the part played by each of the participants. Jerome exploded with anger as he yelled, "I can't believe grown ass men could be so damn stupid!" As he spoke there was a loud banging at the door. I looked out the peep hole and saw that it was Beast.

He entered the flat with his eyes as wide as saucers, and his pistol in his hand. "My woman called me, and begged me to come home. She said that she heard gun shots that sounded like they were coming from up here. What the fuck is going on?" he demanded to know. Jerome led Beast to the bedroom to fill him in, and to discuss what needed to be done.

After a long discussion, they came into the living room where we were waiting, and made a shocking announcement. "We've decided to put Tone in charge of the house, and the day to day operations." From the expression on Sleepy's face, It was quite noticeable as well as obvious by the, I had made a serious enemy for life. You could practically see the steam coming out his ears. To say he was angry would have been a gross understatement, but none of us cared. I received all the perks that came with being in charge of the house. As a result of the promotion, I received a raise of one hundred dollars, and the room with the bed,

The next day I caught up with Slim over my aunt's

house. He had two guys with him that I had never seen. He then introduced me to Gaylord. He was a tall brown skinned man dressed in a suit and tie, and he fancied himself to be a pimp. He didn't wear as many diamond rings as Slim, but he had a fair amount for a pimp.

The other fella was nearly my age. He was only seventeen, and was introduced to me as Bumpy. He had a big forehead, and was also tall. He was light skinned and wore a huge afro hairdo. The afro was a new natural hairstyle. As a matter of fact, it was known as either an afro or a natural. Eventually nearly everyone would wear the natural hairdo, but Bumpy wore the first one I had ever seen. He was sharply dressed, with small black and white checks on his pants, which appeared to be grey from a distance. They were called salt and pepper by street hustlers. He also wore a black luxurious alpaca sweater, with a grey shirt which had a high low collar.

They had come together to complete the final stage of preparation for an armed robbery they had planned to commit that day. The radio was tuned to a jazz station, before they laid back to meditated. After forty-five minutes of meditation, Slim broke the silence by instructing everyone to take off their jewelry, and hand it to me. He explained how a witness could recognize a piece of jewelry, and that piece of jewelry would end up being part of the description. There were no surveillance cameras, so eyewitness descriptions were crucial. After they all had given me their jewelry, they left. "We're either going to come back rich, or die trying." Slim added as they made their exit.

I hung out with my two cousins, waiting on Slims' safe return. Otis was better known as Black Otis, because he was extremely dark skinned. Otis was short and although he was small he walked and carried himself as though he were a swollen body builder. He was only a couple of years younger than me.

Rodger was there also, along with Brian. Brian was doing Rodger's hair. His hair was red, and some called him Red, but close friends and family called him Rodger. He wore his hair conked also. He loved to wear the hairdo called, three to the side. It was called three to the side, because of the three huge waves that were worn to the back, and to one side of the head. As I watched Brian do his hair I couldn't help thinking how this lifestyle wasn't for Rodger. He was caught up in a world that he didn't belong. The only thing that Rodger did that was unlawful was get high. He was a year older than me, but everyone thought we were the same age.

While we were in the middle of doing our rendition of the Temptation's routine for the song My Girl, a sharp knock at the door demanded everyone's undivided attention. Upon answering the door, I was surprise to see that Slim and his crew were back so soon. They calmly walked through the opened door, and they were all smiling.

Bumpy emptied the contents from a brown paper bag onto the coffee table in the living room. I had never seen so much money in one place. They had robbed a credit union, and gotten away with over seventy-five thousand dollars. Gaylord left immediately after receiving his cut and his jewelry. Slim and Bumpy spearheaded a celebration that was talked about for years to come. Slim sent me to get a can of marijuana from Jones. A can is an approximation of an ounce. Rodger's task was to get five bottles of Bali Hi wine, five bottles of Silver Satan wine, and five packs of lemon and grape Kool-Aid.

Once I had scored the weed, Slim sent me to get either Beast or Jerome so he could purchase some uncut heroin. Just like cut heroin was sold in capsules, so was uncut heroin. Uncut heroin was much more expensive. I would have to walk to the spot to get one of them, but it was worth it. He handed Rodger a fist full of money once he realized that we were out of cigarettes, and instructed him to go back to the store and get a pack of cigarettes for everyone. "Don't get any for me" Bumpy shouted out. "Smoking is a big waste. I didn't see what everybody thinks is so cool about it." Slim told Rodger to keep the change, as he walked out the door.

As the regulars arrived, they were amazed at the sight of all the weed, wine, and heroin on the coffee table. "Somebody hit the numbers?" Bernard asked. He added, "Either that, or somebody hit a really good lick." Slim had spent one hundred dollars with Beast, and warned everyone that the heroin was pure. A few guys made some phone calls, and soon after that, some girls joined us. That's when the celebration began. Renee came home accompanied by the members of the Sweet Inspirations, and the celebration was elevated to the level of a party with celebrities in attendance.

Slim made eye contact with me from across the crowded room. He nodded his head in the direction of the empty kitchen, indicating that he wanted me to meet him there. To my surprise, he handed me a thousand dollars, and informed me that he was going to take me downtown the next day. Downtown was where everyone went to shop, so I became very excited. I couldn't wait to tighten up my wardrobe with the money I now had. I had never gone shopping with such a large sum of money.

I met a girl named Kathy at the party that night. Kathy was extremely attractive. She had the type of beauty that made men look twice, and then stare. She was the first woman I had ever seen wearing an afro hairdo. Her hair was jet black and perfectly shaped. Her high yellow skin was flawless, and the contrast between the color of her hair and her skin tone enhanced her strikingly gorgeous features. The colorful mini dress she wore was made of a clinging material that clung to every curve of her slim body. Slim tried to talk to her, but she wasn't a sporting lady, and found no reason to continue the conversation. She was sincerely interested in getting to know me, and remained near me the remainder of the time we were at the party.

She told me to call her Kat. Kat talked fast and cursed a lot. I found her to be quite attractive, but there was a different type of chemistry between us. Eventually I had to leave for work, and she asked if I would mind if she accompanied me. She already knew Jerome and Beast, and felt that this would be the perfect opportunity to check out their new spot. I was elated by the thought of everyone seeing us leave together, and even more excited by the reactions I would receive from those who would witness my entrance with such a knockout looking woman when we arrived. I had money, so although the spot was only four blocks away, I called a taxi cab.

Jerome personally answered the door to let us in once we arrived. He was excited to see Kat and yelled loudly, "Young Tone done brought fine ass young Kat to the house! I was amazed at how popular Kat was. The spot was crowded, but everyone knew who she was.

Jerome had gotten a record player and a couple of albums for the spot. At first, I thought two albums wouldn't be enough to keep us entertained, but how wrong I was. The albums were entitled, Hot Buttered Soul by Isaac Hayes, and Eddie Harris and Les McCann's, Compared to What. She kept me company as I took care of business the entire night. We talked, laughed, snorted heroin, smoked and drank Cold Duck as the music set a peaceful euphoric, atmosphere.

I enjoyed spending time with Kat. She always seemed to notice things that I had never paid any attention too. A good example of that was when she pointed out how Jerome would nod off, when he was high off heroin. It was quite entertaining to watch him asleep on his feet, bent at the waist with his head so low that it was nearly to his knees, all while trying to smoke a cigarette, and hold a conversation. He wasn't completing any of the tasks at hand.

He couldn't stand because he kept nodding off to sleep. The long ash at the end of his cigarette was all the evidence necessary to prove the cigarette in his hand wasn't being smoked. He couldn't hold a conversation because of the continuous pauses in his attempts to form sentences. The pauses came about as a result from effects of the drugs. Occasionally he would complete a sentence, but most of the time he'd fall asleep in midsentence, and would awaken trying to complete the sentence, no matter how long ago the conversation had ended. We found his antics so amusing the word, bent, became the way Kat and I would describe being extremely intoxicated. It wasn't long before nearly everyone was using the word, bent, to describe being extremely intoxicated instead of the word high.

Sleepy tried to talk to Kat, but she cut his lame attempt

into ribbons, with her sharp tongue and quick wit. I couldn't help but to laugh out loud. My laughing wasn't going to help improve our working relationship, but the damage was done. I sensed that he would become my adversary, so I made a mental note to be more cautious in his presence.

As I walked Kat home the next morning, she too expressed concerns about Sleepy. "You watch yourself around that patched eye wearing muthafucka. I don't trust him. I was watching him watching you, and he can't stand yo muthafucken ass!" We walked a little further in silence before she added, "He would fuck you up his muthafucken self, if he believed he had a chance. He's afraid of you, and ain't nothing more dangerous than a coward muthafucka, and I'm telling you he's one.

To my surprise, Kat lived on 128th street across the alley from my Aunt's house. Her mother was on the front porch sweeping, when we walked up. She introduced me to her mother, and as soon as her mother started talking, it was obvious where Kat got her fast talking and witty vocabulary. She talked to Kat like she was a grown woman. I understood why once a cute baby girl came running out of the house. Her arms were stretched out, as she gleefully called out to her mother. Kat smiled broadly, as she lifted the baby into her arms. Kat proudly introduced me to her daughter. That was quite a feat back in the sixties. Having babies out of wedlock was frowned upon. Kat was only one year older than me, and had a very healthy attitude about being a young, single, teen mom. We all entered the house, and Kat introduced me to all five of her brothers and sisters.

Her sister Kari had a birthmark that covered the left side of her face. The mark was a discoloration, and even with the birthmark she was drop dead gorgeous, with full inviting lips. She had a pleasant personality, and was a natural gracious host. She immediately went out of her way to make me feel comfortable and at home. I began to feel like a member of the family as a direct result of her hospitality.

I was fed a hearty bowl of beef stew. It was as filling as it was delicious. We laughed and talked as though I had been there to visit plenty of times before. Kari was into modern dancing, so she put on a black leotard and performed privately for me in the living room, once everyone left us alone. I became very aroused watching her spread her legs into the split position, while rolling her hips to the rhythm and melody of a jazz song by Wes Montgomery entitled, Bumping On the Sunset. I hated to leave, but Slim had promised to take me shopping downtown, and I wasn't about to miss out on it. I promised Kari that I would return, and left out the back door located in the kitchen.

I found Slim waiting for me once I arrived. He was accompanied by a fella that looked exactly like him. The only difference was the guy had a lighter skin tone, and long, dark, naturally curly hair. Slim introduced him to me, "Tone meet my little brother Harold." he said with a nod of his head in Harold's direction. Then he said, "Harold meet Tone." Harold and I exchanged the usual pleasantries that occurred on those rare occurrences when people are genuinely happy to make an acquaintance, and we left. Slims' green Eldorado was parked in front of the house. Although he had told me about his car, it was my first time seeing the car he called his pimpmobile. As I climbed into the backseat of the car Slim asked me, "Did you let that girl georgia you last night?"

"Hell naw!" I responded, as though I found the question insulting. I was familiar with the term georgered. The way it was explained in the Book by Iceberg Slim, georgia was when a whore or a pimp got tricked into having sex for free. A huge smile came across Slims' face, and he chuckled as though he found my answer amusing.

"I'm proud of you man. For a minute, I thought you might be a tender dick muthafucka, or a bust freak." he replied. He truly loved me like I was his younger biological brother. He lit up a joint, started the engine, and pulled away from the curb. We listened to The Jazz Crusaders rendition of the Beatles' popular hit song entitled, Eleanor Rigby, from the Crusaders album, Lighthouse 68, on the radio. Although Slim was twenty-one, and Harold was only eighteen, we all were avid jazz fans. Harold and I became better acquainted as we enjoyed the music, the smooth luxurious ride of the Cadillac, and smoked a couple of more joints of the marijuana, all while Slim maneuvered the car through traffic.

During the ride downtown, Harold and I found out that we shared a lot in common. We both adored Slim, and looked up to him like younger brothers often do. It was quite evident he was our hero.

We went to Cousin's, Louis the Haters', Seblys' Shoes, Stones, Hudson's department store, City Slickers, and most of the popular stores. Every time Slim brought an outfit, he brought one of a different color for me and Harold. Harold and I both had tried to offer to pay on several different occasions, but Slim refused to let us spend one red cent.

He even paid for us to eat steak for dinner at the famous Newport Flames. As we ate dinner, Slim explained to us that all we had were one another. "All we have are each other, but you must never depend on anyone but your damn self. Always find a way to stand on your own two. When you depend on others, you're setting yourself up for a guaranteed disappointment."

I had bags full of the latest fashions, and I still had a pocket full of cash. I was feeling so good that I wanted to talk to Slim about Kari, so I told him all about her. I didn't expect him to respond as harshly, nor to sound so bitter, "Fuck that girlfriend boyfriend bullshit!" he growled. "You were born to pimp hoes, and that's just being real about shit. If you don't learn how to get hoe money, nigga you don't eat. You have to pimp or die! Get that through your fucking head!"

Slim said, "It's time for you to get yourself a bottom hoe, and start building your stable. You do know what those things are don't you?" Once again, Iceberg Slims' book had prepared me for the street jargon. I knew exactly what Slim was talking about. Your bottom hoe was your main woman. Her responsibilities included assisting her pimp in the running of the daily operations of the stable. She also mentored all the new turnouts until they had a feel for the profession. Prostitution is a dangerous profession, and a simple mistake has proven to be a deadly one on many occasions.

Slim continued, "You have to find a sporten lady, and step to her. Ask if she's a sporten lady. If she is indeed in the life, you should tell her that you're a pimp, and pimps and hoes are supposed to be together. Tell her that you like her makeup. Then you catch her off guard. Spread your arms like this." he said as he spread his arm out by his side with the palms of his hands turned up as though he were presenting himself. "Then ask the bitch, 'How do you like mines?' If you're dressed properly, and possess the correct mannerism, she won't have any other choice except to admit she does like your style. Tell the bitch that today is her lucky day, and you're about to open the windows of your mind, and shower her meager existence with unimaginable knowledge and wisdom, if she got choosing money." He turned to me and said, "Now let me hear you try it"

I tried to say it, but I wasn't comfortable with the lyrics. I stumbled over the line, and began laughing at myself. This made Slim extremely angry, and in a serious tone of voice he asked, "How the fuck you expect a bitch to take you seriously, if you can't take yourself seriously? Now stop giggling like a little bitch, and try to deliver the line like you fucken mean the shit! This is work young nigga! If you ain't serious about pimping, don't waste my fucken time!" Needless to say, that was the very last time he ever had to check me about not taking life seriously.

The Spring gave way to a blazing hot Summer, and with it came my birthday. I was turning sixteen, but I was still being haunted by the memories of my twelfth birthday. Any desires I had to celebrate, which happened to reach the surface, were quickly dampened and reburied among the other potential memories. That is until I informed Slim that I had never received oral sex. After overcoming the initial shock, he regained his composure, and promised to celebrate my birthday by making one of his new turnouts give me and all the fellas some head. For the very first time, since being raped, I was able to look forward to my birthday with anticipation. His newest girl was Niki. She was only thirteen, and anxious to prove that she was a thoroughbred. and ready to work the fast tracks for Slim.

It never occurred to me that Slim was a pedophile, because most pimps had teenagers in their stables. It only enhanced their image in our eyes to see pimps with the youngest and prettiest girls in our communities willing to perform unthinkable acts at their whim. To us, they had game, and we considered them to be ultimate players. They seemed to have all the answers to every single question you may have about women, but in fact these men were simply members of an exclusive group of pedophiles, who took advantage of a lot of children. I say most pimps, but there were some pimps who had full grown women stables.

The birthday celebration turned out to be a huge disappointment. We were all unhappy with the way the sessions were conducted, but Niki was Slims' hoe to use as he saw fit. He saw my birthday only as the perfect opportunity to test his newest girl, and he was very pleased with the results.

A few days later, as I was hanging out on the corner shooting dice, my father suddenly drove up. He got out of his car after pulling it on top of the curb, and demanded that I get in his car. I refused, and my world suddenly exploded with a rush of pain on the side of my face. It was a struggle to catch my balance, but I was able to do so, as the realization of my father's actions sunk in. He had struck me. My father and I look a lot alike, and the way he was talking to me, made it was obvious that he was my father, so no one attempted to intervene.

I was furious! I couldn't believe that after all the time which had passed, he still believed he could bully me like I was still a child. My first reaction was to make sure that he understood that he had just committed a costly infraction. I actually growled in a harsh tone, as I made the announcement loud enough for him and everyone in attendance, to clearly hear, "That's your last time putting your muthafucken hands on me." I spun on the ball of my feet, and with a few steps I had broken into a full sprint stride.

I had to get to my aunt's house, but I had to beat my father there. My heart pounded and felt heavy inside my chest as I ran. My only chance of beating my father to the destination would be to take a shot cut through the alley. Slim had begun teaching Bumpy how to pimp also, and I knew Bumpy was there with Sonia, his new potential prostitute. Sonia was his fist prospect for the position of a bottom hoe.

More importantly, I knew a loaded, single barrel, sawed off shotgun was there. I needed to gain possession of the shotgun in order to gun down my father. There was no doubt in my mind what my father's intentions would be. I had a death wish, but I was equally as determined to never lay my life down. I embraced the quote, "Die young and have a good-looking corpse." but not today. It was a perfect day to demand justice, and extract a little revenge from life, and as far as I was concerned, the only way that was going to happen, would be if I lived.

Most days Slim would have been around, and I would've had his pistol in the small of my back, but there was a serial killer stalking prostitutes, and he had to fulfill his responsibilities as the protector of his stable. My father hopped in his car in hot pursuit, but I knew a short cut that was not accessible for motor vehicles. I heard his tires squeal as the car came to a sudden stop, assuring me that I would beat him to my destination.

"Where's the gat?" I yelled to Bumpy as I enter the house. I had tricked my father into following me, and I led him towards an alley that was too threatening for the tires of his vehicle. He was forced to turn around and travel down the street. That gave me enough time to beat him to the house on foot, but I had merely minutes to prepare for his arrival, so every second was precious.

I found Bumpy and Sonia in the bed room barely dressed, and trying to put their clothes back on. "It's under the bed" he answered, "...What's wrong?" Without answering I dove under the bed, and grabbed the shotgun. I heard the tires of my father's car squeal in protest, as he slammed on its' breaks. I positioned myself in front of the entrance, approximately seven feet away from the front door. I could hear my father's footsteps on the creaky wooden porch, as he approached the entrance to the house.

Bumpy peeped out the window and saw a man with such a strong resemblance to me that he knew instinctively that he was my father. He tackled me before I was able to level the weapon, to get a shot off. As my father entered the house he saw us on the floor, as well as the shotgun, and realized instantly what it was I was trying to do. He immediately pounced on me, and began pounding his fist into my face.

I don't know where or how he got possession of an extension cord, but he had one in his hands. Instead of hitting me with the extension cord, he wrapped it around my neck. He was choking me so tightly, it was impossible for me to breath. I was about to pass out when I observed Bumpy picking up the shotgun with my peripheral vision. He put the weapon to my father's head and ordered him to stop. "I didn't stop him from killing you just to allow you to kill him!" he yelled at the top of his lungs. My father stopped choking me as he responded, "Okay! Okay, but I'm taking him to juvenile." "That's cool too, but I'm not going to watch you kill him." Bumpy replied.

My father took me to the County Youth Home, on Junction and Warren, hogtied with the extension cord. The officials were surprised, shocked and amazed by the condition of my face, the way I was being escorted, and welts around my neck, so I was taken into custody. I was given a bar of soap that smelled like laundry detergent, along with some towels. After I had taken a shower, I was given a yellow tee shirt, a pair of blue jeans, a pair of old grey socks, badly in need of elastic, some underwear, a pair of low cut gym shoes, and ordered to get dressed.

After answering some health questions for a beautiful, black, sexy, young nurse, I was escorted to a second-floor housing unit called 2N. The information a male supervisor named Mr. Foster gave me, proved to be quite helpful. He explained how I would be taken to court the next morning to appear before Judge Washington, and at that time the judge would decide if I were to be released into the care of my parent or remain held in custody until the date of my next court appearance.

I had a restless night. I had begun experiencing withdrawal symptoms, and without any heroin there was nothing I could do about it. Eventually the night gave way to the day, and I found myself standing before Judge Washington. I was sweating profusely, and trembling as though I were exposed to an artic chill. It was obvious that I was ill. The judge noticed it also, and ordered that I remain in custody for a month, and brought back before him at that time. Both of my parents were there, and I had never seen my mother look more confused or hurt, as she did when they escorted me from the courtroom.

That evening I became extremely ill after I had been transferred to housing unit 5N. I had a serious addiction to heroin, and I was badly in need of a fix. I felt as though I were coming down with an intensified version of the flu. My nose was running, my head was pounding, I felt chills in my back, all my joints ached, and I couldn't stop throwing up. Between the burning feeling in my esophagus, the regurgitation, and my nose running constantly, I found it very difficult to breath.

I was taken to see the nurse, and as ill as I was, I still looked forward to absorbing her beauty, and inhaling the sweet essence of her perfume. She told me how much she hated to see me suffering, but there was really nothing she could do. She gave me a ten milligrams valium tablet, a couple of aspirin, and some vitamins. It helped a little, but for the next three days I suffered through the agony of the withdrawal symptoms until they eventually subsided.

The County Youth Home was so overcrowded, that it was necessary for some of us to sleep on the floor. Those of us who had to sleep on the floor were referred to as overflow. We had to pile our mattresses up in a closet every morning until someone was released, or a room became available. The wait was never too long. A room usually became available within a couple of weeks at the most. Most of the time a guy's parents would pay the bond to have their son released into their custody.

Since I had been turned in by my father, I wasn't there for any crime I had committed. I was an exception to the rule. My father had placed me in kiddie jail. I was the main topic of conversation among the staff. Everyone wanted to see the heroin addicted kid who was beaten, hogtied, and drugged to the facility to be admitted by his father.

Surprisingly everyone seemed to like me, and came by to tease me daily about my situation. Mr. Foster, Mr. Dyer, Mr.Crowder, Mr. Brewer, and Mr. Ford visited me every day. Mr. Ford took special interest in me. When I asked him why he did so much to help me, his response was that he believed I had a whole lot of potential, and I could achieve some great accomplishments, if I gave myself a chance at living instead of seeking opportunities to risk throwing my life away.

My condition improved, and I regained enough strength to start attending classes. In the mornings, I attended Mr. Green's class. Officially he taught Social Studies and English, but he also gave us life lessons. He taught us things a man should know, and needed to know and understand about his role in society. He would talk to us like we were grown men, but he never passed on an opportunity to point out the fact that we were still boys.

He taught us how people lived in other parts of the world. We learned about customs, and how principals and morals differed, depending upon the culture. He taught us how to break down sentences, and how to recognize the different parts of a sentence. I enjoyed his class, and his teaching techniques immensely. I looked forward to seeing Mr. Green and learning something new every day. He made the world make sense to me. He also rewarded us for perfect scores with candy bars.

In the afternoon, we were fortunate to have Mr. Grant Holcomb for math. He was a college basketball star at State University in the fifties, and played professionally with the Harlem Globe Trotters. He played with the Globe Trotters at the time that Connie Hawkins and Wilt Chamberlin were also members of the team. He told us numerous stories about his playing days, and I enjoyed each and every one of the stories unmeasurably, however, what I enjoyed most was the way he made math fun. First of all, he enlightened us to the fact we knew more about math than we realized. Most of us had worked with measurments when diluting drugs for consumption, solved money issues using math, and in some instances, we used algebra or geometry. Afterwards, we would have an absolute ball learning better ways to solve math problems.

Every day after we had completed our math lessons, Mr. Holcomb would take us to the gym to compete on the basketball court until it was time to go. To make sure we played hard, and to make things interesting we played for candy bars. Mr. Holcomb supplied the candy bars, and we would split up into teams of three, to play three on three half court. Mr. Holcomb would play with us, and he was always a captain with the first pick. He always chose me first, and we always won. I got in great shape, I had plenty of candy bars, and I was being taught the game of basketball by one of the greatest of all time. More importantly was the fact that

I had a renewed interest in education. I not only wanted to attend high school, I wanted to also graduate.

My parents had begun visiting me every weekend. I was very surprised because I didn't expect them to care about me enough to visit. They had purchased a house on 128th Street, and informed me that if I wanted to come home to live, I would be welcomed. I thought that it was great news. I was tired of living like an adult. More than anything I wanted to enjoy being just a high school kid. I had changed, and I was ready for change.

After thirty days, the judge ruled that I be released into the custody of my parents. I was excited about the house once we parked in front of it. The house was huge. It had a full basement and five bedrooms. My mother showed me the room I was to share with my brother Albert, and left me alone to get settled in.

As I walked around the upper level of our new home, I noticed there was a row of windows overlooking the street in front of the house. I was amazed upon looking out the window. There was a long, midnight blue Cadillac limousine parked in front of the house across the street. A tall, fat, light skinned, man walked out of the house with a strikingly beautiful woman on his arm. Her name was Marty Blue, and the man who was escorting her was the famous Blues singer, Johnny Blue. He and his wife had recently been blessed with a baby girl and they named her Tab.

I fell in love with Marty at first sight. She was tall, slim, and very shapely. She was a mulatto, and an extremely sharp dresser. Her hair was very straight, shiny, long and jet black. She wore it pulled back tightly into a ponytail. Whenever she smiled, her pearly white teeth and a gold tooth with a diamond in the center of it were revealed. An explosion of brilliant colored lights would flash from the diamond and enhance the beauty of every one of her smiles. That was the first time I tried to imagine what it would be like to be her boyfriend. I watched as the limousine driver assisted them by holding the door as they climbed into the back seat. I was mesmerized, and I couldn't take my eyes off the limousine until it had turned the corner and was out of my sight.

Snapping out of the blissful state made me want to leave the house for some fresh air. There were things that I needed to do. I had to go up to Clark High School to register, as well as stop by the spot to pick up my clothes. The school was located in a neighborhood that was made up of predominantly Hispanic people, directly across the street from Clark Park.

Upon arriving at the school, I went directly to the administration office. After a brief check a counselor inform me that I had been suspended from all Newport Public Schools. I wasn't going to be admitted to Clark, and would be denied admissions to any Newport public schools. I was totally crushed and disappointed. Mr. Ford had convinced me to return to school, stay off drugs, and to try to do things the right way. I felt as though I had no choice after the encounter other than returning to the life I had become accustom to. I went back to the spot to reclaim my job and my room.

Rodger, Jerome, Beast, Kat and of course Sleepy were all in attendance at the spot when I arrived. They seemed genuinely happy and excited to see me. I mean everybody except Sleepy that is. I was glad that he wasn't trying to fake like he was happy to see me. It saved me the trouble of having to exert the energy that would have been necessary to match his attempt at being deceitful. He had been placed in charge of the house during my absence, however Jerome wasted no time. He quickly announced that since I was back, that I was once again in charge of the house. Sleepy reluctantly turned the sack, the money, and the pistol over to me.

Another development that had occurred during my absence was my cousin Rodger had been hired as a door man. It was my understanding that Jerome would keep both Rodger and Sleepy on as doormen and Rodger would work most of his hours when I was there. I was thrilled with the arrangements and looked forward to working with my cousin. I knew Rodger and I would work well together. I worked until Rodgers shift had ended, then I asked Beast, who had recently arrived, if he would cover for me while I took care of some business. He agreed, but under the conditions that I would sit down with him that night, and allow him to teach me how to cut and cap heroin into capsules. It was impossible for me to conceal the excitement I was overcome with. This was an automatic promotion up to partnership which would mean an increase in my cash flow significantly. I was so distracted and consumed by the joyful emotions that come with accomplishments, that I didn't notice the expression on Sleepy's face. Kat noticed it immediately, and pull me out of hearing range of everyone and warned me once again about Sleepy.

"You better watch that patch eyed muthafucka. I can see the hate for you in his heart. He means you no good." I took her in my arms and hugged her. I kissed her on her cheek, thanked her for sharing her concerns with me, and promised that I would keep one eye on my back, and the other on Sleepy.

Once she realized I was leaving, she insisted upon leaving with me. We left the spot with Rodger, headed to his house. On the way there, we stopped at Bill's beer and wine store. The store was located on the same corner that my father and I had our horrific altercation.

After we had spent some time with Rodger, Black Otis, and Renee getting bent, I realized just how much I missed them all. I told them all about the plans I had, and how everything I had planned fell apart right before my eyes earlier that very day. I was enjoying myself so much that I hated to leave, but I had to take care of myself, which meant I had to get back to work. Beast was covering for me. Besides, tonight would prove to be a very valuable life altering night, once I was able to retain the things that Beast was about to teach me about cutting and capping heroin. Kat and Bumpy refused to allow me to go to work alone. Bumpy called a City taxi cab, and insisted on paying the full fair once we arrived.

Sleepy answered the door, and immediately informed me that Beast was in the bedroom waiting on me. Kat and Bumpy went to the bar to entertain themselves while they waited on me. Beast had unfolded the card table in the room, and was using its' surface as a work station.

A small flour sifter, along with a package wrapped in aluminum foil, sat on a dinner plate upon the table. The table also consisted of two large brown jars, with white labels on them. In bold dark print the word, lactose, was on one of them, and Quinine was printed on the other. A plastic playing card, metal measuring spoons on a ring, and a box of empty red gelatin capsules were the final ingredient to create the penny caps. "Pay close attention to what I'm doing, and how I'm doing it, cause you're going to be doing all of this shit, by yourself from now on." Beast informed me, as he situated the contents on the table. He removed the aluminum package from the sifter, opened it, and by using the plastic playing card like a shovel, he was able to scoop enough of the pure drug to fill the spoon. The spoon was over flowing with the drug. He simply used the playing card's edge, to rake the access drugs off the spoon, thereby leveling its' contents.

After measuring each spoon full he would empty the drugs into the sifter until he had measured out three quarter spoons. He held the sifter about three inches above the plate and tapped on the side of the sifter making the white powder fall onto the plate as he spread it around. Once he emptied the heroin onto the plate, he used the same technique to measure out twenty-seven spoons of lactose. He sat the sifter on the plate, and emptied the lactose inside of it. He repeated the method of making the white powder fall through the sifter by tapping the side of it with the spoon. He measured out three spoons of quinine and repeated the same process.

He used the playing card like a shovel once again. Instead of being used to scoop, it was used like a mixer to fold the ingredients together. The mixture was then run through the sifter several times to assure the ingredients were thoroughly mixed. He turned all of his attention on me and asked, "Do you have any questions so far?" I shook my head to indicate that I had no questions, and I completely understood each step of the process he had demonstrated thus far. A huge smile flashed across Beast's face. I wasn't sure if he was smiling because I was able to retain the lesson, or because he was about to be relieved of the daily chore, or because he enjoyed cutting and capping the drugs. The mixture was known by a few names in the city. One of the names was scrambled eggs, but most street people called it mixed jive, or dog food.

When I first became addicted to heroin, I didn't even know what it was. That was because it was called by so many different names, other than heroin, but it wasn't called heroin. The white powdery substance had names such as Smack, Horse, Boy, Skagg, Strong, Dog food, Pee... et

The Italian gangsters of Newport flooded the streets of the urban dwellers with cheap heroin, as they had done in most urban communities across America, with devastating results. Many black men, including myself, sold the poison in our own communities. Our neighbors, members of our own families, and friends, in hopes of making enough money to escape the devastating horrors and powerful grip of poverty. All we actually succeed in doing, was destroying the lives of many of our people, while annihilating the structure as well as the very foundation of our communities and families. The trend continued, as the white man's pockets were once again lined, by exploiting black people. Some say these were gangsters, but I say they all were gangsters... Including the United States government

Beast removed an empty capsule from the box. He separated it, opened his mouth wide, and breathed into the opened end of the capsule. He pressed the opened end of the capsule down on top of the mixture over and over again. The moisture from his breath made the drugs stick to the inside the capsule, and he repeatedly pressed the capsule on the pile of drugs until it had filled. He then put the capsule together again, and placed the filled capsule inside the empty sifter.

"You think you can do that?" he asked. "That's easy!" I answered with confidence.He watched me closely as I made a few, from the beginning to completion. After being satisfied I was capable of completing the task at hand, he stood and said, "Come get me when you're done." He left the room, and closed the door behind himself. It didn't take long at all for me to complete the task, and rejoin everyone. I enjoyed the company, and making money the rest of the night.

After cutting and capping the drugs on my own a few times, Jerome and Beast showed me where in the closet the drugs were hidden. They also taught me how to keep an accurate account of everything. I was warned to never allow anyone admittance into the bedroom, and to keep it locked whenever I left the house with a combination lock they provided. Sleepy had a few expensive articles of clothing that he wanted to keep in the bedroom closet as oppose to keeping them in the hall closet where everyone had open access, and the opportunity to steal them. I allowed him to keep a few things in the bedroom closet, with the understanding that I would retrieve anything he needed.

Slim surfaced after a couple of weeks. The serial killer had been apprehended, so it was alright for him to venture away from the track, and leave his stable unattended. We went to my aunt's house, because he insisted we had a serious issue to resolve. There was a hint of the smellt of burning leaves in the evening air, but othere than that, the evening air was refreshingly cool and crisps. The leaves on the trees had already completed their annual color changing ritual, which made even the most seasoned travelers among us, gaze in star struck amazement and appreciation. The entire state is especially beautiful during the fall, when the leaves have changed colors. On this particular sunny day, Mother Nature was showing off her brilliance as well as her creativity.

Bumpy was standing on the corner talking to a couple of guys when we walked up. Upon recognizing me, he flashed a broad smile, and his eyes lit up like headlights. He walked up to me and gave me a warm welcoming embrace. "Are you alright?" he asked. I'm fine now that I'm out. How you've been?" I asked. He slowly released me from his grip, and while doing so, he continued to stare into my eyes. He apologized for stopping me from killing my father. I stopped him in his tracks right there, and assured him I wasn't upset or disappointed by the actions he had taken at all. I then made him understand how thankful I was to have not murdered my father in premeditated, cold blooded murder.

Bumpy had some marijuana, and suggested that we went to the house to get high. I thought it was an excellent idea, and laughed at the humor that Kat interjected by correcting me and reminding me, "We don't get high. We get bent!" Bumpy and Rodger had puzzled expressions on their faces, because they had no idea what was so funny to me and Kat. Getting bent was still an inside joke between us at that time.

After we arrived at the house, Bumpy addressed me and Kat by asking, "What's going on between ya'll? Ya'll go together or something?" Kat quickly responded, "No! That's my brother." Bumpy added, "That's my brother too, so I guess that makes us all family." I admired and adored them both. The way they both had claimed me as a family member made me feel extremely special.

I couldn't wait to see Slim. Bumpy told me that Slim was upset with him when he heard about what had happened to me. He was extremely angry with Bumpy, but I assured Bumpy that as far as I was concerned, that wasn't the case. Not only was I not upset, I was very thankful that his actions had prevented me from killing my father. During my incarceration, I was enlightened to a fact. Even though my father and I found it difficult to coexist, or to get along for that matter, we didn't hate each other. We shared a hostile love, and sometimes our love bore strange fruit. We both demanded the utmost respect, and because of our stubbornness, we would go beyond clashing. We would often collide, and serious, heated battles would occur.

After a few days Slim came by the spot to see me. "I thought I was grooming you to be my pimping partner, and now I hear you're a dope man! What's up?" he asked. I laughed and tried to explain to him how I wasn't trying to get into the dope business, it just happened. He added, "Even Bumpy done gave up pimping, and is concentrating on selling dope."

"Damn!" was my initial reaction, then I thought of Sonia. "What happened to that hoe he turned out?" I asked. "Who she with?" I continued. I seriously wanted to know. Slim quickly responded, "She's an outlaw now." An outlaw was a prostitute working without a pimp. I had noticed her staring at me on several different occasions. According to the rules of the game, a working prostitute is in violation if she holds eye contact with a pimp, other than her own. The violation is called being caught out of pocket. Since she was Bumpy's hoe, I never called her out on it.

Slim informed me that Bumpy had fallen in love with a girl named Brandy. She lived right next door to Kat with her mother on 128th street. She also has a new born baby boy. I had just seen Bumpy, and he failed to mention anything about these latest developments. I made a mental note to find Sonia, and knock her off. There was no doubt in my mind, she wanted to belong to me. It was in her eyes. There was something about the way she stared at me.

"I've got another job for you and Bernard, if you still want to get down like that." I could tell by the way Slim asked the question that he was testing the waters, so to speak, to see if I still wanted to become an accomplished stick up man. "Hell yeah!" I replied. The holiday season was upon us, and I had to get my bankroll together, so I could do it up in the grandest of style possible. I hopped in the front passenger's seat, better known as the shotgun seat. Slim turned the keys in the ignition, and steered the car from the curb. We had to find Bernard. There was money to be taken!

We found Bernard at his parent's apartment. The job was easy, and I received eight hundred dollars as my share of the take. All we had to do was rob a beer delivery truck. Afterwards Slim had to return to work, so I had him drop me off at Style's barber shop to get my hair done. Bernard wanted to be dropped off back at his parent's apartment. I was dropped off first since the barber shop was closer, and along the way.

That's when I first met Ape Simmons. He was well known as the beast of the west side. Many believed that he could whip Beast if they were to get into it. I was counted amongst them. A fella once shot Ape five times in the chest with a twenty-two pistol. Ape took away the pistol and pistol whipped the guy to death.

He turned and faced the crowd afterwards, and proclaimed that he was god. He was transported to Penny hospital where he was admitted, and released a few days later. Many who saw him upon his released swore he looked so fit you couldn't tell he was recovering from gunshot wounds to his chest.

He was so huge, that even me being at my size, he referred to me as "Little nigga", and it seemed appropriate. We were sitting next to one another waiting to get our hair done when he turned to me and asked, "Hey little nigga. What's cracken?" I was surprised that he had greeted me. He asked me if I were Slim's younger brother out loud, for everyone to hear the question, as though he already knew what the answer was.

"Yeah." I answered. "How did you know?" I asked.

"I know everything little nigga. Your name is Tone, right?" I was completely astonished by the question, because it proved that he knew who I was, and he was acknowledging me in front of everyone inside the most popular barber shop on the west side. We were talking about weed just before it was his turn to get his hair done. Ron, which was short for Ronald, was Ape's best friend, and since he was the number one barber at that establishment, Ron kept Ape's hair together.

I got my hair done, and caught a cab to the playground where everybody hung out. A lot of the guys my age was playing tackle football without equipment. I was invited to join them, but because of my fresh hairdo, I was forced to decline. I had paid fifteen dollars to get it done, and I wasn't about to throw it all away just to play some ball.

The game was beginning to become quite entertaining. The girls' presence motivated the guys, and they were putting on quite a show of athleticism when suddenly all hell broke loose. Ape Simmons showed up. Some of the guys took off running in order to avoid being free picked by Ape to engage in a physical confrontation. A few decided to gamble on not being picked, and they had remained behind. Ape climbed on top of a picnic table and announced that the playground was closed. Most of the kids found their way to the exits, while most of the guys who stayed behind ended up getting slapped around, and humiliated.

He was headed in my direction when he suddenly recognized me. "Tone! My nigga! Hey man, show me where I can get some of that weed you were telling me about at the shop." I was more than happy to show him, so I agreed to do it. There was no reason to stick around. Ape had disrupted the game and the atmosphere.

Ron drove a 1968 convertible Cadillac Coup Deville. He sat behind the wheel, and three beautiful young girls were in the backseat when Ape and I waked up to the car. He opened the door, and held the seat forward to assist me in getting in the backseat. One of the girls asked if I were his little brother. He flashed a broad smile and answered, "Naw. That's Slims' little brother." The girls all asked in unison, "Slim the pimp?" Ape answered, "Yeah the pimp." They all squealed like excited pigs. I was beginning to get use to the reaction Slim had on women. It happened all the time.

Ape was so popular that whenever anyone mentioned him, you always felt like you knew him personally, because you had heard so much about him. Now I was known as Slims' younger brother, and a close friend of Ape Simmons. He was a huge young man. He stood six feet two, weighed two hundred and sixty-five pounds, of pure muscles. He was only twenty-one years old.

I took him to Preston's place to get the weed, and when we drove up, I noticed Preston's 1970 Fleetwood Cadillac parked in front of the house. Preston was happy to see me. Ape had given me a ten dollar bill, and instructed me to get a nickel bag for both of us. Preston served me himself, and walked out with me to let Ape know that this was his spot. As it turned out, they were good friends and had gotten so busy living their own lives, they had gotten out of touch. They talked for what seemed like hours trying to catch up. We all eventually had to go our separate ways. We were serious hustlers with traps to check, places to go and people to see.

Bumpy and an older guy by the name of Peppers had become partners. Peppers had just been released from prison, and had opened a spot that was very popular among a lot of teenage boys, located on 130th Street and Rich. He and Bumpy went into business together on a spot that was located on 128th Street, next door to Kat's family. I had some spare time on this particular day, so I decided to stop by and check him out. I also wanted information on how to get in touch with Sonia. I wanted to find out for myself, if he truly was indeed in love. Slim had already told me that he was, and it wasn't that I didn't believe him. I always investigate anything that I'm told, regardless of who's the source of the information.

Before I could say a word, I noticed a concerned

expression on his face. He asked, "Man, what you do to Beast?" without even first greeting me. I had no idea what it was he was talking about, so he informed me that Beast had been looking for me, and he was mad as hell. He told me Beast was over Peppers' main spot on 130th, and suggested I immediately catch up with Beast, and find out what was the deal. I had no idea why Beast would be upset with me. I thought that it may have had something to do with the business, so I left and sought him out immediately. I was trying to think of a possible explanation for the urgency, and couldn't think of one solitary reason for Beast to be upset with me.

When I arrived at Pepper's place, Beast was in the kitchen. As always, there were a lot of teenage boys, trying to be thugs, hanging out in the house. They all were in my age range, and even though we seldom hung out together, we had ultimate respect, and genuine concern for the welfare of one another. We were beyond peers. We were comrades. Ours' wasn't a relationship forged by negotiation. Game recognizes game, and we had the qualities of developed conscience minds at an extremely young age. We were able to recognize one another. It was as though we were swept into a pile together involuntarily, and became bonded by fate. This being the case, they all warned me that Beast was in the kitchen asking Peppers questions about how to find me. They had never seen him as upset, and his anger was directed towards me.

The walk to the kitchen seemed like a mile. I had so many unanswered questions running through my mind. When I saw the expression on Beast's face, all the talk I'd heard of his anger towards me was confirmed. He was visibly trying to contain himself as he spoke, "I love you Tone, and I'm not mad at you. A nigga got you to knock on my door the other day. He told you to tell my woman, he wanted her to come outside. He was waiting on the side of the house, and he wanted to talk to her. All I want to know is who that nigga was? That's all." I had absolutely no idea what it was he was talking about, and I told him so.

Peppers spoke up, "Look Tone, it makes no sense to get fucked up trying to protect this nigga, whoever the fuck he is." Once again, I insisted that I didn't know what it was they were talking about. I told Beast that I had never knocked on his door. I made sure that I put emphasis on the word, never.

Beast's responded, "Okay, meet me at my house in an hour. If my old lady says you did knock on our door, and told her a nigga wanted to see her on the side of the house, I'm gonna fuck you up. It's gonna break my heart cause, I loved Roderick, but I'm gonna fuck you up."

All I could do was continue to insist that I was innocent of the allegations, and give my word that I would meet him at his house in an hour. "Don't make me have to come looking fo yo ass neither." he said in a threatening tone of voice that I found offensive as well as insulting.

I assured him once again that I would keep the appointment. "I'll be there. I have nothing to hide. It wasn't me." I could not believe what was happening. As I was leaving the house everyone was begging me to tell Beast who the guy was. Absolutely no one seemed to believe me. I was certain I couldn't beat Beast in a fist fight. I would fight him, but I didn't think I could win. I was afraid, but I wasn't about to run from any man to avoid a fight. It could have been Muhammad Ail threatening to whip my ass, and even the champ would've had to prove to me that he could fulfill that prophecy.

I went to my aunt's house, and some of my cousins were there. My older cousin Lil Ed was there. Because he could shoot pool so well, everyone called him Fast. That was short for Fast Eddie, the legendary pool hustler. My cousin was a tenacious pool hustler, and he also had the skills to fit the name. He stood six feet two inches tall, and weighed well over two hundred and sixty pounds. Rodger, Renee, and Otis were also there. After I informed them of the events that had occurred, they all suggested that I run. We all agreed that I had to be crazy to believe that I could fight Beast, and finish the fight whole. I let them all know that under no terms was I going to run. "If he fucks me up I'd just be fucked up, but I refuse to run from a muthafucka!"

I hung with them until it was time to go. No one volunteered to go with me, and I didn't ask anyone to. We all knew that if they were present during a physical confrontation between me and Beast, and if Beast was beating me badly, they would be looked upon as cowards by the entire neighborhood, if they didn't assist me. I understood, and I didn't want to put any of them in that position, so I struck out to face my problems on my own two feet.

Beast was standing on the front porch when I arrived. He asked if I was sure I wanted to do this. I looked deeply into his eyes and nodded my head. I knew for certain I wasn't lying, so it wasn't too difficult to muster the necessary courage to conceal the emotional turmoil I was in, as a result of the situation. I refused to allow him, or anyone else for that matter, to ever detect fear in me. My plan was to fight, if it became necessary.

The situation made me think of Chance, and how he and his play brother, Chris, once started a fight with the Crane gang. We had just finished watching a new televison series entitled, The Green Hornet, which showcased Bruce Lee demonstrating martial arts. As we were walking and talking about how we had never seen anything like that style of fighting, we came across Clarence. Clarence was the younger brother of Charles Pryor, a high ranking, member of the Crane gang. He was approaching us, walking on the same side of the street, and once we met up, Chance and Chris erupted into a flurry of punches and kicks to various parts of his body. Clarence collapsed to the ground as his body absorbed the blows from the vicious, unexpected attack. Clarence was a meek, humble, passive individual who did nothing to provoke ill feelings from anyone. I refused to join in on the melee.

The Crane gang's name derived from the name of the street the members lived on. Crane was one block from Fisherman. After they had finished beating Clarence, I knew we would face serious consequences because of their actions. That wasn't the reason I didn't join in on the attack though. I genuinely liked Clarence, and I felt as though they had chosen him because they knew he would be an easy victim to attack. In my soul I felt it was a cowardly act provoked by Chris.

The next morning the Crane gang caught Chance and I trying to return home after leaving the A&P market that was located on Main and Crane. Chance didn't want to go, however, his mother insisted that he patronize that particular market, because of their everyday low prices. I didn't have to go, but Chance didn't want to go alone, so he asked me to join him. The same courage I found within myself to accompany him to the market on Crane that morning, was the same courage I summoned to face Beast.

Chance told me to run when we noticed that the gang had spotted us, and were approaching us at a fast pace, but I refused. I wasn't going to leave him to fight the gang alone. I remained by his side, and we gallantly fought as more and more members of the gang continued to arrive and join in on the mayhem.

Suddenly Chance yelled to me "Run!" and once again I responded by letting him know that I wasn't going to leave him. To my surprise, Chance saw a small break in the traffic, and bolted across Main. He made it across the street safely, just as the congested traffic returned, and prohibited the gang's pursuit. He had left me to fight the entire gang alone.

I was only thirteen at the time, but I fought so well even their best fighters weren't able to get me off my feet, and some of them were actually full grown young men. Eventually I realized there were just too many of them for me to fight alone, so I took off running. They caught me a few blocks away by hitting me with a car. While I was laying on the ground, they stomped me and beat me with their baseball bats, but I was used to beatings, and I survived. My father had severely beaten me, and I had survived. What could Beast do to me that hadn't already been done? I believed because I was able to survive fighting an entire gang by myself, at the age of thirteen, I was certainly capable of fighting Beast. The thought of me winning or losing has never be a determining factor in deciding should I fight our not. Making sure I did my best to send that ass to the cemetery, was and will always be considered my only option, as far as I was concerned. No easy victories here.

After Beast and I walked through the door, he led me to a room with an arched entrance. A curtain hung across the door entrance to assure privacy. Beast pulled back the curtain, and a huge bed, which took up the majority of the available space in the room, came into view. Beast's woman was already undressed, and in the bed. Beast asked if I was the guy who knocked on the door that night.

She rose to a sitting position, in order to get a better look at me. Once I saw her face, I knew I had never seen this woman. She was an extremely slim woman with short nappy hair. She wore a white slip with no bra. Her small, firm breast stood up against the pull of gravity with ease. I don't know if her nipples were hard or not, but they were quite visible. She was so ugly I mentally gave her the benefit of the doubt, and imagined that it was possible for her to improve upon her appearance. We had just caught her at a bad moment.

She shook her head and said, "Naw Beast. It was a man, much older than this boy. They don't even look alike."

I was relieved, and when I looked at Beast I noticed that he too had just experienced an exhale moment. I instinctively realized that he was relived not to have to fight his deceased, best friend's cousin, for more reasons than one. From that moment on, Beast had a whole new respect for me. He too had sensed that this was going to be one hell of a fight. He was no longer as certain he was able to predict the outcome of such an encounter.

I asked him what had happened to make him so sure that

it was me who knocked on his door. The way he explained it to me, Sleepy told him that he had witnessed me knocking on the door that night. Sleepy also said he seen the guy, but didn't recognize who he was, but he believed I knew who the guy was, because he saw us talking to one another.

Beast apologized, and stated, "I should've thought about Sleepy's feelings about you before I believed anything he had to say." I accepted his apology, however I was puzzled as to why Beast wasn't as upset with Sleepy as he had been with me. Why wasn't he displaying the same threatening, hostile attitude that he had presented to me? I began to believe that Beast had reservations about getting into it with Sleepy.

Beast and I left his house, headed upstairs. When we stepped outside we both noticed there were people staring out the windows upstairs. Once we got upstairs they all informed us that they were looking out the window because Sleepy had informed them all that Beast and I were going to fight. He had orchestrated the entire situation. I decided at that very moment to make an example out of Sleepy by taking his life at the very first opportunity I got. The proverbial straw had finally broken the camel's back.

I returned to my aunt's house to let my cousins know I was alright. I also gave them a detailed account of the incident. I was still quite upset, and I told them of my plans to eliminate Sleepy. I found their attitudes about the subject amazing. It was as though they thought I was simply venting.

I was disappointed and disgusted by their attitudes. They doubted my assessment of the situation would lead me to the point I would actually commit the ultimate act of violence. I knew their attitudes would soon change, and everyone who thought they knew me, would have to do a reassessment of their opinions. They truly had no clue as to how far I was willing to go.

I was in a hurry to get back to work, and to Sleepy, so I said my good -byes. In order to take advantage of my first opportunity to kill Sleepy, I would have to spend more time there than I usually did. A sacrifice I didn't mind making at all The sooner I was able to take care of the issue, the better, as far as I was concerned

When I arrived, I found Angela there with Kevin. Kevin was there to do Sleepy's hair. Kevin was an excellent barber, and his reputation was solid. Angela was waiting to see me. She and I had flirted with each other from the first time we met, and it wasn't long before she expressed a desire to have sex with me. I felt the same way, and we became lovers. The only time she ever came around was when she wanted to get high and have sex with me. I was happy to see her, but I doubted that I'd have her this night.

Jerome and Beast were also there. Everyone was in the living room watching the Ed Sullivan Show on television. He was introducing a young new singing group named the Jackson Five. A ten year old kid was the lead singer, and they performed two songs. The first song was entitled, I Want You Back. It was already experiencing a lot of attention on the radio. The second song entitled, Who's Loving Who, put the viewing public on notice. The ten year old kid sung the song with so much emotion, that it was hard to believe his heart was too young to have actually experienced the gut wrenching heart ache the song was describing. The future child star was Michael Jackson and his brothers. We all marveled over his brilliant performance and agreed that the kid was headed to the top of the music world.

Beast and Jerome left together headed for The Twenty Grand. The Twenty Grand was a popular night club on 112th where you could go to enjoy some live entertainment, drinks, flirting women on the prowl, and network with other street hustlers. Kevin was doing Sleepy's hair in the bathroom, and Angela and I were on the couch making out. Angela was an amazingly good kisser. We used to make out for hours at a time. She once confessed to how much she loved kissing, and she truly believed that the key to being a great kisser, was to love kissing. She told me I was the best kisser she had ever kissed, and I love kissing. I guess that would give some credence to her statement.

Once Kevin had finished doing Sleepy's hair, Sleepy informed me that he wanted a shirt out of the closet. He was already disappointed that his plan to get Beast upset enough to hurt me had failed. Kevin pulled me to the side, and informed me that while he was doing Sleepy's hair, all he talked about was how he was going to kick my ass himself.

After Sleepy informed me that he wanted a shirt from the closet, he started walking towards the room as though he was going to retrieve the shirt himself. I walked at a quick enough pace to intercept him, and made a maneuver to block his path, all before he actually made it to the room's entrance.

Sleepy pushed me in an attempt to get me out his way, and at the same time pick a fight with me, if I offered any resistance. He pushed me hard enough to knock me off balance. For some reason I thought about that bastard who raped me on my birthday, because I was a child unable to defend myself. I thought about my father beating my ass and choking me damn near to death, and again, it was because I was a defenseless child. I was still a child, but now I was a far cry from being defenseless. I fought to regain my balance, and after doing so, I pulled the .32 Beretta from the small of my back. It seemed like everything happened in slow motion afterwards. Something inside of me was fighting to prevent me from pulling the trigger. I fought off my self-accusing spirit, and leveled the weapon, all while still struggling to pull the trigger.

Eventually the weapon exploded, and sent a slug ripping through his neck, which caused his blood to begin squirting from the mangled wound on the side of his neck. With an expression of shock, horror and disbelief he yelled, "He shot me!" while he ran down the hall towards the living room. A fresh coat of blood splattered on the walls with each and every step he took. To make sure he was dead, I followed him, and continued to pull the trigger until the weapon made the click sound it makes when the hammer hits an empty chamber. I had emptied the majority of the remaining bullets into his body.

I looked around and wondered realistically if it truly were possible to clean up all the blood. Kevin and Angela had locked themselves in the bathroom. They were absolutely convinced that I was going to kill them next, so they locked themselves in the bathroom, and begged me to spare their lives by shouting through the door. That puzzled me, because I was tremendously fond of the both of them. I was even looking forward to letting Kevin do my hair. I wouldn't have to go anywhere. He would come to me where ever I was, just as he had come to Sleepy.

I was also looking forward to having more sex with Angela. I had never had sex with anyone who could move her body the way Angela could. I'm at a loss for words to describe the magnificent pleasures I've experienced with each and every sexual encounter with her. She always made her buttocks twirl in circles while we were doing it. That alone was enough to prevent me from having any thoughts of harming her. She obviously had no idea of how much our sexual encounters meant to me.

The eerie silence was eventually broken with a sudden knock at the door. My heart beat quickened as a sense of panic attempted to sweep over me. I walked to the door as quietly as I could, to make sure that I wouldn't be heard by whoever it was on the other side of the door. I slowly moved the card to the side and peeped out the peephole, and became overjoyed to see it was Rodger.

I quickly let him in, and responded boastfully, more out of nervousness than cockiness, "I believe I killed Sleepy just like I told ya'll I would!" As I led Rodger to the body, I suggested that he help me clean up the blood. While visibly struggling to contain his composure. "Man, we can't clean up all this blood!", he uttered just as a gargling sound escaped Sleepy's limp body. "He's still alive!" Rodger yelled with joy, and to my obvious disappointment. I had no more bullets.

Another knock at the door made the feelings of panic I had just experienced when Rodger knocked. Once again, I quietly peeped out the peephole. It was Beast and my mother's cousin, Chester. I quickly let them in, and I felt a small sense of relief. I was overwhelmed and had no idea of what I should be doing. He had come by to let me know he was leaving. He was moving to Florida to live that very night. Chester knew the streets, and he would know exactly what to do.

The very first thing he did was coxed Angela and Kevin out of the bathroom, and comforted them by assuring them that the shooting was over, and made sure they understood how imperative it was for them to keep what they knew to themselves. Secondly, he made me understand that because of the gun shots, we couldn't possibly know if someone had heard the shots, and called the police or not. Therefore, we couldn't possibly know how much time we had to clean up, before the police would arrive. We all had to get out of there as quickly as possible, to avoid running into the police, and getting interrogated.

"Give me the gun you shot him with. That bitch is going to Florida with me and I'm going to get rid of it down there." I handed him the murder weapon, and he shouted, "Everybody get the fuck out of here! This fool ain't got long to live. John Law might be here any second now."

As we were leaving Monique was standing on her porch motioning for me to come to her house. She lived directly across the street. Everyone continued to go their separate ways, or at least I felt that way, because it seemed like they all were trying to get some distance between us in a hurry. It was a cold winter's night, and Monique wasn't dressed for the weather. She hurried me inside the house, once I had climbed the steps to her front porch.

"You did it didn't you?" she asked as she led me up the stairs that led to the attic.

"Did what?" I asked. She continued, "Kat told me Sleepy has been fucking with you, and he has no idea who he's fucking with. She said that she's afraid you are going to kill Sleepy any day now, and she begged me to look out for you.

Monique was gorgeous. Everybody in the hood had positive things to say about her as a person, and amazing things to say about her beauty. None of the things said were exaggerated. "There's a window in the attic that overlooks the street. We can watch the house from up here." She stated more than suggested. After climbing the stairs, she took a seat, and pointed towards the window.

The belt to her heavy, Blue, terrycloth robe came loose, fell open, and exposed her firm, curvy body, and creamy skin. Monique and I had flirted with one another on many different occasions, and the chemistry between us was undeniable.

My heart was racing, and I was sweating. It was the direct result of the belief I may have just killed a full-grown man for underestimating my ability to defend myself. Monique seemed to get more and more turned on as the events of the possible homicide were unfolding.

The police came, and I wondered out loud, "How will I know if he's dead or not." My mother once told me that they carry dead bodies out from a house, feet first. Because the door was in the back of the house, it was out of my view, and I wouldn't be able to see them exit the house. Monique responded to the question even though she knew the question wasn't directed towards her. "If his face is covered up while they're carrying him on the stretcher, then that means he's dead."

We both stared out the window attentively when they eventually carried him to the ambulance with his face covered. It had taken them so long to bring him out that we both sort of knew that he was dead. When she seen his face covered she couldn't contain herself any longer, but the only thing I could think of at that point was finding Slim. He would know exactly what it was I needed to be doing at that point. I would have to catch up with Monique some other time. I explained to her that I had to go catch up with Slim. She kissed me deeply, and her tongue tasted as sweet as candy. She purred into my ear, in a sultry, very seductive tone of voice, "But I want you to stay."

Too much had happened, and I felt overwhelmed. The only things I was sure of, was my wanting to put as much distance between me and that location as I possibly could, and I was desperate to talk to Slim. Monique stood in her doorway and waved to me as I left on foot. The kitchen light which illuminated from behind her, gave justice to her silhouette, and I wondered why an opportunity to ravish such a stunning woman had to come at such an inopportune moment. The timing couldn't have been worse.

I stopped at Kat's house first. I didn't think he would be there, but I wanted to solicit Kat's valuable assistance in finding him. Kat wasn't home, but Kari was there. From the way she was responding to me, I could tell she hadn't heard anything about the incident. I told her I needed Kat's help because I was in trouble, and I needed to find my brother. "Slims' your brother, right?" she asked.

"Yeah, do you know where he is?" I asked. She explained in detail how she had overheard Kat talking to Brandy about Bumpy, and according to their conversation, Slim and Bumpy were looking for me, but couldn't find me. They had decided to take a break, and were right next door. I left immediately, and found them both there. Bumpy answered the door, while Slim sat at the kitchen table near the door. He had a huge smile on his face. He turned to Bumpy and said, "I told you if we sat still, he would find us."

"I'm glad to see you are alright little bro!" he said as I entered the kitchen. Then he asked, "Why didn't you tell me that there was static between you and Big Beast?" According to the rumors on the streets, I was going to fight Beast. He and Bumpy thought I had already fought Beast, and seeing me appearing not to have so much as a scratch on me, made them even more curious. They wanted to know the whole story, but they had no idea so much had happened.

I told them the whole story, including everything about the confrontation between me and Beast. I explained how that issue had led to the final confrontation between me and Sleepy. They both listened attentively. After I had finished, Slim calmly stated, "You should be cool for tonight, because it just happened, but not much longer after that. There are a lot of guys named Tone in this city, but we have no idea how long it will be before some snitching muthafucka connect the dots, and rat you out. You just need to stay out of circulation until we find out what they know.

He took me to Lauren's apartment. She was one of his new hoes, and he informed her that I would be staying with her for a while. I reminded Slim that I had to leave all my clothes. I didn't take the time to pack before I left. I only took time to retrieve the drugs. I kept all the money because of Beast's continuous insistence, but I gave him all the drugs. Slim told me not to concern myself with the clothes I left behind. He then reminded me that Beast lived downstairs and as soon as the police wrap up their investigation, Beast could easily go upstairs and get my clothes for me. He warned me not to go anywhere, for any reason, unless I wanted to risk going to the penitentiary for the rest of my life.

As soon as he left, Lauren changed into a robe and panties. She stood about five foot ten, with medium size breast and a frame accentuated by thick hips and thighs. Her hair was red, long, and wavy. She wore it down her back, with a part in the middle. She was a beautiful girl, and you truly couldn't tell if it were her hazel eyes or her full lips that enhanced her loveliness. She had a large buttock that was shaped like a black woman's rump, so I asked, "Do you have some black in you?" She looked into my eyes, smiled and answered, "No."

She made it quite obvious when she leaned forward, and slid her tongue into my mouth that she intended to lay with me for days. I began kissing her on her neck between bouts of sucking on her tongue. The more I kissed her, the more relaxed I became. My thoughts and feelings from all of the day's activities began to fade. She suggested we retire to the bedroom.

Her bedroom had a box spring and a mattress on the floor stacked on top of one another to serve as a bed. The bed was queen size with dark Blue sheets on it. There was a Blue and red comforter with an abstract design on the makeshift bed. A couple of milk crates stacked on top of each other served as night stands on each side of the bed. A small screen television also sat on milk crates which served as a television stand in one corner of the room. There was a stereo system next to a window that consisted of a turntable and a radio. She turned the radio on, and left the room to get some wine from the kitchen. On the floor was an album cover with a white substance on it that I recognized as heroin. When she returned to the room, she was carrying a bottle of wine and a couple of plastic cups. Isaac Hayes was singing, Shaft, on the radio.

She had observed my heightened interest in the powder on the album cover. "You want to smoke some weed, or snort some blow?" she asked. I responded by informing her I had a strong taste for both. A sly smile came across her face as she stated, "We're going to have some fun! Now get out of those clothes, and get ready for bed.. What are you waiting for, an invitation?"

I preferred injecting heroin, to calm the complaining, gnawing, grumbling, giant monkey I carried around on my back, but I would settle for blowing. I knew it was best that I got the drugs into my system by any method that was available, to avoid getting ill.

I took my clothes off and almost as soon as I sat on the bed, Amy's eyes widened with excitement. She noticed the needle marks on my arms. "You're a shooter!" she asked as she jumped up, ran to the closet and pulled out a shoe box. When she opened the box, I saw the box was full of all the paraphernalia necessary to inject heroin. I too became excited. There was a rubber tube to be used as a tourniquet. The pressure makes the veins stand out, and therefore easier to pierce with a needle. She also had several eyedroppers with a rubber band tightly wrapped around the base of the dropper to reinforce it. There were at least five needles of different sizes. A couple of silver spoons, a candle and a pack of matches concluded the collection.

She tied the rubber tube around her forearm, slapped the back of her hand, and attentively searched for a bulging vein. We had already place a sizeable amount of heroin in a spoon, added a few drops of water, and heated the drugs and water with a match until it came to a boil. We now had a brown potent liquid, which smelled like vinegar, but could easily be drawn up into the eyedropper.

Now we had to make sure we would be able to successfully pierce a vein. We did this with a method known as a water hit. The dropper was filled half way with water, and a needle was placed on its' end. That brought us to the point where it was time to pierce the vein we had located bulging on the back of her hand.

"Can you hit me?" she asked. She was asking me could I administer the drugs into her veins. There were dangers that one had to look out for that amateurs aren't aware of. You had to be conscience of the effect the drug is having on the individual being injected. It is best to inject the drug very slowly to avoid missing any signs that the individual may be having an episode. The last thing you want is to have what was intended to be a good time, turn into an overdose that could possibly result in a death. You also had to be very careful not to inject any air into the veins. Urban legend has it that if you should have some air injected into your veins, the pocket of air would travel to your heart and kill you.

"Of course, I can hit you." I stated as I took the makeshift syringe with the water in it and laid the needle's point on top of her vein. I thumped the bub on the eyedropper with my middle finger, and the needle successfully pierced the vein. The blood oozed into the stem of the makeshift syringe indicating the vein had been penetrated. I slowly but carefully separated the needle from the syringe, rolled a small piece of toilet tissue between my thumb and forefinger until it had twisted into a point and inserted it into the opened end of the needle to soak up the blood, and prevent making a bloody mess.

I remove the bloody water from the syringe by squirting it into a piece of balled up toilet tissue. I took a piece of cotton from a cigarette's filter, and shredded it until I was able to roll it into a small ball, and placed the cotton ball in the spoon with the drugs. I placed the opened end of the eyedropper on the cotton and drew the heroin up into the syringe using the cotton ball as a filter. I removed the tissue from the needle, and very carefully reinserted the eyedropper into the opened end, while being very careful not to compromise its' location.

Once the dark red blood oozed into the syringe, indicating that its' location hadn't been compromised, I applied pressure to the bub and squeezed the drugs into her veins very slowly. As the drug took affect her eyes slowly closed and her head appeared heavy as it slowly dropped. "Are you alright?" I asked. There was still a small amount of heroin left in the syringe, but I decided against giving it to her. She was so high that she was already barely responsive. I removed the syringe from her arm and took it to the bathroom to be cleaned with running water in the sink.

With no A.I.D.S, or H.I.V. to be concerned about, sharing needles was a common practice among intravenous drug users. After I cleaned everything, I injected myself. I closed my eyes, and began nodding off as I felt the drug taking affect.

Over the next few days all we did was sleep together, eat, watch television, smoke weed, drank wine, listen to music, and inject heroin. We enjoyed each other immensely, and I would often forget I was hiding out!

After a week passed, Slim and Bumpy showed up at the apartment with my clothes. Slim looked at me and laughed before saying, "There's no way you can convince me that you've been sleeping on the couch for a whole week, and haven't georgered my bitch." I admitted that I had never slept on the couch as a matter of fact. He laughed and called me a, "… tender dick muthafucka."

Slim had a job for me but it was different from any job he had ever pulled my coat to. Kat had an uncle named Lucky. He believed that with the influence I had on the youngsters in the neighborhood, I could put a group together that would terrorize a neighborhood bar that was frequented by a white clientele. He was waiting at Kat's house to meet me, and go over the details. It was Friday night, and although I loved hanging out with Lauren, I was developing a server case of claustrophobia. I had heeded Slims' prophecy about what would happen to me if I left the house for any reason. I was ready to get out of the apartment, no matter where we were going. I got dressed, and rode with Slim and Bumpy to meet Lucky.

Lucky was an older man in his early forties. He was very bright in complexion and intelligence. He and Kat's mother looked so much alike there was no need to tell anyone they were related. The way he explained it, he knew the owner of a bar, and if we could frighten his white clientele enough, they would discontinue patronizing the establishment and the owner would jump at his first opportunity to hire him as the new manager. He in turn would change the bar into a black bar simply by changing the music in the jukebox to the type of music liked by the black people in the community were the bar was located.

Back in those days, country music and a confederate flag hanging on a wall in a recreational establishment in a black community had the same effect as a Jim Crow sign. The music is a beautiful form of art, which has proven to possess mass appeal by crossing over to many different categories of music, and winning awards. Unfortunately, the music and the Confederate flag were adopted by several bigoted organizations, and we in the African American community had come to the point we associated the two as signs to be aware of. It has cost many of black people their lives, simply because they failed to notice these signs, and take heed, until it was too late. Intolerance and alcohol don't mix well.

The owner of the bar was a Mexican named Julio. He owned the bar and the liquor license. Lucky told me he would pay me two thousand dollars, if I could get the place shot up. I promised him the job would be taken care of as soon as possible.

Slim told me to be careful, and told Bumpy to call him once I was ready to go back to the apartment. I thought Bumpy was going with me, but I was mistaken. Brandy lived right next door and that was his sole destination.

Bumpy and Peppers' spot had become the location where a lot of the youngsters hung out. That made things easier for me, since I wouldn't have to travel in order to locate them. They were right next door. When I got there, I received a hero's welcome from the fellas. The last time they saw me, I displayed no fear in the face of the possibly of fighting Beast. The word was out. They heard I had also killed Sleepy.

They listened attentively as I explained to them, "It is time we ran those pink muthfuckas out of the hood. I find it insulting when they come down here to do their dirt. They buy some dope, and trash our streets. How many of ya'll done had a white man pull up alongside you, in an expensive car, only to ask you if you knew where he could find a black girl? We all know what the fuck that means!" The fellas started grumbling in agreement, and were beginning to show signs of getting fired up. "How long are we going to allow them to come here to our neighborhoods, and drink in peace? Can you go to the white neighborhood in peace? Hell naw! They'll lock yo black ass up. Go to Lakeview, Gross Island, or Bakersfield if you think I'm lying."

They were more than grumbling now. They had been incited, and were completely fired up. They were joining in and shared stories to collaborate the statements I made. We all became fired up and determined to carry out the mission. We gathered all of our weapons together, and after a quick inventory found that we had five pistols, three sawed off shotguns, and two rifles. We armed ourselves and gathered in front of the bar. The bar was crowded which wasn't unusual for a Friday night. I picked up a large tree branch I found on the ground under a tree, and hurled it through the bar's picture window. Afterwards we opened fired on the bar, through the broken window, and then shot up all of their parked cars.

Just as we had planned, we all ran to my aunt's house down the street, and hid out until the police came and left. It had been hours before we went back to the bar and found some men trying to board up the broken window. We opened fire on the crew, and sent them scrambling for cover.

A few of the people were shot, but we didn't kill anyone. The manager was sure to quit, and Lucky was a sure in. He gave me the agreed upon amount in full, and I in turn gave each of my fellas one hundred dollars apiece. They had done the job without expecting any financial compensation, so they were very surprised, and happy, to receive the money.

I brought a can of weed from Sharon, and five bottles of M.D. 20/20. M.D. was the initials for Morgan David, the name of the winery, but we called it Mad Dog 20/20, and for tonight it had become our choice for a celebration drink. It was so potent it could dull your senses, and make you numb. We were all over Bumpy's spot, waiting on him to come tell me when Slim was coming.

The conversation was of the typical hypothetical variety when the subject eventually got around to the elephant sitting in the living room. Everyone truly wanted to know if the rumors were true, and had I committed murder. Finally, JB couldn't take the waiting, or the not knowing any longer, so he asked, "Did you kill that bitch nigga Sleepy?" I was among my people, and I felt comfortable enough to share even my darkest, and innermost secrets with them. I was about to answer the question when Chucky interrupted, "Don't answer that question man! JB, you the fuckin police or what nigga? " His attention returned to me, "Tone I've never killed anyone in my life, but from what I've been taught, you should never discuss that shit with no fuckin body. That especially includes niggas, like JB, who can't do a damn thing for you, except put your fuckin business in the street. There's no statue of limitations on bodies, my nigga!"

Chucky was my age, and my size. He was tall, dark skinned, and handsome. He was also the undisputed leader of his clique. Even his older brother Obie yielded to his leadership. Chucky, as we called him, could light up a room with his smile, and his charisma was undeniable. I gave him an extra hundred dollars, and some marijuana for himself. He had displayed genuine concern for my wellbeing, and that led us to becoming the best of friends.

Bumpy came by just to inform me he had talked to Slim, and he said he was on his way to pick me up. He left immediately after he had delivered the message, and introduced me to his girlfriend, Brandy. Upon seeing her I understood completely why he had fallen in love with the chocolate beauty. Bumpy had admitted to me that he was in love with Brandy, so it satisfied my curiosity to finally meet her. There was nothing disappointing about her physical appearance, and that was for sure.

I wanted to ask Kari if it was alright for me to visit her, so I said my good-byes and headed next door. I hadn't talked to Kari privately since I had killed Sleepy, and I wanted to know her feelings. She wanted to talk to me privately when I got there, but Lucky was still there, and he seemed to be as happy as everybody else.

"Call me Uncle Lucky from now on young man. My niece speaks very highly of you, and she considers you her brother. I have some big plans, and after the leadership ability you displayed tonight, I'm determined to make you a part. The distinct sound of a Cadillac horn interrupted our conversation. It turned out to be Slim, and he was waiting for me to come out to the car. I said my goodbyes to everyone, and promised Kari I'd be back to spend some time with her. She blushed and said, "You better keep that promise, Tone Dog."

As soon as I got in the car I got the bad news. I was a little disappointed when Slim informed me that everyone on the streets believed I killed Sleepy, but I was a little gleeful also. Now the entire neighborhood had been put on notice. There was a new player in town, and there was no reason to have any doubt, if he promised to send your soul to meet its' maker. It meant that I had to go back into hiding for a while, but I didn't mind at all. As a matter of fact, I looked forward to spending more time with Lauren.

Once I got to the apartment I sent Lauren out to get twenty-five caps of the heroin we had been using. The potency was amazing. She wasn't gone for too long of a time, before she returned. I was astonished when she informed me she had been purchasing the product from, of all people, Bumpy! I could've done that myself. I had been cutting heroin for months, and had become quite knowledgeable with the art of diluting the heroin with various substances. I had no idea Bumpy and Peppers had such an amazing product. There was no doubt about it. They were on the path to prosperity.

A couple of days later, I caught a cab to see Kari. I had hoped she would be happy to see me, and she was. Kat was there with a friend of her's named Ella. She and Kat were in Kat's bedroom, and the rest of the family was in the living room watching American Bandstand. Kari suggested we go to her bedroom for some privacy, and lead me there by the hand.

Once we were settled in her bedroom, I told her the whole story. I thought no one except Kari could hear my words, but I was wrong. There was a heat vent that was connected to both Kari's, and Kat's rooms. If the flaps were in the open position in both bedrooms, private conversations could easily be overheard.

Kat had left Ella alone in her bedroom while she took an important telephone call in another room. While Kat was away, Ella took the opportunity to be nosey, and eavesdropped in on our conversion. She knew I thought Kari and I were alone, and no one else could hear my confession. Chucky had warned me, never to discuss anything with anybody about any murder. I should have listened, and took heed. I didn't know it at that time, but she was the next-door neighbor of Sleepy's parents.

I was having a great time with Kari. I was doing my best to convince her to put her leotard on, and dance for me, when Kat came in the room. She asked had we seen Ella. We hadn't paid much attention to anything other than each other, so we were unable to provide her with any additional information.

With a confused expression on her face she said more to herself than to anyone who may have been listening, "That's some strange shit the way that bitch just up and left like that. She didn't even let me know she was leaving."

"Is anything missing?" Kari asked. "I don't know. I better go check that shit out. If this muthafucken bitch done took anything of mine, I'm fuckin her bitch ass up on sight." she continued to mumble something under her breath, as she stormed out the room.

It was getting late, and I could feel the weight of my personal monkey beginning to mount my back. I had to get back to Lauren's apartment before I became ill. I called a cab, and said my goodbyes when the cab arrived. As I walked down the steps, a voice in the night called out my entire birth name in an authoritative tone. Armed uniformed police officers approached me from the side of the house with their weapons drawn. "You are under arrest. You have the right to remain silent. Anything you say can and will be used against you in a court of law. You have a right to an attorney. If you can't afford an attorney, one will be provided for you. Do you understand these rights?"

I was arrested for murder, and carrying a concealed weapon, but I was a minor, so they weren't allowed to interrogate me. I found myself spending the night on 2N, waiting to be brought before a judge once again. I had no idea what the judge was going to do the last time I was brought before him, but this time there was no doubt in my mind. The thought of having to stay in the facility, and the monkey which had found a comfortable seat for the ride on my back, all made me nauseous. So nauseous in fact, I was forced to rush to the restroom, without permission, to empty my stomach on several occasions.

After surviving a long night, the next morning several supervisors came by to see me. Mr. Ford was the first to deliver a message that was repeated by them all throughout the early morning hours. "Don't discuss your case with anyone." Even the lawyer assigned to represent me had nothing new to add. I couldn't wait to tell Chucky the advice, which he was the first to give me, was repeated over and over again by professionals.

When I went to court, I was pleasantly surprised to see my parents in attendance. I tried to do things the correct way, but the establishment had what appeared to be insurmountable obstacles in the form of rules and policies designed to prevent me from re-entering school. Maybe I should've been more diligent in my efforts to re-enter the educational system, however, I was an uneducated child going up against educated, professional adults, intended on keeping me out. I detected fear in my mother, and it wasn't because she was afraid for herself. It was for me that she was afraid. She had witnessed firsthand how hard I had tried to get back into school. She was also very aware of the fact that being a street hustler was my alternate choice for an occupation, and most street hustlers ended up dead or incarcerated. I was already on the path whereas facing death, or incarceration would be an inevitable consequence for my actions.

There weren't any surprises when the judge ordered that I be held in custody until the case was resolved. I was transferred to housing unit 6C. 6C was used for segregation. High profile, and protective custody cases were also housed on unit 6C. Some guys were housed there temporarily for disciplinary reasons, but after a few days they were transferred back into general population. The murder charge, however, fitted the criteria to classify me to the high profiled category. Therefore, I was placed in segregation to reside there for the duration of my stay. On top of everything I was concerned about, I couldn't help worrying about the hearing being held for the judge to decide if I was to be waved over to the adult justice system to be tried as adult.

For the first three days I was there, I had a serious bout with withdrawals, so it didn't matter where they kept me. Once again, I went through a regiment that consisted of valium, vitamins, and aspirin. Eventually I kicked, but it seemed the withdrawal symptoms were much more intense this time. I figured it was because my habit was much bigger than it was the last time I kicked. Therefore, the bigger the habit is, the more severe the withdrawal symptoms will be.

In segregation, I remained locked in a single man cell for twenty-three hours of the day. There were speakers in the ceilings of the cells, as well as throughout the entire housing unit. Other than the supervisors using the speakers to make announcements through the P.A. system, the speakers were used to pipe music. Most of the time, the radio was on the jazz station, W.C.H.D. 105.9. They let us out of our cells two at a time for one hour out of the day, and during that hour we were allowed to watch television, take a shower or play ping pong.

For months, all I did all day was pray, sleep, eat, workout, listened to music, masturbated, and wept. I had gotten so good at playing ping pong I had no opponents willing to play me. The time I was outside my cell was spent mostly watching television after I took a shower. One day while we were watching television with our supervisor, old man Mr. Dyer, he fell asleep. It wasn't a big deal to me, because he did it all the time, but this time a white kid had decided to take advantage of a possible opportunity to escape.

The chairs were built to last from solid oak. The boy stood, and then picked up his chair. He raised the chair above his head, and slowly tiptoed in Mr. Dyer's direction. As watched, I realized there was no way, in good conscience, I could sit idly by, and witness a white kid potentially kill a black man, and do nothing. Mr. Dyer was an old man nearing retirement. He had survived during the times when lynches and other dehumanizing acts forced upon black people, by white people, were considered acceptable, and were quite prevalent. There was no way, as far as I could see, for him to have a chance of surviving such a blow.

I sprung to my feet and caught the chair in my hands just before it was about to descend upon its intended target, which was Mr. Dyer' head. The commotion woke Mr. Dyer up, and he thought the white boy and I were fighting. He ordered us to stop and to return to our cells, and that was the end of it.

The next morning a couple of supervisors were observing the video tapes of the incident from a monitor. They saw I had actually prevented Mr. Dyer from getting seriously injured, if not killed. To the staff, I became an instant hero.

They all began doing things to spoil me. Mr. Dyer had a son who also worked at the facility, and he seemed to never pass on an opportunity to show his gratitude. He would come by my cell everyday he worked just to say, "Thank you for saving my dad." and to give me something special. I kept telling him it wasn't necessary, but he continuously insisted, and would not allow my modesty to prevent him from giving me things.

They all would bring me cigarettes and matches, candy bars, food and comic books. Whichever supervisor we got to run our unit for that day, would let me out my cell to pass out the meal trays. I was in charge of all the extra trays, so I passed out extra food at the end of every meal. I was allowed to stay out of my cell for hours, playing ping pong against various supervisors during their scheduled lunch breaks.

Mr. Brewer used to bring me all of his expensive shoes, and I would spend an entire morning or afternoon shining them in my cell. We weren't allowed to have cigarettes or to smoke, but Mr. Brewer would give me a whole pack of cigarettes and two books of matches for shining his shoes.

Time seemed to be flying by, and before I knew it six months had passed. It was already the day before the wavier hearing. I didn't fear much, but for some reason the thought of that hearing always gave me an overwhelming sense of doom. That night I prayed, and begged God to save me. I knew if I got waved I could possibly spend the rest of my life in prison. I didn't know what to asked for, so I prayed for guidance.

All of a sudden, the entire cell turned into a bright, pure white light. All I could see was white, and I felt The Most High's presence. There wasn't a voice for me to hear, but I felt His words. The words were placed on my heart, as He instructed me to tell the truth. Of course, I had been contemplating lying. I thought it was my only option, but He promised me that if I placed my faith in Him, He would deliver me from the clutches of despair. I don't even remember going to bed, or falling asleep. I was awakened by a supervisor the next morning, instructing me to get ready to go to court.

It seemed like every supervisor that worked that morning stopped by my cell to wish me good luck. Mr. Ford had visited my parents, and went up to Clark High School to get the necessary documents to prove I had tried to get back in school. He had a long meeting with Judge Washington on my behalf. He fought to keep me from going to prison, and becoming just another statistic. He communicated with my lawyer consistently, and he did all this on his on time. I asked him why he was fighting so hard on my behalf. I really was a bad, problematic child, and because of that, I couldn't understand why he cared. He told me he did it all because he believed in me, and felt that if I had a fair chance in life, I would prove to be something very special. He said if I could only see myself through his eyes, I would recognize my potential, and begin believing in myself. In that conversation he taught me the importance of a man believing in himself. Before you can achieve anything that leads to basking in the emotional thrills of lofty accomplishments, one must first believe in him or herself. It is imperative, because you are who you believe you are.

Four of us were led to a waiting room, better known as the bull pen. We were all being brought before Judge Washington for him to decide should we be tried as adults or not. Anthony Burch was charged with bank robbery. Anthony was off the eastside, and we knew each other very well. I knew robbing banks was his hustle. The young brother was extremely cool, and smooth. He was a sharp dresser, and always kept a huge wad of money, which appeared to be crispy, brand new bills.

Quincy Weiner was one of the other guys waiting to go before the judge, and he was charged with armed robbery. Quincy was off the west side, and his hustle was robbing supermarkets. He had approached me about doing some jobs with him. He lived on the other side of West Grand Boulevard in the neighborhood. Quincy was a free spirit, but many considered him to be a loose cannon.

The other guy was Clint Morris, and he was charged with rape. He had gotten involved with some unsavory older boys. They had raped a girl one day while they were hanging out, and told Clint that he had to have sex with her too, in order for them to believe he wouldn't tell. The older boys were already old enough to be tried as adults, so they were already being held in custody at the County Jail.

Of course, this information made me extremely nervous, because I was charged with the most serious offense of all. We all were charged with offenses that carried a penalty of up to life in prison, yet I was the only one the staff felt it was necessary to house in segregation. I truly didn't have a clue as to how dangerous the authorities believed I had become.

Anthony was the first to be escorted into the courtroom to face Judge Washington. After a short while he reappeared from the courtroom being escorted by two white men in dark colored suites. We watched as they led him down the hall in handcuffs. We were told by the bailiff that Anthony had been waved, and the men were federal marshals taking him into custody.

Quincy was the next one to emerged from the courtroom escorted in handcuffs. Two sheriff deputies, were transporting him to the County Jail. He didn't seem to be upset at all. He had told me that he wanted to get waved, so he could get a bond, and get released. He was smiling as he was being led away.

Clint was led into the courtroom next. By now I had become so nervous I decided it would be best for me to pray. I got on my knees, and begged God to intervene, and not to permit me to be waved. Even though I had witnessed two boys with charges not as serious as my own get waved, I still believed with all my heart that God would save me from such a fate. As I got up off my knees I saw Clint in tears as he was being led away in handcuffs. He had been waved, and was being escorted by sheriff deputies.

It was my turn to be escorted into the courtroom by the bailiff. I was so nervous I could barely walk. The Bailiff had to assist me by holding me up by my arm. I was led to the table where my lawyer was seated. I recognized him although I had seen him only once the whole time I had been locked up.

He stood and gave me a firm handshake before using a gesture to indicate he wanted me to take a seat in the empty chair next to his own. After I had been seated, I watched as my parents entered the courtroom. They took a seat on the bench behind the table where I was seated, and spoke to me. They hadn't visit me while I was locked up this time, so it was our first time seeing each other in six months.

They too were visibly shaken with nerves. I was called to the stand, and the bailiff swore me in with a Bible before I took a seat. I was much more nervous now than I had been. I looked over the faces present before turning all my attention towards the judge as he spoke. The judge instructed me to tell the court exactly what had happened, in my own words. I informed the judge that I cussed a lot, and I wanted to know if he really meant for me to use my own words. The entire courtroom erupted into laughter. It was as though the tension was too thick in the air, and everyone was looking for an excuse to loosen up. The laughter was a nervous laughter, but as relief swept over everyone, I realized this wasn't an ordinary nervousness. The sound of laughter couldn't have been more welcomed. Even Judge Washington had to laugh before he replied, "Okay, I understand, but please refrain from cussing while you're using your own words in my courtroom."

I was afraid to tell the truth. I wanted to lie, and

swear that I was innocent. I had everyone's undivided attention, yet at that moment I had never felt more alone. I was overwhelmed with relief once the white, bright, light from the night before reappeared. I couldn't see anyone or anything in the small court room. All I could see was the same white, bright light I had seen in my room the night before.

Just as He had appeared when I was in my cell the night before, I felt God's presence. Once again, He placed it on my heart, "Trust me. Tell the truth." I was frightened, and I wasn't sure how everyone would feel about me afterwards, but I did as my Lord had instructed me. I told the truth, the whole truth, and nothing but the truth. It was difficult, but knowing that my God was literally with me, gave me the fortitude, and the strength to truthfully complete my testimony.

When I concluded my testimony, the light went away, and I could see the tears and horror on everyone's face. Judge Washington broke the silence, "Wow! This child has never had a chance in his life. If I were to wave him today, he would more than likely get convicted of at the very least, second degree murder, and that's based upon the testimony he has given under oath here today. I'm not going to wave this boy, and deny him a chance in his life. Instead of that, as of now I'm ordering that he be made a ward of the state, and that he be committed to State's Boys Training School, where he will remain under their jurisdiction until the age of nineteen. Good luck young man. I hope you realize what an opportunity this is I'm offering you, and you take full advantage of it. He then lowered his gavel upon the block, and announced that court had been adjourned. There wasn't a dry eye in the courtroom.

I was so happy that I began to cry. It seemed even the bailiff was wiping tears from his eyes with a handkerchief, as he led me away. I had never in my life experienced such happiness. I was overwhelmed to tears at that moment, and was my Creator whom deserved all the praise. I was smiling, and crying all at once. My legs felt like noodles, and once again I needed the bailiff's assistance to walk.

I still had to return to segregation, so I had to wait on 2N until a supervisor became available to escort me back upstairs. All the supervisors came by 2N to see me, shake my hand, hug me and congratulate me. They pretended be too busy to take me back upstairs. That way I was able to stay out of my cell, play ping pong, watch television, play cards, and just enjoy being a kid around some kids.

None of the boys understood how I could be so joyful about going to Boys Training school. It was the worst case scenario, for almost every one of them. Mr. Ford noticed their confusion, and explained to them why I was so happy to receive what they were trying to avoid. When they were informed that I was facing life for murder, they understood.

That night I prayed, and thanked God for the awesome demonstration of love displayed in my life that day. It was The Creator who offered me the guidance necessary to avoid ruining my life, and blessed me with a team of dedicated supporters. For the first time in my life, I realized I was important, and special to The Most-High. He always saves me when I make huge mistakes.

I only say "He" because its' how most people refer to our Creator. God is neither a man, nor a woman. I will not even attempt to say what The Most High is. Some say that God is The Creative Spirit. The only thing I will bear witness to is that The Most High is the Creator, and everything else is creation. There is no way our minds can comprehend the complexity, or the magnitude of our Creator, with the experiences of our meager existence, yet there is more than enough evidence to support The Most High's existence.

Chapter 4

A few days later I was transferred to Four Rivers, the city where A.J. Maxie, and Brown Oaks were located. These were state institutions, governed by the state for juvenile delinquents. Once in the system the average stay was about six months, but first we had to be quarantined, so we could be intellectually tested and be given a complete medical physical. There was a section of the facility for boys in transit, and once the evaluations were completed, a staff used the results to determine which facility would be your final destination. This process took approximately thirty days.

A.J. Maxie was a brand new, facility built from the ground up. The felid house was a top notched, state of the art facility. They also had an Olympic size swimming pool, complete with diving boards and diving platforms. You had your own bedroom with windows that you had the option of either opening or closing. We were allowed to walk all around the compound unsupervised, unless you were in transit. Four Rivers was in a rural area of the state. Most of the boys were from the urban areas of the state, which translated means the black area. I had never lived away from the hustle and bustle of the city, and I found the beautiful manicured landscape soul stirring.

Now Brown Oaks was another story all together. Brown Oaks was a locked down unit, which meant you weren't allowed to roam unsupervised. It had bedrooms with windows incased in steel frames with steel screens. That prohibited access and disallowed the ability to open or close the windows. The facility was also used to temporarily house boys for disciplinary reasons. There was a twelve, foot high fence, topped with barbwire, surrounding the grounds of the entire facility, yet some had managed to escape.

There were a couple of camps in other cities, but everyone seemed to genuinely prefer Holt's Boys Training School. The juvenile facility was located literally next door to Western High School, in the middle of an urban area, as opposed to a rural setting. Students from State University were frequent visitors to the facility implementing experimental programs. The institution participated and competed in high school athletics with high schools in the surrounding small towns. They even traveled to the other schools for away games. You could also get your barber's license or a certification for operating metal machinery from the technology classes they offered.

I believed there was no way I would be selected to go to Holt. Offenders who have committed serious offenses get a red tag placed on their folders. This is to alert the staff, of the individual they're dealing with. Red tagged individuals where sent to Brown Oaks for at least a year. I hoped for Maxie, but I prepared myself mentally for Brown Oaks.

All the meals served at Four Rivers were prepared in the kitchen of A.J. Maxie, and that included Brown Oaks. The food was unbelievably delicious! We were allowed to eat as much as we wanted, but there was a no garbage rule for seconds. If you got seconds and didn't eat it, you would be threatened with a written disciplinary report.

All the facilities, except Brown Oaks, allowed offenders to earn weekend home visits. Towards the end of our incarceration, we could earn a home visit for an entire week. According to the guidelines, all indications seemed to reinforce the point there was a high probability I would be sent to Brown Oaks.

Coach King was in charge of all the activities we participated in. We swam, raced, and played a lot of basketball. Most mornings and afternoons we were taking test. We were instructed to do our very best because they were accredited, and whatever grade level we tested in, would be the grade we'd be placed in. The fact that I had not attended school in years didn't matter. We were informed that we could be placed in a grade as high as the tenth. Of course, I tested beyond the tenth grade.

The month we were there was a very pleasant stay, and I prayed every night that I wouldn't be sent to Brown Oaks. I walked into the room to face the classification committee, and find out where I was going. I was nervous, but I had faced so much by this time I wasn't as nervous as I had anticipated.

The committee members sat in wooden chairs behind a long white portable table. Coach King did all the talking, and informed me that I had been selected by the committee to do my time in Holt. He said there was an excellent possibility I could earn a scholarship, and it would be great for the program if I were to earn a scholarship.

Coach King went on to explain his reasoning for feeling that way, "You are so fundamentally sound, you would be an asset to any team that is fortunate enough to get you." I thought of Mr. Holcomb when he said that. Mr. Holcomb had taught me the fundamentals while I was in the youth home, and it paid off. Mr. Green and Mr. Holcomb were great teachers, and they taught me well. I tested at the eleventh grade, level

I was transferred to Holt the very next day. When we arrived, I noticed there were actually residential homes on the same street that the facility was located. As we exited the station wagon, and were being led to the control center, I noticed how ancient the buildings were. A.J. Maxie was a fairly new facility, but Holt was so old the contras was astonishing.

The first thing I noticed was the majority of the staff was comprised of African Americans. They were surprisingly quite cordial, which is very unusual. Most of the time, African Americans in the position of authority, fear appearing as though they are showing favoritism towards their own race, so they overcompensate to the point their hostile actions could easily be considered cruel.

Our sizes were taken, and we were outfitted with brand new clothes, and shoes. They weren't the latest fashion, but after spending six months in a uniform it was a welcomed change. We were issued a pair of dress shoes, and a pair of gym shoes. We were warned that the gym shoes we had been issued were to only be worn during athletic activities, there would be serious repercussions if we did not comply with that particular rule.

As we were leaving, we passed through a hall which had an awful stench emitting from it. There was a roll of five empty cells, and they proved to be the source of the overwhelming stench. We were informed by our escort that if you escape and were caught. you would have to spend five days in one of these cells. That is why they called it Five; not because there were five cells. Five was dark, filthy and resembled a dungeon. The walls were covered with so much graffiti and filth that it appeared to have never been attended.

I was concerned about the conditions of Five, but not for myself. There was nothing that could happened to make me even contemplate the idea of trying to escape. The consequences of getting caught were not the same for me as they were for most offenders who were captured. I was red tagged, so I would be taken straight to the County Jail to face not only an escape charge as an adult, but also the murder. The idea that children were forced to sleep in such a place was horrifying, as well as appalling. What made matters even worst, was the fact that Five was infested with roaches, ants, and mice.

Today three of us were being escorted, but it felt like we were being ushered into a world within a world. The housing units were called cottages, and were named after the states. I was the first to be dropped off. I was assigned to a cottage named California, where the oldest boys resided. The escort introduced me to my housing supervisors. Their official titles were cottage parents. Ms. Little and Mr. Morris were their names.

Mr. Morris was a big man with a powerful presence. His demeanor spoke volumes for him. He was definitely a no nonsense man, without a single sign of meanies. He was once a high school basketball star in the city of Chicago. He was happy to take the time out and tell me all about his playing days. He even promised to bring all his newspaper clippings in, and to go over them with me. He told me he had been informed about me and briefed, before my arrival. The plan was for me to play football, basketball, and run track. I was also blessed to have a cottage father who was sincerely interested in me.

Ms Little was of medium height, slim, dark skinned, and wore a stylish wig. Her wearing a wig was not surprising at all. Most of the women who wore full wigs back then, truly preferred weaves or getting their hair done, but simply could not afford it. She was very pretty, and used to smile every time Mr. Morris flirted with her. She was very self-conscious of her crooked teeth, and she would cover her mouth with her fingers while smiling, to prevent exposing them. The gesture always made her appear as though she were shyly blushing.

Mr. Morris pulled my file from his desk, and fingered through it before asking me if I was aware of the fact, I was a red tag. I assured him I was well aware of that fact. "Did you do it?" he asked. He studied my facial expressions, and body langue as I replied. "Yes sir," I was trying my best not to sound, nor appear proud of it.

I had been congratulated, and received numerous pats on my back from my peers, but this was different. This was a staff member, and it didn't take a genius to understand this was a different world, and boasting about a homicide would be frowned upon. I didn't want to appear as though I were a proud killer.

I explained that it wasn't a robbery, and it was a matter of either he would kill me, or I would kill him. "I'm from Chicago, and I know how crazy the fuckin streets can get, man." he added before asking, "It is my understanding that you like being called Red Top?" He stood up and came from behind his desk as I told him that was a nick name that somehow had stuck with me. My peers in the youth home had started calling me Red Top because my hair was damaged from neglect, and became a bright color red.

He instructed me to follow him, so I could put my things away and get settled in. He led me down the stairs to the basement, and then we entered a large recreation room with a grey cement floor and yellow brick walls. In the center of the room, a couple of guy were playing ping pong on the regulation size table. On one side of the room lockers lined the wall. A record player sat on top of a small table in a corner of the room with several boys seated around it. They were smoking cigarettes and singing along with Stevie Wonder's latest hit, "Signed, Sealed, Delivered, I'm yours".

I recognized a few of the boys from the youth home, and that's when Travis walked up to me, and offered me a cigarette. We were both thrilled to see each other. We had become close when I had to stay in the youth home the first time. I lit the cigarette with the candle that sat on a desk near the entrance.

"If you don't mind sir, I can show Red Top his locker and bed." Travis asked.

"I don't mind at all" he said as he handed me a Master's lock in a box and handed Travis a sheet of paper with my locker assignment, and bed assignment typed on it. Mr. Morris instructed me to check everything on the list before returning the paper to him signed, once I was settled in, and my bed was made. He didn't hesitate to leave immediately to get back to the company of Ms. Little

I placed all of my things in the locker except one outfit. It was time to change into some real clothes. I was about to lock my locker when Travis stopped me. "What you doing man? We don't have to lock our shit up! Most muthafuckas hope that nobody steals their shit, but not us. We wish a muthafucka would try it, so we could fuck his bitch ass up. You're doing time for murder. You'll never have to worry about that kind of petty shit here. Ain't nobody stupid enough to fuck with you, bro!"

He explained all the rules I needed to know, like we were allowed to smoke cigarettes only in the basement. He waited for me to finish smoking my cigarette as he introduced me to everybody. Afterwards we climb the stairs to the top floor of the three story building, and entered the dorm area.

The dorm held a lot of bunk beds. The beds that were occupied were made up uniformly, in a military style. It looked a lot like an army barracks. I had a lot of trouble trying to duplicate the military style of making my bed, so Travis showed me how. The secret was to make hospital corners, and keeping both the sheets and the blanket as tightly drawn as possible. Once we had successfully completed the task, Travis took a quarter from his pocket, and checked to see if the quarter would bounce when dropped on the bed. He said when they conducted inspections they always checked the beds by using a quarter. If it didn't bounce, you failed inspection. Failing inspection too often could result in you being withheld from the many enjoyable special activities they held. The quarter bounce with ease, therefore, I was ready to sign and return the papers to Mr. Morris.

Travis gave me the complete run down on the place. "It's truly sweet here. You want to walk to the store?" he asked.

"Huh?" was all I was able to say in response. I had heard him correctly. I just found it difficult to believe what I had heard. He was laughing as I asked, "You telling me, we can actually leave here walking to the store?"

"Come on. I can show you better than I can tell you." he answered as he headed for the stairwell. I quickly followed. I wanted to see if what he had suggested was in fact a possibility. I had been locked down for more than seven months, so a stroll down the street would have been an amazing treat for me, even if it wasn't the streets of Newport.

We walked into the room where Mr. Morris sat behind the desk beside Ms. Little. It was a large room with six card tables, each surrounded with four chairs. There was also a bumper pool table in the middle of the room.

After I had signed the inventory paper, Travis simply asked, "Mr. Morris, can we walk to the store?" Mr. Morris was acting like he wanted us to hurry up and leave, so he could be alone with Ms. Little. "You guys got any doe?" he asked. Travis showed him a five dollar bill, and Mr. Morris gave us the nod.

Travis told me that there was an all- girl's home directly across the street. We stopped over there, so I could check it out. To my surprise, some very nice looking girls lived there. The girls couldn't come out at that time, but we were allowed to wait until it was time for them to come out, and go to the park next door to the home. Unfortunately, we didn't have enough time to wait. We only had a short amount of time before we would be expected back.

At the small corner party store, located on Pennsylvania

and Saginaw, we purchased a pack of Kool cigarettes, a couple of Nu grape sodas, and some candy. Travis told me that we weren't allowed to have more than five dollars in our possession at once, but most of the boys broke that rule all the time.

A couple of days after I arrived, I celebrated my seventeenth birthday. I was becoming more and more comfortable as time passed, and football season was quickly approaching. I had to play football, basketball, and run track. That was the reason I had been sent to Holt instead of Brown Oaks. I was a little nervous because I had never played organized ball before, but I was looking forward to the challenge. I relished the opportunity to test my skills against those who were considered the best among my peers.

The institution was buzzing with excitement because of the hired of Mr. Ernie Patterson, and Mr. Scott Long as the new football coaches. They both were members of the 1966 State University's National Championship team. They shared the title because their opponent had the opportunity to go for a touchdown to capture the title, but elected to go for a tie instead, by kicking a field goal. The game was labeled the game of the century, although many of the fans were left very disappointed. Many felt the opponent's coach was a coward, because he decided to play for the tie. One of the games commentators said it left him with a bad feeling. He concluded by adding, "It's like kissing your sister."

Mr. Patterson was the starting fullback, and Mr. Long was the starting inside linebacker on State's team during that time. It was like being coached by celebrities. During those days, they played semiprofessional football for the undefeated Holt All Stars. All of their home games were played at Western's High School's football Stadium, and they took us to every single home game. That way they were able to teach us as well as show us how the game was meant to be played.

As a result of their coaching, I was selected to the Conference All-Star team as a defensive back, and running back. I had managed to accumulate one hundred yards or more rushing every single game. I even ran a ninety-eight yard touchdown from scrimmage, and set a state record. I received the trophy reserved for the team's best back at our team's football banquet, and was rewarded an offer of a full ride scholarship at Eastern University. My bunkmate was George Lincoln Jr., and he also was named to the Conference All-Star team as an offensive tackle. He was awarded the trophy reserved for the team's best lineman. He also received an offer for a full scholarship from the University of Minnesota. The entire staff was so proud of us that they often congratulated us, and gave us the newspaper clippings they found with articles about us.

The first time I was in the newspaper, Mr. Patterson was extremely proud of me. He came to me, and handed me the newspaper article and said, "You've got some ink!" I had never experienced anything like that before in my life. I had received several copies from the staff, so I mailed them home to my family. George and I were treated like celebrities everywhere we went.

The winter term started, and I was sent to attend Western high school next door. It was a major adjustment for me to attend a predominantly white school. It was my first time being a member of the minority in school.

I tried out for the school's varsity basketball team which

was rated number one in the state, and I made the team. The first game we played after I made the team was against Martin L. King. A predominantly black team that was rated number three in the state. It was a tightly contested game, and we lost by one point.

King had a senior by the name of Walter Davy, who dominated the game offensively, and a junior by the name of Cory Dungee who dominated the game defensively. They both made the necessary plays down the stretch to secure the victory. There were only three black players on our team, including myself, and none of us played in the game. At the time, I understood why I didn't get a chance to play. I was new to the team, and I didn't know all the plays yet, but the other two black players said it was because we were black. I didn't agree. The best players played, and we only lost by one point. We were then dropped in the ratings to number three.

Our next game was against Central. They were rated number six in the state. Their home games were played at Western University's field house. I was excited to have the opportunity to play on an official college basketball court. We were winning the game with a little over five minutes left to play. Central was predominantly White. The crowd became rowdy and began chanting, "Put the nigga in. Put the nigga in. Put the nigga in."

Coach Harper looked down the bench, and motioned for me to check into the game. I immediately stood up, and ran to the table before removing my warm ups, and took a knee. The crowd exploded into a roar of laughter. I was certain they were laughing because I was about to enter the game. I felt a draft, and after looking down, I was horrified to I discover that I had accidently removed my uniform shorts as well. My entire buttock was exposed to the crowd. All I had on from the waist down was a jockey strap and foot gear. It was clearly the most embarrassing moment of my life! I put my uniform shorts back on, and quickly found myself a seat at the far end of the bench. The coach kept motioning for me to check into the game, but I ignored him. All I wanted to do was disappear. I scooted down in my seat as far as I could, and tried my best to become as less visible as possible. The game couldn't end quickly enough for me. I was never able to live the moment down.

Track season began, and we proved to have an amazingly talented team. We won nearly every track meet we participated in, including all our dual meets. I participated in the hundred-yard dash, the long jump, the mile relay, and the eight hundred, and eighty-yard relay. At the state finals, to my surprise, Adam was there to compete in the hundred-yard dash, representing Hill Top high school. We were excited to see each other again. It had been years since we had last seen each other. We grew up on Fisherman together, and we raced every single night that the weather permitted. I had never beaten Adam in a foot race, and here we were competing against each other in the state finals.

As it turned out, neither one of us took first place. I did finally beat Adam, but I only took second place, and Adam took third. First place was won by a kid named of Wendell Harrison. He was representing Northern. He later went on to make the United States Olympic team, and received a gold medal on the way to setting a world's record while attending State University his freshmen year.

We almost won the eight hundred, and eighty-yard relay, but our third leg, pulled a quad muscle in the middle of his leg of the race. He bravely finished his leg, and our anchor was able to pull out a second, place finish. He caught everyone, except Harrison.

The last meet was the city meet. I was a member of the first place eight hundred, and eighty, yard relay team, and the first place, mile relay team. I took second place in the long jump competition, because I was unable to concentrate. I couldn't get the hundred-yard dash off my mind. I had beaten my teammate at the state championship meet, and everyone came out to see if I could do it again. place behind my teammate Ambrose in the hundred-yard, dash. Of course, we won the City Track Meet's team title. At the end of the meet I did as I always did. I never kept anything, except gold medals. All of the silver and bronze medals I won, I always threw into my crowd of fans. The number fans grew as did my popularity. I was flying higher than I had ever flown before, and I loved it. I was doing my very best to prove I was worthy of the opportunity I'd been given.

Chapter 5

Mr. Morris had been trying very hard, but he seemed to be faced with an impossible task when it came convincing the staff to allow me to go home for a visit. My parents came to visit me once, and it was very nice. I showed them around the grounds and they were truly impressed. In their wildest dreams, I don't think they ever imagined a day would come that I would be held in such high esteem.

Mr. Morris tried to use the fact that my parents had visited as leverage to force their hand, but the staff still refused to consider it. He insisted that I needed a visit to reconnect with my family to no avail.

Everyone else in the cottage was allowed to go home, and I envied none of them. They all thought of me while they were home, and brought a lot of good things back with them to share with me. Things like cigarettes, clothes to wear to school, food, record albums, and of course marijuana.

One night while lying in on our bunks, we were having a discussion about the things we missed about home. I admitted that I missed getting so high off heroin that I had to vomit. That's when I realized how much I missed vomiting. My bunk mate George, and our friend who slept across from us named Frank, also realized and admitted that they too missed vomiting.

Whenever heroin is strong, once it is consumed, it will make you nausea, and you will spill the contents of your stomach. Once the vomiting has ceased, you would feel extremely intoxicated. We all realized and admitted that there was something very wrong with enjoying vomiting. That's when we made a pack among ourselves to never use heroin again. It turned out to be the best decisions I've ever made in my life. I never used again.

On Mr. Morris's and Ms. Little's off days, Mr. Sterling, and Mr. Jordan worked our cottage. They too played football for State when they won a share of the title. They also played for the Holt All- Stars along with our coaches. A couple of times a month they would get permission to take some of us off grounds to the show. Once we were off grounds they would ask us to vote on going to the show, or to a party at State. We always elected to go to the party. At the parties, there were always a lot of students smoking marijuana, drinking, and taking acid. They only insisted that we did not drink, or take acid. If a girl wanted to have sex with us, it wasn't a problem. None of us ever came close to getting a girl, but we always had a ball.

The students we met at the parties began coming to the facility implementing programs. They started a black history class, and opened the doors to a whole new world for me. Most of us were from Newport, and had experienced the effects of racism first hand without realizing it. We were all old enough to remember the riots, and were asked to tell the class what it was we remembered about the riot.

I was excited about the opportunity to talk about my

riot experiences. Everything in Newport changed after the riot. There was an entirely different culture that emerged as a direct result of the violence, and the sheer need for the community to unite in order to survive.

I remembered standing on the corner of Vinewood and Harper listening to the jazz station on my transistor radio. It was a Sunday afternoon and gospel dominated the airwaves. I didn't want to listen to gospel, but the only other choice I had other than jazz was the station C.K.L.W. which aired out of Canada, and played mixed music.

I was hanging out with Chance, Greg, and Terrell when we all heard an unbelievable announcement. There had been a disturbance that occurred on the city's west side the night before, after the police raided an illegal establishment that offered prostitution, gambling, food, and alcohol after hours. These places were better known as blind pigs. It was actually after two o'clock in the morning, but black people always considered it night if the Sun hadn't risen. The blind pig was located on 112th street, and when a police officer slapped a black woman the situation escalated into a full blown civil disturbance. All the police who worked our streets during those days were white, so the racial disharmony was quite prevalent. The announcement was for every police officer to report to the location of the disturbance, rather they were on or off duty. It didn't take us long to realize that if every single police officer was on the west side, then there couldn't be any on the east side.

Alarms began blaring, along with the sound of glass being smashed as people began breaking store windows. They had obviously heard the same announcement as we had, and they boldly climbed through the broken windows and were exiting the stores with looted goods. We quickly made the transition from spectators to participants. There was no time to shop. You simply had to grab an arm full of whatever you could carry off. You didn't even have to run.

Chance, Terrell, and I all lived on the same block, so it was easy for us to use our garages for stash spots between trips. It didn't take long before all our garages were filled. My father even got in on the action. He had gotten a lot of food, and some expensive Finder and Gibson electric guitars. More importantly he got a floor model hi fi with a built in, color television. Color televisions were rare during those days in the black community. Most streets had only one family with a color television, and that family would invite their neighbors over to watch special programs. It was truly a special event. All the adults and children would gather in one room, and share the special moment. The looting from the riot changed all of that. Nearly everyone had their own color television after the riot.

That night the mayor ordered the police not to shoot any looters, but the disturbance escalated, and lasted for five days. After the third day, the riot turned deadly for everyone. A lot of innocent black people, who had nothing to do with the activities, were gunned down by the National Guards who were sent to Newport by the Governor. They were white, and with them came an ugly brand of brutal racism. They saw this as a great opportunity to shoot a bunch of black folk, and took full advantage of it. They addressed us as niggers, and gunned us down without hesitation.

The president sent U.S. Army troops to Newport, and a lot of them were black. They patrolled the streets in tanks and jeeps with their guns ready, and enforced an 8:00 pm curfew, with orders to shoot first and ask questions later. The black soldier's presence, and in many cases intervention, prevented a lot of racial brutality, and murders. As a result of the military actions, forty-three men, women and children were killed, and one thousand, one hundred and eighty nine were injured. Seven thousand, two hundred were arrested. Two thousand buildings were destroyed. Some of the buildings were destroyed by fire as snipers fired upon the firemen trying to fight the flames, as the crowd chanted, "Burn baby burn!"

The large parking lots of department stores were turned into forts. It wasn't unusual to see and hear tanks rolling down the streets with their barrels ready to blast at a moment's notice. The tanks were so heavy, they literally torn the streets up

Chance had gotten captured in the basement of a furniture store, and was taken to the extremely overcrowded County Youth Home, along with over seven hundred juveniles who had been arrested; mostly for curfew violation.

I was only a block away from home when a Jeep full of white National Guardsmen pulled up beside me. One of the soldiers asked me where I was headed. I remember feeling relieved that they were asking me questions instead of shooting me. "Hee haw, let's shoot that coon!" one of them yelled. "That would be fun." one of the others added. "Let's make him run down the alley, and see who has the best shot."

To say I was frightened would've been a gross understatement. I began to cry. I was only fourteen, and believed with all my heart, I was about to be murdered for sport. One of them yelled, "Run nigger!" I was about to take off when another Jeep pulled up with a young black Army captain behind the wheel. He asked harshly, "What the fuck is going on here." I saw him as my savior, so I answered as quickly as I could, "They want me to run down the alley, so they can shoot in the back."

In a low harsh growl, without concealing his anger, he ordered them to leave the premises. He seemed like a no nonsense officer, and the Jeep loaded with National Guardsmen got the message, and backed down. They roared with laughter as their Jeep pulled away from the curb, and sped down the street.

"Where do you live?" the officer asked. I informed him that I lived one block away. He instructed me to get in the Jeep, so he could take me home. When he dropped me off, I realized that the anonymous young black captain had just saved my life, and I thanked him whole heartedly.

Everyone in the classroom stared at me with their mouths opened in shock and horror, except Mark. Mark was a young dynamic black student in charge of all the Black History programs implemented. He was tall, handsome, and smart. He was the most popular student at State, and all of the students made him their undisputed leader. He asked us if we remembered how the government came into our communities after the riot, and cut down a lot of trees, and trimmed the ones they left standing. After being sure that we were aware of the action, he explained why it was done.

The way he explained it to us, it was because the helicopters were unable to patrol the streets during the riots from the air, because the trees blocked their view. After the riots, the trees were cut down, and trimmed in most U.S. urban cities to prevent it from ever happening again.

He also explained that Newport only had two major highways, and that caused the military a lot of difficulty getting into the interior of the city, and maneuvering. After the riots, Newport constructed three new freeways. Mark told us they were actually military highways, and their construction was designed to prevent such an obstruction from ever being a hindrance, prohibiting them from being able to quickly take control of the city.

He also told us about one man who was training to become an F.B.I., and another who was training to become a C.I.A. agent. They both stole sensitive training Joes, manuals and documents before they deserted. They had undisputable proof that the F.B.I. was trying to infiltrate the Black Panther Party, and that they had provided the Nation of Islam with the information necessary to bring about the assassination of Malcolm X. The Joe from the C.I.A. had a lot of information about what they expected to encounter during an urban conflict, or civil disturbance. The organization of students, that Mark was the leader of, were hiding the two men, which gave them total access to all the stolen material.

Unlike the food prepared at A.J. Maxie, the food at Holt was the total opposite. Horrible is not a meaningful enough expression to describe the food. It's still hard to believe they served that garbage to children, but they had gotten away with it for years. Upon having the opportunity to see firsthand how bad the food was, Mark suggested that we go on a hunger strike. Once we agreed to try, he organized us, and appointed me to be the spokesman for our group. He made out a list of demands for us to present. Closing down Five and better food, was at the top of our list of demands.

We passed the word around the compound that we weren't going to eat. We would get our food, and leave it on the table, and walk out. None of the other cottages complied, but everyone in our cottage held firm. Because we stood firm, Mark arranged for food to be smuggled in to us during the nights, through the back. He also contacted the local media, and gave them the scoop. There wasn't much going on news worthy during that time, so our peaceful demonstration turned out to be the headline story.

The administration instructed Mr. Morris not to bring us to the chow hall any more, since we were the only cottage participating in the hunger strike. All the local television stations, and a few state representatives, were given a tour of the facility. They were appalled by what they found. They took still pictures, and film footage of the chow hall, and Five, before coming to our cottage to hear directly from us. None of us had ever been involved in a news conference, but we knew we wanted to make it as dramatic as possible. We brought the record player upstairs, and played the Temptation's latest hit "Ball of Confusion" while they entered our cottage. While they were setting up and getting seated in the chairs behind the conference table we had provided, we played The Chi-Lites latest hit, "For God's Sake Give More Power to the People".

I stood before my audience, and read our demands. To my surprise, they were attentive, and very receptive. At the end of everything, we were granted far more than we had asked for. Five was shut down immediately, and Michigan, the cottage that served as a disciplinary cottage, was changed into a general population cottage. There were vast improvements made in the way the food was prepared, and served. Some of the meals were actually tasty, after the hunger strike. The biggest surprise of all was the planning stages had begun to close the facility down completely. As it turned out, the place was over a hundred years old. It was an amazing demonstration of what unity could accomplish, and the lessons we learned stayed with all of us.

The students from State continued to come and teach us. We all looked up to Roy. He was responsible for every activity we participated in. They brought in literature for us to read, and albums for us to listen to. We listened to everything the Last Poets released. We even listened to a lot of Malcolm X's speeches, such as "The Ballot or the Bullet, and Message to the Grassroots". We read, "Die Nigga Die" by H. Rap Brown, "The Autobiography of Malcolm X" by Alex Haley, "Before the Mayflower" by Lerone Bennentt Jr., "Superman to Man" by Jole Augustus Rodgers, and of course "The Making of a Slave" by Willie Lynch. We also read poems by Nikki Giovanni. It was like taking a crash course in black history.

Mark instructed us to choose a hero, and to try to live our lives in a way that would honor our proud heroes. I chose Malcolm X. George chose Marcus Garvey. Frank chose Nat Turner. We all were tempted to choose Allen Page. He was an all-pro defensive end for the Minnesota Vikings, and a lawyer. Today he is a Federal judge.

One day while I was playing basketball in the field house Mr. Morris sent for me to return to the cottage immediately. I had no idea what it was he wanted, but since he had never sent for me like that before, I knew it had to be very important. Once I saw him, the first thing I noticed was how pleased he seemed to be.

He informed me that a kid in Texas cottage named Lance Stone, who was also a red tag serving time for murder, brother had been found murdered. The administration had granted him a home visit, to allow him to attend the funeral. He told me that if all went well, and Lance returned without incident, it would open the door for all red tags to receive home visits.

I knew Lance as Rabbit. I immediately went to him to offer my condolences. He told me he was not going to risk being sent to prison to serve time for murder as an adult, by escaping. He also had been informed that if he returned without incident he would be allowed to go home every sixty days, like everyone else.

That's what eventually opened the door for me. Shortly after Rabbit's return, I was approved and granted a home visit. I was to catch a Greyhound bus to Newport that Friday, and my father was to bring me back that Sunday.

I was so excited when I was on the bus on my way to Newport! I couldn't believe it was actually happening. When we arrived at the bus station in Newport I used the payphone to call home. My mother was very excited when she heard my voice. She said, "We're on our way baby!" and hung up the phone. I didn't even have a chance to tell her where I would be waiting.

When I got home, the very first thing I noticed was Marty walking down the steps. I stopped on the front porch to get a good close look at her. She was far more beautiful than I remembered. I told myself that one day I was going to hold that woman in my arms, but for right now I had to call Darla and make plans to see her. To my surprise, Darla insisted on seeing me that very night.

I found out, as family members dropped by, that I was no longer considered the black sheep of the family. Everyone heard how I had gotten back in school, and they had read the many newspaper clippings I had mailed home to my mother. There were football, basketball, and track clippings. My parents had also received letters from several colleges expressing interest in offering me scholarships. I enjoyed the positive attention, but I really missed Darla, and the time couldn't pass quickly enough for me to see her. Darla always dressed up for me, and I could not wait to see my girlfriend.

I stopped by Aunt Elizabeth's house, to visit Rodger, Renee, Otis, Steven, and of course Aunt Elizabeth. After letting me in, my aunt pulled me to the side for a quick, private conversation. She informed me that Otis wasn't attending school, and Renee had dropped out her senior year. I couldn't understand why, and she never went back. Steven was in elementary school, and excelling in every subject. She asked me to talk to them, and see if I might be able to influence them to return to school. I promised her I would, and I did try.

They were all happy to see me, but they weren't interested in any talk about them returning to school. I still smoked weed, and drank wine, but I had no desire to inject heroin. Rodger had begun injecting heroin, and Renee was snorting it. Some of their friends came by, and they both left the house.

Aunt Elizabeth was playing a record over and over again by the Stable Singers entitled, "Respect Yourself". Otis took the opportunity we had alone to tell me about his friend Victor McDonald. Victor was incarcerated at the House of Corrections, and Otis showed me letters that Victor had written to him. I read a couple of the many letters, and it was obvious that Otis had been corresponding back and forth with this guy. It hurt me because, I had been writing Otis letters the entire time I had been away, and he never answered a single letter. I suppressed the emotions I was feeling, and never allowed him to know how deeply hurt I was. I can't express how thrilled I was when the time had passed, and it was time for me to meet up with Darla. She alone had written to me, and several of her letters expressed her undying love for me, and I did still love her.

When I arrived at her home, her nephew led me to the living room. "Pumpkin will be right down." he announced before leaving me alone. Darla's nick name was Pumpkin, and Pumpkin always made an entrance. She would always walk slowly down the staircase, stop at the floor model hi-fi to select a stack of singles to be played automatically. She always stopped in front of the mirror, which hung over the white fire place, to admire herself. That's when she'd turn towards me, making eye contact for the first time, and slowly walk towards me, as she song along with whatever song the record player was playing.

She was so lovely, but there was something different about her. I was seventeen going on eighteen now, and she was twenty, and we both had changed physically. I had grown facial hair, and she had developed breast. We kissed as she gently stroked my chest. Her eyes widened as she stated, "Damn, you've grown!" As I was holding her tightly in my arms I stated, "So have you!" We giggled with delight as we continued making out.

That night we kissed, and talked until we had exhausted every possible subject. We listened to all the music that had been released while I was away that she knew I would like. We smoked cigarettes, and bumped and grind till our hearts were content. She made me ejaculate in my pants at least three times. She would giggle with delight every time she could feel my penis throbbing in my pants. Her entire family was in the house, so we really couldn't do much more than we did. Darla was always scared to death of getting pregnant, so at that point we had not done more than a lot of kissing, bumping and grinding.

I was happy to get back to Holt. I was beginning to realize how much I enjoyed living the simple life of a high school kid. I was happy to see my family again, but I was anxious to return to school. Mr. Morris had missed me too. He wouldn't say it with words, but he became very playful with me, and began treating me like he was my proud father. He even took me to the field house, and patiently taught me the fine art of rebounding. After perfecting the footwork, and the art of manuvering as well as jocking for position for the anticipated rebound, I couldn't wait for the next time I played against my peers. I wanted to try out the things he had taught me.

On our walk to the cottage from the field house, Mr. Morris told me he could help us get extra days for our home visits, but he needed our help to make it happen. I was curious, and since I had had such a great time on my visit, the thought of getting longer visits was quite intriguing. "What can we do to help?" I asked.

"All we have to do is go two months without any escapes from our cottage, and we'll be allowed to implement a program whereas you could earn as many as three extra days for all home visits. That includes the seven-day home visit also. Can you imagine being allowed to spend as many as ten days at home?" Mr. Morris studied my face to see what type of reaction the information he had just given would have on me, and waited for my response.

"I don't know what we can do to prevent boys from escaping Mr. Morris."

He said, "You guys are some smart boys. Get together with the fellas when we get back, and have a meeting. I'm sure ya'll will come up with something workable to get more time to spend on home visits. I know if I was in the situation ya'll are in, I would think of something." He was right. I had to at least inform everyone, and see if we truly were smart enough to come up with a workable plan.

Once we arrived at the cottage, I called an emergency cottage meeting, so I could share the amazing news with my peers. We needed to brainstorm, and come up with a plan. One thing we all agreed upon was that we didn't want to take on the role of being like the police, trying to prevent boys from escaping, if that's what they felt was best course of action for them. After a serious discussion, which got quite heated at times, we came up with a plan that everyone agreed upon. It was a great plan. The majority of the boys, who attempt to escape, are often captured before they make it out of the city limits, because they didn't have the necessary transportation to assure a successful escape. To eliminate the problem, we would seek the assistance of the college students from State to provide the transportation.

We all agreed that if anyone wanted to escape, we would help them. However, if anyone elected to stay, they had to stay for at least two months. We had to be assured by the students that we had their full support, and they would assist us. It was a huge hurdle to cross, because the students could get into serious trouble if they were caught assisting an escapee.

We waited until Mr. Morris's off day, and then we got permission from Mr. Sterling and Mr. Jordan to allow the girls from Mark's organization to enter the cottage from the rear, so they wouldn't be detected by the administration. We informed them of our plan to go two months without any escapes, and how we had planned to accomplish such a feat. They were all for the idea, and Mr. Jordan explained to us that according to the new program the administration had implemented, the residents in the cottage with the fewest escapes, would be rewarded an extra day for each good work report, school evaluation, and good behavior. We could be rewarded as much as three extra days. The staff of that particular cottage would receive a cash bonus. That explained why Mr. Morris was so passionate about winning.

Chance had a girlfriend name Veronica when he was killed, and her brother Timothy came to our cottage for car thief. He could have been released as early as six months, based upon his behavior. I was excited because I hoped he would stay and take advantage of the opportunity to spend time with me, and change his life, but he elected to leave. I was very disappointed, but it was his life and his choice. All the escapes we planned were executed smoothly, and we were well on our way to establishing the reputation of being the cottage with the least escapes.

Things were going pretty well, although I missed attending school at the training school. There was a teacher by the name of Kathy Walters. I used to love standing in the hall outside her classroom admiring her amazing body.

She was a red head with the perkiest breast I had ever laid eyes on. Her waist was so small that it appeared that she was wearing a girdle of some sort. When the term childbearing hips was coined, it must have been because of her wide hips. Her buttock looked as though she was carrying around a couple of volleyballs under her clothes. Her thighs were thick, and she had big creamy perfectly shaped legs to match. I believe to this day that she is the reason I prefer thick women. She would always notice me gazing at her, full of lust, and she would always flash her big pearly white smile, while waving at me.

She had left her boyfriend, who was the assistant coach at Tri City Central, and taken up with Charlies Bradford. Mr. Bradford was an employee at the facility, and was also a member of the State football team that won two National Championships in a roll. He was a first team All- American linebacker. Ms. Walters was white, and Mr. Bradford was black, so their relationship was very controversial during those times. I believe that's why their relationship didn't last but a very brief moment.

Whenever I had a chance I would go up to the school just to see her and talk. I knew without any doubt that she was aware of the huge lustful crush I had on her. If I believed that there was a chance she would say yes, I would've dropped to my knees and begged her for her hand, but I was just a boy. We talked about a lot of different subjects, and we soon became very good friends.

She started back talking to her old boyfriend after she broke up with Mr. Bradford, and told him all about me. I had no idea that they had researched my situation, and were actively trying to have me released, until I received a surprise visit from him. His name was Chip Kelso. He drove a brand new, black 1971 Pontiac Granville, with red leather interior. There were some eight- track tapes on the passenger's seat, and I noticed they were all the latest R & B releases. I thought to myself how cool he must be to listen to that kind of music. He was young, but he was already bald on the top of his head. He wore a brown, buffalo skin suit that looked just like soft leather. He told me that he had just returned from Peru. As dark as his tan was, it wasn't hard to believe.

He held a lit cigarette loosely between his lips as he spoke to me. He asked me, "How would you like to get out, come live with me and play football, basketball, and run track for Tri City Central?" It caught me totally off guard, but I had to be realistic about the offer. I hadn't spent any time at all in Tri City so I wasn't sure, and I explained that to him. Although I wanted to get out badly, I had to make sure the move was the right move for me. At that time, I had been through a lot to turn my life around, and I was determined to stay on course to graduate. After hearing my concerns, he promised to make the arrangements for me to visit with him for a weekend, so I would have a chance to check the city out. He reassured me that I was going to love the city, before we said our good-byes.

I was so excited that I could hardly contain myself. I could barely wait for Monday to arrive, so I could speak to Ms. Walters and get her opinion. I thought the time would drag and it did. When I finally had the opportunity to speak with her, she informed me that she already knew. She told me she didn't have to convince him to try to get me out. As it turned out George and I had become quite a hot commodity.

Several schools throughout the state were interested in us, and had openly asked for permission to speak with us. Jackson Parkway was also interested in both of us, but because I had competed on the highest level of competition I was better known, and wanted by more schools. Tri City Central, Bloomfield high and Huron Southern had all expressed interest in having me attend their schools.

Ms. Walters told she had plans to come see me while I. She had just received a Porch she ordered, and thought it would be the perfect opportunity to break in the engine. My counselor had purchased a Mercedes Benz. He told me that each of their cars had cost more than a Cadillac Fleetwood. I was amazed, and wondered out loud, "Why would anyone choose to purchase these cars, instead of a Cadillac Fleetwood." That turned out to be my introduction to foreign luxury automobiles.

The following Friday coach Kelso came to Holt to pick me up. To my surprise, he was driving an orange Volkswagen Beatle. I had to be back that Sunday evening, so Coach told me that we would come back Saturday night, and catch a movie with Ms. Walters and spend the night at her apartment to make sure we were back in time. The truth became obvious as time passed that the only thing he was trying to make sure of was that he had the chance to spend the night with Ms. Walters.

Once we arrived at his house, he gave me the grand tour of his home. It was a nice size duplex with an upstairs, main floor, and a basement. He led me to a room upstairs at the front of the house, and told me that if I elected to stay with him that this would be my bedroom. I was a very nice sized room, but it was totally empty. He promised to get me a new bedroom set If I stayed. There was another bedroom that belonged to him, and a television room with a love seat and a couple of chairs. In the room next to it, there was a bathroom, complete with a tub and shower. I had never lived in a house with a shower before. All the showers I had ever taken were either in school, or a juvenile detention facility.

The main floor had sunset orange painted walls, a semi open floor plan with the conventional living room, and dining room furniture. The kitchen was huge with pale Blue painted walls, outdated cabinets, and a half bath near the back door. Off the dining area there was room that was used as a music entertainment room. There was a huge poster of Che Guevara on the wall, with a black light and black light posters. This made the posters seem to light up the room. There were a couple of beanbags on the floor to fulfill the purpose of seats, and a topnotch component set, with amazing speakers. His collection of music was also very impressive. He was obviously a huge jazz fan.

A guy close to my age named Joe stopped by to meet me. He was not quite six feet tall, was dark skinned, wore a huge afro, and had a muscular build. He had accepted the responsibility of showing me around town.

An older guy, who was a close friend of the coach, also stopped by. He was introduced to me as Huey. Huey was about five foot ten, dark skinned and slim. I noticed he carried a thirty, two pistol in his back pocket. He and Joe both called Mr. Kelso, Coach. I took a mental note to also start calling him Coach.

Huey was carrying a shoe box under his arm as he entered the house. He asked Coach to give him some old newspaper, and once he had the paper, he spread the paper out on the floor. We all watched his every move, and it became obvious to me that neither Joe nor Coach had ever seen Huey perform this task before. Our curiosity got the better of us, and we watched his every move attentively as he removed a brick of marijuana from the shoe box. He broke the brick up into buds, and offered Joe and I some of the buds to smoke. We both took a little. I had never seen so much marijuana in my life! Huey pulled a pack of Tops cigarette papers from his pocket, and handed me a few sheets. We rolled a couple of joints and went to the music room. I placed George Benson's album entitled, "The Other Side of Abby Road on, and Joe and I smoked the weed, and listened to the smooth new sounds of jazz.

As Huey and Coach talked I gathered from their conversation that a group of guys had used Coach to smuggle kilos of cocaine into the country, and Coach was waiting to receive his share of the proceeds. His partners lived in Newport, and they were supposed to sell the drugs there and share the profits with him. The things I learned about Coach that day should've made me run, but I was too young, and far too impressionable to recognize the red flags, or the contract I was signing with a devil's emp. There was still a part of me that admired gangsters, and all the evidence of large amounts of marijuana and cocaine amused me. I had been raised in the streets, so I viewed it as a potential opportunity to become involved with big time drug dealers. It was a dream come true for many struggling young boys growing up on the streets at that time, and I was no exception to the rule.

Our grade principle at Central was a man by the name of Mr. Robert Philpot. He was very close to Coach, and he had stopped by to visit for a while. As it turned out, he also had invested in the cocaine Coach had smuggled into the country, and was also waiting on his share of the profits. He didn't mind that we were smoking marijuana in his presence, or that we were listening to them openly discuss the trip they had taken to Peru together. I stepped outside on the front porch because I wanted to see what type of car Mr. Philpot drove. Mr. Philpot was a short, overweight, light skinned black man, with a huge black afro. He was a very sharp dresser, and I was shocked when I saw his car. It was the very same Pontiac Grandville that Coach had driven when he first came to visit me. He never told me that the car was his, but he knew I thought it was, and he allowed me to continue thinking so. He accepted the compliments I had given him on the car that day. It was another red flag that I wasn't experienced enough to recognize. He misrepresented himself to impress me and mislead me. It worked.

After listening in on their conversation, I realized that I knew Mr. Philpot's estranged wife. She was a close friend of Mr. Jordan's and I met her at his apartment in Holt. She was a strikingly beautiful, full figured woman, and the chemistry between us was undeniable. We were both very attracted to one another, but she insisted that I was just a little too young. I could sense her fighting desperately to resist my advances. I had her in my arms, with my tongue in her mouth, before she came to her senses and pulled away.

She asked me if I had ever heard of William Simmons, the super star basketball player. Of course, I had heard of him. He was dunking so hard that he was tearing down backboards in high schools. He was fighting the professionals for the right to come out of college early, so he could enter the league. She told me that she was his foster sister. When I tell you, she was drop dead gorgeous, that would be a serious understatement. She had left Mr. Philpot, and filed for divorce.

I broke in on the conversation, and told Mr. Philpot I knew his estranged wife. After he asked me a few questions, he was sure that we were talking about the same woman. I never told him about the kiss, or how hard she had to fight to resist me. I never told him how disappointed I was to find out that she had moved from Tri City. She even left their child, a baby boy, with him.

Coach told Joe that Anita Tate was my date for that night, and she planned to take me to a party. Joe told me that Anita was extremely fine. I couldn't wait to meet her and see for myself.

After everyone left, Coach showed me where the towels were kept, and how the shower worked. I got busy getting ready for the party. I had been to the parties students gave at State, but I hadn't been to a party with kids my own age in years. I wondered how I would be accepted, and how much did they know about me.

Anita arrived a short time later, and she was just as beautiful as everyone said she was. I liked her a lot, and I could tell that the feelings were mutual, but right from the start I could tell that there just was no chemistry between us. She took me to a party in a housing project, and I was happy to see Joe there. He was there with two of his uncles. They were his mother's brothers, and they looked a lot alike. The older one was named David, and he drove a gold Pontiac Grand Prix. The younger one's name was Benny, and he and Joe were the same age.

Anita vanished while we were talking, but I didn't mind. Everything was within walking distance in Tri City, and the party was only four blocks from the house. David and Benny all lived together with their older brother name Smokey, just two blocks away from the party, on Wood street. David brought us a couple of bottles of Cold Duck to drink, and I brought some cigarettes. We sat on the front porch of the house while we got high, and got better acquainted. We joked and talked for hours, before calling it a night.

That night Coach showed me how to move the coffee table out of the way, and let the sofa bed out. We talked a little about the party, and Anita. I told him that I liked her a lot, but only as a friend. He was really interested in knowing what I knew about Mr. Bradford, but all I told him were things I knew he was already was aware of. For instance, he was a big bad dude, you wouldn't want to fuck with. I didn't tell him he was one of my heroes! Why wouldn't he be? He was a fist team all – American inside linebacker from a national championship team. A black male role model, with a college degree. He worked with us kids as our supervisor. He loved us, but he didn't take shit off nobody. Even his bosses were intimidated by the mere mentioning of his name, and he gave us permission to use his name, whenever he gave us of the permission to do something. It had been a long day and once he realized that I was having trouble staying awake, he said good-night, and headed up the stairs.

The next afternoon after we ate steak and eggs for breakfast, he gave me a piece of paper with a name and phone number written on it. It was a girl named Phillis

Washington. He told me that she had just had a baby, and wondered if I was interested in girls that had babies. I assured him that I had no problem with girls that had babies. As a matter of fact, I preferred girls with babies, and bad reputations for obvious reasons.

I called her and we talked for a long time, before she suggested that I come to her house. She lived only a half of a block away on Oaklawn. I agreed, and after telling Coach my plans, I left the house on my own in the city for the very first time. wanted to spend some time with this girl. She had flirted with me over the phone, and I became anxious to see the face behind that sexy voice. She expressed excitement about seeing me face to face also.

I was not disappointed when I saw Phillis. She was a dark skinned, full figured beauty. She had big juicy full lips, and the way she licked her lips as she looked at me, I could tell that I wasn't the only one looking forward to being alone. I couldn't wait to hold this girl in my arms with her lips planted firmly on mine. I longed to kiss her, taste her, and feel the taste buds on her tongue rubbing against my own.

Her parents were sitting in the living room watching television, so we joined them for a little while. After a while, she asked me if I was hot. After admitting I was, she suggested that we go out on the enclosed front porch, and cool off. Her new born baby was a cute baby boy name Delvito. She picked him up, and carried him as she led me out to the porch. I wondered what it was she expected to do on the porch with her baby in one arm, and her parents in the living room. I wanted to get close to her, and I wanted her right at that very moment.

There was a blind spot on the porch that prevented her parents from seeing us, and as she held the baby in one arm, she began kissing me. After a while, I asked her to be my girl, but she insisted I waited until I was sure I was going to stay in Tri City. She said, "Even if you were sure that you wanted to stay here, I still would want you to wait until school starts, so you can see the other girls, and know for sure that I am who you want." I told her that I was sure that I was going to stay, and I was sure about what I wanted, and it was her. Phillis was playing for keeps, and unbeknown to me, it was working like a charm. I knew at that moment I was going to choose Tri City.

Coach called and told Phillis to let me know it was time to go. I had a very enjoyable afternoon. I liked Phillis a lot, and I was pretty certain I wouldn't want any other girl. I wondered how Coach was going to get me out. After all, the judge had sentenced me to be a ward of the state until the age of nineteen, and I was only eighteen. I kissed Phillis, and promised her that I would return.

I had made up my mind, and when I saw Coach I told him so. I expressed my concerns, and doubts about his ability to have me released. He told me to concentrate on sports and school, and he would handle all the details to make it happen. Although he was wild, young, and unpredictable I trusted him. He was going to be one of my coaches, and my legal guardian. Even though he was only twenty-seven years old, he was very mature for his age, and like I said, he had earned my confidence.

Ms. Walters pulled up in the driveway while we were talking. She was driving what I thought was a small sports car, and once again I was puzzled about the fact that this small sports car cost as much as three Cadillac Fleetwoods. She was looking so sexy that it took my maximum effort not to stare at her. I knew she was aware of my lust for her, but I didn't want to make Coach aware of it. He was excited by the fact that he was about to spend the night with her, and I didn't want to spoil it.

We were all going to ride to Holt in her new Porch, so we loaded up in the car. I was in the back seat, and I must admit that it was the most uncomfortable ride I had ever taken in my life. I remember thinking that although there was a backseat, I couldn't bring myself to believe the manufacturer had truly designed the backseat with the intentions of it serving the purpose of seating two passengers.

Ms. Walters had traveled all the way to Belgium, Germany to purchase the expensive vehicle, and had it shipped to the United States. I asked her why did she go all the way to Germany to purchase the vehicle, and she explained that there were many advantages to traveling abroad, to purchase the Porch. First of all, it will cut the waiting period, and secondly, Germany has no speed limits. Therefore, she was able to test the car's limits as well as her own. "I did 120 miles an hour for more than ten miles!" she confessed with glee.

They chose to check out a new movie released entitled, "The French Connection". It was a pretty good movie about how a determined police officer discovered exactly how a heroin ring was smuggling heroin into the United States. It was based on a true story. That night I sensed that Ms. Walters wasn't comfortable having sex with me around, but she had sexual intercourse with him all the same. The moans, groans, and the sounds of the bed springs did not escape me. The entire encounter was less than five minutes, and the sound of the bed springs lasted for less than two minutes. I couldn't believe they were finished that quickly. I could even hear Coach snoring! I was jealous, because I felt he was the luckiest man alive. It was difficult, but I managed to endure the unsettling emotions.

When I was in the Youth Home Mr. Green had talked to us about the art of making love to women. He said, "There are some women who actually enjoy a minute man, but that is very rare. You have to caress her, kiss her, touch her in the right places, and compliment her to warm her up. When you insert your penis, it is actually the beginning of the end, so do your best to prolong the foreplay for as long as necessary. Allow her to let you know when she wants you to do more. Be very attentive to the messages her body will give you as she response to the things you are doing to her. Learn about the different parts of her body. It is very important to make yourself familiar with the different parts of a woman's body, to ensure you are able to deliver pleasure. You are ready for a woman, once you truly are interested in making sure every sexual encounter you have, is one ending with the goal of mutual gratification being met.

If you don't understand that, you are still a boy, and you'll make love like a boy. A real woman wants a real man." Maybe it was because I was jealous, but that night I knew that Coach made love like a boy, and I wished Ms. Walters would come to me while he was asleep, so I could've shown her the good time she wanted and deserved.

True to his word, I was released on probation two weeks later. He was now my legal guardian. After a brief meeting with my probation officer, we went to my new home. When we pulled into the driveway I saw Joe was already there waiting on us. He was sitting on the front porch talking to Tommy. Tommy lived in the other unit in the duplex. Coach introduced us, and Tommy's wife, Joyce, came out to meet me. They were a young handsome couple. Tommy was tall, brown skinned, good-looking and muscular. His wife was gorgeous! She also was brown skinned, and tall. She was so beautiful that I thought she was a professional model. She had long, straight, dark brown, flowing shoulder length hair, and keen facial features that resembled the famous image of Queen Nefertiti. They both made me feel welcomed. They also had a huge albino German Shepherd they called Sheba.

Joe was happy that I was back, and after I was settled in, we went to the park to kick it, and shoot some hoops. The park was on Wood, and his uncle's house was so close by you could see it from the park. Guys saw us shooting hoops, and joined us. It seemed like everybody either already knew who I was, or had heard about me. They knew I had done time for murder, but that didn't make a difference to any of them.

I had a good day on the basketball court, and made it obvious that I planned to not only make the team, but also make a serious impact. I had a short guy on my team, and we dominated. His name was Larry. He was a short chunky fella, with a huge afro. He suggested that we all walk to the store to get something to drink.

As we walked to the store I was briefed on the pedigree of Tri City. It turned out that Tri City was not a soft city. There were several thoroughbred gangsters residing in the city. I was introduced to Alvin Raff. He was the second youngest in a large family of older brothers. They not only demanded respect, they received it. He lived next door to

Larry, and since we all lived in such close proximity, a bond was immediately formed. Alvin was tall, good-looking and had the biggest afro I had ever seen on a dude. A lot of people who were either new in town, or observed him when he ventured out of town, thought it was a wig. There was never a single hair out of place. He wore his hair braided most of the time, so all the hometown people knew it was his natural hair.

He invited me to his house. His brothers had heard about me, and he wanted them to meet me. We walked the few blocks to his house, and I was introduced to all of them. They all liked me after we had talked briefly. Harold said, "Game recognizes game, and this kid is already a man. He's a young thoroughbred!" It became understood, if you messed with any of us, you had a problem with all of us.

That night I slept on the sofa bed. I was awakened early the next morning by Larry Whitter knocking on the front door. Coach let him in and introduced us. He was the captain, and starting quarterback of the varsity football team. Larry was a tall very handsome white kid with Blue eyes, and blond hair. He had a muscular body, and a delightful personality. He was nothing like I thought he would be at first glance. The very first thing I noticed about him was how sincere and genuine he was. He had come by to welcome me to Tri City, and to tell me if I needed him for anything, to let him know. He lived next door to Alvin. The next thing I noticed about him was he didn't have a prejudice cell in his body. He didn't try to talk by using black lingo our physical gestures like most white people do when they try to fit in with black people, and prove they were hip to the ways of our culture. I appreciated that he was cool just being himself, and we soon became extremely close. He didn't smoke weed or drink, but I enjoyed hanging out with him all the same. He knew that I drank alcohol, smoked cigarettes and marijuana, but he was not judgmental, and never told a soul.

We spent the entire morning talking, and eating a breakfast that consisted of steaks and eggs, prepared by Coach. Eventually Larry Banks and Alvin came by. Soon after that, Joe arrived with his cousin Gerald Dickerson. Coach jokingly named us, "The wild Bunch" and the name stuck with us, and our numbers grew.

Gerald's nick name was Weed. Although I learned differently from his mother, I had thought they called him weed because of the amount of marijuana he smoked. We were both seniors, and he was the starting wide receiver on the varsity football team. He 3also ran the high hurdles on the track team. He enjoyed smoking weed as much as I did, but the reason they called him Weed was because of the pace he grew.

When the school year began, I found out that Weed's mother worked at the high school. She was the Bear's Den coordinator. The Tri City Central's mascot was a bear, so they named this particular room the Bear's Den. I have no idea why they called it a Den. It was as large as any dance hall I had ever been to. The Bear's Den contained four pool tables, two ping pong tables, a dance floor, picnic tables with benches attached, and a juke box with all the latest R&B releases. It was like a continuous party began before the first hour classes began, and ended once the school was closed for the day. You were only allowed to enter the bearcat room during your lunch hour, your free hour, or your study hour.

There was soul music played over the intercom system in the halls and the classrooms. A student store sold snacks and soft drinks before classes began every morning. I had never seen or heard of anything like this school, and the more I learned about the school the more I was pleased with my choice.

The school was built like a college campus. There was a main building were most classes were held. Across the street from the main building they had a complete football stadium with a quarter mile track built around the football field, and a large parking lot so students with cars parked, free of charge. Down the street from the football stadium they had a three story, field house which also contained an Olympic size pool, bowling alleys, basketball court, weightlifting facility, and offices for the coaches. On the main street where the school was located, there was a library building. A separate building was a huge auditorium. Everything had the Wheeler's logo on it, and was the best that money could buy. Wheeler was a factory in town that made wheels.

Weed's mother was such a beautiful and sweet person that I fell madly in love with her. She loved me too, and insisted that I called her Momma, and I never called her anything else. Every student addressed her as Momma Dickerson, but I addressed her as Momma. She was always there for me. I could talk to her about anything. I didn't have to pretend with her. She knew my situation, and adopted me right away. Since Weed and I were the same age, she called us her twins.

They already had football tryouts, but they held a special tryout for me. It was a no brainer for them. I easily made the team. Al Ford was the starting running back and the starting safety. He was just that talented. The problem was we both played the same positions, so I wasn't allowed the playing time I felt I deserved. In order to be a running back on the team, Central had a rule you had to run a mile under six minutes. I had never run the mile before, so Larry Whitter volunteered to run it with me, in order to pace me. I finished the mile in time thanks to Larry, but I pulled my groin. That prohibit me from performing at full strength, but I got plenty of playing time at practice. There was a buzz throughout the city, and everyone I met, told me that they would be at the game to see me play.

Our first game was against Northern, and although I had never practiced on the special teams, I was put in the game as a gunner. I wasn't familiar with the position that was double teamed, and I didn't do well at all. I managed to make one touchdown saving tackle for the entire game, and we lost 26 to nothing. It was an embarrassing moment.

I quit because I didn't like the way the coaching staff used me. I didn't have anyone filling the role as a father figure, even though that was the role Coach was supposed to fulfill for me. I needed a man to get in my face, and demand that I not start developing the characteristics of a quitter. When I tried talking to Coach about it, he was unconcerned and complacent. He offered nothing by the way of advice, and thus I made a huge mistake. A mistake that I could've avoided, and I regretted that decision for the rest of my life. It was my senior year, and my last chance to prove that I was worthy of a football scholarship. All the offers I had received were withdrawn, because I was viewed as a quitter, and rightfully so.

I decided to concentrate on basketball. Coach, was the Junior Varsity basketball coach, and although he had lost two starting players to the varsity team, they were still expected to finish the season undefeated. My quitting the football team and joining the basketball team eliminated the possibility of him losing a third player to the varsity team. Bo Gilliam had been penciled in as his starting center. Because of my amazing jumping ability, I was penciled in as the starting center for the varsity team, even though I was only six foot two at the time.

After a couple of weeks Al Ford blew his knee out. If I hadn't quit, I would have gotten my chance to play. Al began hanging out with us every day. He enjoyed smoking marijuana and partying too. We nick named him X. X was six foot even, very handsome, and the girls were crazy about him. He was brown skinned, and wore a medium size afro.

Coach began spending no time at all at home. He spent every night in Holt with Ms. Walters. He was actually making an hour commute from Holt. He would visit me on the weekends long enough to stock the kitchen with food, and pick up his mail. It was my responsibility to cook for myself, do my homework, keep the house clean, and make sure I made it to school daily. I didn't mind it at all, because I wanted to be grown, even though it was quite obvious that I still needed parental guidance.

I was spending a lot of time with Phillis, but I also spent time with other girls. I met a girl by the name of Violet. She actually came to my house to meet me. She had graduated from Central the year before, and was the captain of the cheer leading squad while she was there. She was now a freshman at the Community College. It wasn't long before we were in the music room making out. Violet came to my house that Friday, Saturday and Sunday and we spent the whole time listening to music, entertaining the members of the wild bunch, and making out every chance we got. Violet was a very good kisser.

Joe told me that Violet had just broken up with Butch, and that Sunday evening he came to my house looking for her. He asked her to come outside, and talk to him, but I felt that he was going to assault her, and I told her so. I also told her that all she had to say was that she was with me now, and stay in the house, but she elected to leave with Butch against my wishes. The next day he came to my house with some Boone's Farm apple wine, and some marijuana as a peace offering. He told me that he had assaulted Violet, and by doing so he had broken her entire face. He apologized for bringing the drama to my house, and we became tight. His nick name was Colonel Klink, and he proudly became a member of the Wild Bunch. Violet was in the hospital for weeks.

The crowd that hung out at my house grew. Not only did the wild bunch continue to expand, but an entourage of girls from Central developed. We had a party at my crib every single day. I always did my homework to make sure I kept better than average grades. I had a 3.4 grade point average, and I did everything that I felt was necessary to keep it that way. I was a senior, and I was determined to graduate with good grades.

Even though there was a lot of chaos at the house, and there were times I found it difficult to get away, I always seemed to somehow make sure I spent time with Phillis. I was absolutely crazy about the girl. Our chemistry was undeniable, as well as growing unbelievably stronger. I kept telling her that she was the one, but she insisted on remaining just one of the many girls I dealt with.

During my entire senior year, not one single girl could say I was her boyfriend. I was always in the halls, the stairwells, and the empty classrooms, kissing, and hugging with some willing girl. I was making out with several girls. They all knew it, and they all knew each other. I wasn't cheating, because I belonged to none of them, but at the same time I belonged to all of them. Some of them had boyfriends, but I didn't care. I kept their secrets, and enjoyed the benefits.

Phillis was a different story all together. She seemed clueless about what she truly meant to me. If she had agreed to be my girl, I would've gladly dropped every one of those girls for her. She did everything for me that a girlfriend was supposed to do for her boyfriend. I could never understand why she wouldn't be my girl.

Coach never did buy the bedroom set for me like he had promised. The living room was my bedroom the entire time I lived with him. I received fifty dollars every two weeks from the state, and Coach kept it for me. He said he was saving it for me, so I could purchase a car to go to college with. I wanted to use some of the money, so I could buy a comfortable bed, but Coach would have none of that. He promised me that once I was a college student with a car, I would appreciate not touching the money.

The football season ended, and basketball season began. To my surprise, I was elected to be one of the co-captains, along with Larry Whitter. It was a great honor, and it was very humbling to have undisputable proof of what my peers thought of me. I loved playing basketball, but it was while

I was participating on the school's basketball team that I learned one of Central's darkest secrets.

There had been a race riot the year before, and Central was paying several black students, whom they considered trouble makers, not to attend regular classes. They met in a classroom located in the field house, and weren't allowed to come to the main building. They only had to go to class for a couple of hours a day. Those who participated in the program would graduate, but they couldn't participate in any of the special activities. Some of the school's best basketball players were in the program, and were not allowed to play. Richard Miller was an excellent ball handler, and he had great size for a guard. Lorenzo Edwards was about six feet six, with tremendous athleticism. He would have been a handful for any center in the state, and Darrius Dixon and I were the same size. He hung out at my house every day. His presence would have given us the type of depth that would have allowed us to put on a full court press the entire game.

The Bear's Den, the student store, and the music over the intercom were all concessions awarded to the student body to pacify them. The students that did the most damage during the riots were targeted for the program, and they all received diplomas except of course Lorenzo. He was arrested for committing a murder that occurred while we were out of town playing a basketball game. Had he been allowed to attend regular classes, he would have been eligible to play. We were informed about the murder which occurred at a dance given at the Black Racondo's building upon our return. He should've been with us instead of at that dance.

I was reminded once again how unpredictable life can be. Your whole life could change in a split second, as well as end. You must remain mindful of this fact, at all times. How many do you think were prepared for it all to end? We have to live each moment of our lives, with this in the forefront of our minds. We have a very powerful enemy, whom we often underestimate. Trust me, White Supremacy is not a myth, and their laws, policies, and education are all nothing, but traps and obstacles embedded into the very fiber of this culture designed to impede the progress of our people. This was just an example of one young brother who got caught up.

We had a fair basketball season, and we wanted to do something to celebrate. Darrius' decision to join the Navy. He was leaving that Sunday to report. He came by, and suggested that we put our money together to buy a ten-dollar bag of marijuana. Larry Banks had five dollars, and he quickly gave it to me. I in turn handed the five-dollar bill to Darrius, and I didn't hear anything more from him, or about him for next four days. What I heard made me burst into laughter. Darrius had failed the test, so the Navy rejected him, and was sending him home. I would see him again, and soon. I had made a promise to myself to seek retribution.

Joe had a baby by Darrius' sister. They weren't involved with one another anymore. In fact, they barely spoke. It was as if they hated each other. I didn't agree with the way he refused to spend time with his son, simply because he didn't get along with his mother. I couldn't understand how Joe could turn his back on his son, or Brenda. I always had a serious crush on Brenda. She was enchantingly beautiful. Legendary beautiful was a perfect description of her. She was a redbone with a huge, naturally curly red afro. She had a body that was chiseled to perfection, and a face so pretty you could never tire from absorbing the image. She was a knock out. I wanted her badly, but alas she was Joe's baby's mother, and because of their hostile relationship she avoided all of us.

I saw her in the school hall, and I told her, "I'm gonna to beat your brother's ass wherever I see him." She was so angry that she cussed me out. I can't remember to this very day anything she said. The whole time she was cussing me out, all I could think about was how fine she was, and how much I adored her. I do remember her saying, "You ain't gone do a shit to my brother!" I just shook my head and walked away.

As I was walking down the steps, I saw Darrius talking to the assistant principle, Mr. Townsend. I walked up to them, and punched Darrius in the face with a straight right cross. He was knocked out cold, as he slid down the wall he was standing next to. Blood was gushing from his nose, and there was a loud roar from the crowd of students in the hall who had witnessed, and been impressed by the assault.

I was taken to the principal's office, and the discussions began to determine if I should be suspended. That is when I discovered I already had accumulated enough credits to graduate at the end of the previous semester. I should have been given my diploma at that time. That information had been withheld from me, because they weren't sure how I would've responded to the news. They needed me to continue playing basketball for the school. Since I was not running track at that time, due to a serious injury, I wasn't of any use to the team nor the school, so I was told not to return until graduation.

Coach was furious and appalled that I had actually

assaulted a student in front of Mr. Townsend. Those days he seemed to be angry and bitter all the time, even though he had guided the junior varsity team thru an undefeated season. Ms. Walters had broken up with him once again. It also became painfully obvious by this time, the guys whom he had smuggled the coke for, were not going to give him one red cent.

He was so angry with me that he had me packed, and shipped back to Newport that very day. While I was in Newport, someone broke into his house, and stole his expensive, state of the art, component set. He called me, to tell me all about it. I sensed he blamed me, and he hasn't really had anything to do with me since.

I came back with my parents for the graduation commencement exercises, and to my surprise Mr. Ford from the youth home was in attendance. He was beaming with pride when I walked across the stage, and received my diploma. True to form, he had great advice for me. He didn't use many words, but he convinced me that I shouldn't wait until the fall to go to college. We both agreed that staying in Newport, while waiting to go to school in the fall, wouldn't be a bright idea. I decided right then and there to go to college for the summer term.

We all stopped by Coach's crib after the ceremony, and that was the last time I saw his face, or even heard his voice. He kept all of my money that he claimed he had been saving for me to get a car, and used it to replace his component set. I was so hurt! Particularly since I had absolutely nothing to do with the theft of his property.

I trusted the man, and had a lot of love in my heart for him. I just let it go, and went on with my life. I kept up with his whereabouts, and his accomplishments over the years. I even tried to reach out to him on several different occasions, but all my efforts were for naught. I always got the same results. He had clearly used me to fulfill his personal hidden agendas. His drinking, drug use, and lack of guidance had a tremendous effect on my life in so many ways, and on so many levels. I'm sorry that it had to end the way it did. I had a ball living in Tri City, and I got a diploma out the deal.

I went back to Newport to spend a few weeks before school started. I had been accepted at State University, and they were willing to pay for everything. I decided to spend as much time as I could with Darla. I was crazy about Darla, but I knew I would have to leave her soon, and go to school. As a result of spending so much time with her, she got pregnant. She told me that I was the father, and I had no doubts about that being the truth. I had tested Darla on many occasions, and her love for me had never wavered. When I was strung out on heroin, I did everything I could to convenience her that I was not worthy of her precious love. I even became physically abusive, and she still refused to leave my side.

She insisted we get married immediatlly, but I told her she would have to wait until I got settled in school first. She didn't like the idea, but what kind of life could we live, and what type of future would we have, if I didn't return to school? We both had graduated from high school, and she had begun working at a nursing home making minimum wage. Realistically, there was no way we could have survived on her salary, even though she insisted that we give it a try before riling it out.

I put my foot down and insisted that we wait. I was

certain she would wait. She had waited for me to get off heroin. She had waited until I did time for murder. She had waited until I graduated from high school. Why should I believe that she wouldn't continue to wait a little longer with all the potential our future held?

One day she called me, and told me she had met a guy on the bus, on her way home from work, and he looked just like me. A few weeks later she informed me that they were getting married that very Friday, even though she was huge, because of the pregnancy. I didn't believe her. In fact, I thought it was a ploy on her part to pressure me into marrying her before the baby was born. I decided to stop by her house to make sure she understood that I truly did love and adore her, and it was my intentions to marry her. I wanted to explore the possibilities as well as go over our options as a couple. Maybe getting married before I graduated was a possibility, but first I would have to leave Newport and get settled in.

I walked to her house, and to my astonishment when I arrived, there was a huge crowd there celebrating their wedding. They were holding their wedding reception at her mother's house. I never entered the house. The entire scene between us took place in the doorway. With tears in my eyes, I stated more than asked, "Oh no! What have you done?" She was also crying when she said to me, "Kiss the bride.", and when I did, she stuck her sweet tongue in my mouth, for the very last time. She was crying so hard I could actually taste her salty tears, during the seemingly endless kiss. We both knew this would be our last kiss, and neither one of us wanted to be the one to end it. I eventually began to wonder to myself, "How could she do this to us?" The pain the thought caused, was enough to help me tear myself away from her.

I never actually entered the house. I was too embarrassed by the unwanted attention I received from the crowd, by being the jilted baby's father and all. Everyone knew the baby was mine, including the groom. I stood in the opened doorway the entire time before eventually leaving.

I was crushed, and although I tried my best to fight back the tears, I was unsuccessful at doing so. It was hard to believe that she hadn't waited for me. It was hard to believe that this guy actually married her, knowing that she loved me, and was carrying my child. I cried a lot, and got drunk a lot over the next couple of days, until I heard they had plans to name the baby after her new husband. It was a pretty sobering experience, and I had to pull myself together, and go on with my life.

A few days later I heard the rumors that Theresa Burks, of Tri City had just had a baby girl, and she looked just like me. Her boyfriend was Earl. He was my friend X's brother. Theresa lived three blocks from me when I lived in Tri City, and she would visit me late at night at least once or twice a week.

A couple of months after that, I heard rumors that she was pregnant. She sat next to me in our geometry class, so I asked her about the rumors. She confirmed that the rumors were in deed true, but in that same conversation she assured me that her boyfriend was the father. Here it was now a year later, and I found the rumors about her baby looking just like me very unsettling. The combination of the experience with Darla, and Theresa, sent me into a tailspin. I had to get away from it all. In such a short span of time, everything seemed to unravel, and I had no idea what the future held for me. I believed I had become the father of two children, and I was pretty sure that both of their mothers were doing their best to deny me any access into their lives. I decided that it was time to do exactly what Mr. Ford had suggested, and go to school early. I needed to get away as soon as possible and State University needed me. As it turned out, because of Affirmative Action, they had a quota to fulfill, and it was a difficult task to find young black men eligible to enroll. I caught the bus the next day to Hudsonville. A representative from the school were waiting at the station to give me a ride to school. She was holding a sign with my name on it, and she had a beautiful smile.

Chapter 6

I had barely gotten settled in before I realized I had come to college grossly unprepared. All I brought with me were clothes. I didn't bring any throw rugs, a record player, a radio, a television, a typewriter, any sheets, blankets or towels. I had no idea what would be needed to live on campus. I tried to contact Coach. He had been hired as the head basketball coach of a nearby high school, so he was very close by. I wrote letters to him, and left messages in his office, but that actually was the beginning of a pattern he would establish of never responding to me.

I had sought no one's advice, whom had campus life experience, so my underestimation of what would be needed was entirely my fault. I was breaking ice and new ground for our family. Everyone in my family was happy I had turned my life around, and was the first in our family to go to college. That alone was considered quite an accomplishment for the one who had once been considered the black sheep. It was a huge, positive step in the right direction for our family.

The food in the cafeteria was exactly like most schools. The only true difference was the wider variety to choose from, and you could eat as much as you wanted, if you resided in the dorms. If you were on the football team during spring training or during preseason you were also allowed to eat as much as you wanted. All you had to do to eat, was present your school's identification card.

I was on my way to my room when I noticed a huge black guy moving into a room down the hall from me. He was the very first black student I had seen. In those days when a black person saw another black person, where our numbers were few, it was a great comfort for most of us. Some of us preferred being the only black person, but neither one of us were like that. We were both very happy to see one another.

His name was Jeffery Rayon, but he told me that preferred being called Gator. He was six feet two and weighed two hundred and eighty, five pounds. I was excited when he told me that he was from Monroe. That was a suburb of Newport. He told me that he had also just been released from State Prison. The prison was better known as the State Reformatory, or Gladiator's school. There was an edge to his delivery. He was frightening to some people, but he was cool to me. We had a lot in common. He loved listening to jazz, and he genuinely enjoyed talking about jazz tunes. Smoking marijuana was as much of a passion with Gator, as it was with me. He loved playing and watching football, basketball, and boxing. We both enjoyed being the center of attention at parties. We could drink, dance, and smoke with the best of them. He had a lot of penitentiary stories that he shared with me, and he was a great storyteller. He would describe every detail vividly. He could make you feel like you were actually there. He told me there would be others coming to State straight from prison, and gave me a complete rundown all about them.

The campus grounds were breath taking beautiful. It was a small campus with three dormitories on one side of the campus, and six apartment buildings on the other. Hudsonville, with a population estimation of nearly one hundred thousand, was a very small town. All the town consisted of was a drive-in movie theater, a bowling gallery, and a tavern on campus that doubled as a pizzeria. Everything was only minutes apart. The tavern delivered everything they sold, except the beer and wine.

We were allowed to drink legally. Congress had lowered the drinking age from twenty-one to eighteen, and there was a lot of drinking going on. The Viet Nam war was going on during that time, so the justification for the drinking age being lowered was, if we are old enough to get drafted, and die fighting for our country, then we were old enough to have a drink in our country.

Gator had told me all about Pierre Lane, Demetrius Collins, and Patrick Jennings, and I was truly looking forward to meeting every one of them. Pierre's nick name was Box. Demetrius' nick name was Meme, and Patrick was called Day Day.

The first to arrive was Box and Meme. Box was dark skinned, about five feet ten inches tall, with a slender build. He wore a short afro, and had an all business attitude. As you could tell by his name, Meme was selfish, and he too had a slender built. He also wore a short afro. They both were strictly old school with old souls, and already had associate degrees. They were very serious about life, and I respected and admired their self-discipline. Day Day was to come the following term. I was told that he was six feet tall, but he didn't play basketball at all. He was a bodybuilder, and the light heavyweight boxing champion in prison. He was a running back that loved football contact, and absolutely loved to workout. I couldn't wait to meet him. Out of them all, he was the youngest.

That summer was a fun summer. You could hear songs from Donnie Hathaway's latest album entitled "Everything is Everything" everywhere you went. The songs were "Little Ghetto Boy", "The Ghetto", To Be Young Gifted and Black", and of course the title tune "Everything is Everything".

Stevie Wonder had an album entitled "The Talking Book" out at that time, so of course you heard "Superwoman", Visions", "Creep", "Too High" and "Where Were You When I Needed You". Donnie Hathaway also team up with Roberta Flack, and the collaboration produced the number one single, "Where is the Love". The Temptations were proving to still be relevant by singing the song, "Poppa Was a Rolling Stone", and Curtis Mayfield had released the sound track to the movie, "Superfly". The album consisted of many hit tunes, such as "Pusher Man", "Fred is Dead", "Give Me your Love" and of course the title track "Superfly". It was an unbelievable time for music, and the perfect sound track for our summer.

Towards the end of the summer I met two guys at a party they were giving. We became extremely close. They shared an apartment, and they enjoyed all the things that I loved. I began spending all of my time with them. I was practically living there, and we were going through girls like a hot knife through butter. One of them was Miquel Nelson and he was born and raised in Tri City. We knew a lot of the same people. Miquel's nick name was Flash. The other guy was Samuel Tate. His nick name was Hands, and he was born and raised in Hudsonville. He had a nephew who was boxing by the name of David Tate. If the name sounds familiar, it's because his son is David Tate Jr., was the undisputed welterweight champion of the World. David Sr. was an amateur welterweight during that time, and we all were so very proud of him.

I had gotten to the point I wasn't attending any of my classes at all. All I did was throw parties, and looked good attending them. I went to football practice every day, and amazed the coaching staff with my speed. Speed is something that can't be taught. Either you have speed, or you don't. It's a pure blessing, and every day the coaches made me prove to everyone that there was no one on the team nearly as fast as me. At the end of each practice the head coach would have me line up on the five-yard line. Then he would instruct the entire team to line up at the goal line behind me, and told them if anyone could catch me, and tackle me, before I reached the end zone at the other end of the field, they wouldn't have to run any wind sprints. No one ever even came close to catching me. After a few times of beating everyone with such ease, I began to wonder if they were truly trying.

The entire coaching staff loved me. I became the starting safety, even though I was only a freshman. The coaches loved Gator too, and they made him the starting offensive guard, even though he also was just a freshman. We were so popular it seemed like we were celebrities, and the season hadn't even begun.

One day while leaving football practice, I noticed some basketball players sitting on the bleachers accompanied by some gorgeous cheerleaders. Cold weather comes early in the north, and it was already wet and freezing cold. I had already developed a tendency to quit whenever I found the going not to my liking, so I quit football to concentrate on basketball. I had no guidance, and I listened to absolutely no one. There was no way I should have quit a starting position on a varsity football team in collage. I would have gotten a scholarship, and maybe the attention of the pros. The lack of guidance showed in my decision making, and my judgment.

As the Fall term was coming to a close, Flash, Hands, and I were experiencing some financially trying times. We seemed to always be hungry. I was alright because I could always go to the cafeteria to eat, but Hands and Flash couldn't. Hands came up with a plan. He suggested that we rob a store in Cedar Springs, that he knew was an easy target, and use the money to purchase some marijuana to sell on campus.

It was an excellent plan. With my experience, we were able to plan and rob the store without any problems. We already knew where to purchase the marijuana, so we brought a pound. The marijuana was much stronger than we had anticipated. We quickly became everyone's favorite source for marijuana on and off campus. The money began flowing in like water from a flowing stream. Things couldn't have been going any better.

I had a dorm room, but I hardly ever stayed there. I kept some of the marijuana in my room, so I wouldn't have to transport it across campus to the dorms in order to make sells there. There was a chubby white girl by the name of Ruby who worked behind the desk of the dorm my room was in, and she controlled the electronic door which allowed you to enter after visiting hours. If you didn't have a key, she was the one to buzz you in. Once she allowed you entrance into the building, you were required to sign a log book, and whomever you were visiting had to come down to the desk to escort you up to their room.

I had to make a sell one night, and I saw she was working. Ruby wasn't great looking, but she had a thick, curvy body I enjoyed pleasing on many occasions. She had long brown hair, a sexy persona, and an extremely provocative walk. She loved smoking marijuana, and whenever we smoked marijuana together, we both would become extremely horny, and we spend the night fulfilling our lustful desires. I loved the way she always wrapped her big shapely legs around my back, and squeezed me tightly between her thighs, in an attempt to either stop me from banging so hard and deep, or to prevent me from pulling out.

We spent that night together in her dorm room. It was a very enjoyable night, plus she spent fifty dollars with me. I wasn't comfortable smoking the same marijuana with her that I had just sold her, but she insisted that it was her pleasure. "I know you'll be sure to come see me often, if I give money to you, as well as some good pussy. The white guys call me a nigga lover now, because they've figured out that we are lovers. The only way I can get laid now, is with you." I gave it some thought, and made a mental note to make sure I visited her at least a couple of times a week.

The next morning when I arrived at the apartment, I found Flash and Hands highly upset and agitated. I could tell from their body language that they were nervous, and worried. They told me that the landlord was attempting to move another student in the apartment. Even though the apartment had two bedrooms, the landlord was always trying to lease the apartment out to four students. He had twin beds in each bedroom. We sold weed from my dorm room, and from the apartment. We couldn't afford to let a stranger move into the apartment for obvious reason.

Hands and Flash had talked to the brother, and he informed them that he had just finished a tour of duty in Viet Nam, and all he wanted to do was attend school, so he could better provide for his family. Hands and Flash had enjoyed not having to share their bedrooms with any other students for a whole year, but it looked like things were about to change.

After we had exhausted the subject, we went our separate ways to take care of our clientele on campus. I went back to my dorm room to take care of my regulars, and when I got there I found Flash's friend, Toni, waiting for me. I was surprised to see her waiting for me. I thought she and Flash were an item. When I asked her what she wanted she said, "I want to know why everyone respects you so much, and I'm willing to do anything you want me to, to find out."

I found the statement shocking, so I responded by stating, "I thought you were Flash's girl. I don't fuck around with my friend's women." She tried to assure me that she was not Flash's girl, but I reminded her of my presence a few nights that she and Flash had spent together having sexual intercourse. She insisted that they were only friends with benefits, and her interest in me ran much deeper than that. She also told me that she had expressed her interest in me to Flash, and he had failed to keep his promise to inform me of her feelings, so she was taking it upon herself to do so.

We spent the entire day together. She accompanied me on every marijuana delivery I made, and hung around to watch me during practice. Afterwards we went to her dorm room. She wanted me to know where her room was, in case I needed or wanted her. It was a co-ed dorm and although the genders lived on different floors, we shared the same building. My room was also in the same building, one floor below hers'.

We laid down on her bunk bed, and smoked marijuana, while we listened to Donald Byrd's newest album entitled "Black Bird". Eventually we began kissing, and I discovered what a great kisser she was. I couldn't get enough! The way she clung to me, was all the proof I needed to know she enjoyed it as well. Her roommate came home, so Toni suggested we take the party to my room, and continue what we had started.

To my disappointment, we found my roommate also was in. Toni quickly climbed on to my bunk. Since I seldom slept in my room, my roommate slept on the bottom bunk. I joined her on my bunk. I was thinking if my roommate were to fall asleep, he wouldn't know what we were doing in the bunk above him. Toni wanted to have sexual intercourse right then, and there. In no time at all, we were engaged in an intense sexual encounter. The fact my roommate was awake, only heighten the already intense, lustful experience. We made love until I had nothing left to give, and passed out with her in my arms.

The next morning when I woke up, my roommate was gone. I began kissing Toni to wake her, and she responded by kissing me back. She told me she would do anything for me. I laughed, and informed her that I was raised in Newport by pimps and drug dealers, so she should be very mindful making such promises to me. Once again, she insisted that she was not overstating a fact. "Would you sell pussy for me?" I asked. I was sure I had mentioned something she wouldn't be willing to do.

"Are you kidding me?" she asked. "With the respect, and attention you receive from the ladies, you don't think that I've considered the fact that you may have aspirations of becoming a pimp, and that you might want to make me one of your hoes? Of course, I would sell pussy for you. If that's what you wanted me to do. I belong to you.!"

Toni was an amazingly beautiful red bone. She wore a big red afro, and had big, bright, pretty, Betty Davis eyes. Her lips were full, and beyond tempting. She always wore lip stick, and it made her appear as though she were made up for a magazine cover girl shoot. Whenever she wore eye makeup, it made her eyes mesmerizing. Her body was thick and tight, without a scar or a blemish. The way she kissed and made love, enhanced her loveliness. She also had one of the most pleasing personality to match.

One day I decided to test her to find out if she were truly willing to sell pussy for me. Meme had always expressed a strong interest in having sex with Toni. He talked about her like she was a goddess. I gave him one hundred dollars, and told him I had made arrangements for him to have sex with her. All he had to do was to give her the money had given him. Instead of sticking to the agreement, Meme went off script, and told her I had read a book by Robert Beck, and now I wanted to be a pimp, because of the influence the book had on me. He even told her I had given him the money to test her with. Toni became enraged, and threw him out. She was very upset with me also.

I couldn't understand why Meme would practically

beg me to let him know if I were ever able to successfully convince Toni to sell pussy for me, and then turn right around and deliberately sabotage the opportunity to realize his fantasy of having sexual intercourse with her, at no cost to him. I finally came to the conclusion that he was trying to be Captain Save a Hoe, and it backfired on him. I almost lost Toni after that stunt. She wasn't upset that I wanted to be a pimp. She was upset with me, because I didn't believe her when she told me she would do anything for me. It took a few hours, but I eventually was able to calm her down.

I'm not sure of when it happened, but the next day I began to feel differently about her. It made me treat her differently too. I saw her sitting alone in the student center, and there are no words to describe how lovely she looked.to me. I was caught up in her rapture when my thoughts were interrupted by Gator. He had to tell me what happened the night before. Hands and Flash came to his apartment about three o'clock in the morning seeking his sawed-off shotgun, because some guy was chasing them with machete.

They had tried to convince the guy from the military that there was no way they were going to allow him to move in, but he was as equally determined to show them how serious he was about moving into the apartment. Gator's saw off shotgun changed his mind. He decided it was best for him to commute, instead of dealing with all the drama. We had our spot to ourselves again, but I had missed out on all the excitement. Then suddenly without notice Gator whispered to me, "There he is right there!" and pointed in a dark skinned, stocky guy's direction.

I immediately sprung into action. We were in the section of the student center where six pool tables were located, so

I picked up a pool stick. The walls were made of concrete cement, and had a rough unfinished appearance. That was the decorative design, and it was quite attractive. There was another wall, which separated the dining area from the pool room, made entirely of thick glass, from the ceiling to the floor.

I walked up behind him, with more than three hundred students looking on, and tapped him on his shoulder with the heavy end of the pool stick and said, "I hear we've got a problem with the living arrangements." He told me there was no problem, and turned his back to walk away from the trouble I was attempting to create. This time I tapped him on the top of his head with the pool stick, and told him, "Don't ever fuck with my friends again."

He became enraged, and came after me. I dropped the pool stick, and put my dukes up. He walked right into a flurry of my punches. I grabbed him around his neck, and raked the side of his head against the unfinished concrete wall. He got loose from my grip, and picked up his briefcase. I perceived his actions as an indication that he wanted to end the fight, but I was wrong. He opened his briefcase, and pulled out the now infamous machete.

He raised the machete above his head, and the ceiling lights caught the menacing blade. The reflection lit up the entire room, and panic gripped the crowd as everyone scattered in different directions among shouts of, "He's got a knife!" I had my back up against the wall, when I noticed the blade headed downward towards my exposed chest. All of a sudden, the whole room turned into the bright, pure white light, and I felt The Most High's presence. There were no words nor message this time. When the white light cleared, my body had been turned, and my left shoulder was press firmly against the wall.

The machete had missed me completely, and unfortunately for him, his head was left exposed, and in the perfect position to receive a straight right to his temple. I threw the punch with all the strength I could muster. I had run to the other side of a pool table, once I realized the punch had not made him release the weapon from his tight grip. I snatched some pool balls from the pool table with both hands, and began hurling them at his head. Every ball found its' mark, and struck him directly upside his head or in his face. I was doing so well hitting him with the solid balls, that he dropped his machete, and tried his hand at throwing balls at me.

He was not the athlete I was, so he was unable to throw or duck as accurately. I ducked, and one of his ill thrown balls smashed into the glass wall behind me, and the glass wall shattered. Once everyone realized what the commotion was all about, the crowd began reacting. Someone shouted out, "Here come the fuzz!" Upon hearing that, we both stopped fighting, and walked briskly in opposite direction of one another.

The police went after him, and arrested him, because witnesses stated he was armed with a knife. I had managed to elude their capture, but when they took their suspect to the hospital to receive medical attention, he had to receive more than forty stiches. That's when they made the decision to come after me. I wasn't trying to hide, so when they were ready to question me about the incident, they simply notified the campus police, and instructed them to pick me up.

That Friday the campus police approached me, and I denied being who they were looking for. I even presented identification that stated my name was Robert Love. I didn't believe it would work, because I was extremely popular, and I believed they knew who I was. They were white officers, and believed it was possible another black guy could look like me. To avoid making such an embarrassing mistake, they allowed me to walk away.

I walked straight into the dorm, and proceeded directly to my room to retrieve the marijuana from the drawer I kept it in. I thought there was a strong possibility the police would obtain a warrant to search my room, and I didn't want them stumbling upon my stash. From there I went to Toni's room. Her roommate had gone home for the weekend, so we had the room to ourselves.

Back in those days, if you were arrested during the weekend, you had to remain in custody until the following Monday before you were brought before a sitting judge. The thought of spending the weekend in jail was not appealing to me at all. I spent the entire weekend hidden in Toni's room. The girls on the floor thought it was so romantic, they helped us out. They would clear the restroom, so I could use the bathroom, and take showers. We made love all weekend. Like I said earlier, my attitude towards Toni had changed. Everybody on campus knew Toni was my girl, and I was proud to be known as her man.

The police kept the building surrounded with officers at every exit, and just as I had anticipated, a warrant had been issued, and my room was search. I walked out the front door that Monday morning prepared to face the situation. I had no plans of pressing any charges, or cooperating with the authorities. I was hoping that our soldier felt the same way about the police as I did. During those times the police were considered pigs, and most college students were antiestablishment. Total rebellion was considered cool. He did feel the same way, so the pursuit of charges was drop.

I had to hitch hike a ride home. The county jail, and court house were in the same building located in Big Heaven. Hudsonville was too great of a distance to walk back to the school. As a matter of fact, it was about a thirty-minute ride in a car. When I walked to the side of road, I saw a truck approaching from a short distance away. I stuck my thumb out, hoping to hitch a ride home, but the truck sped by. I watch in horror as the truck driver lost control, and the trailer turned over on its' side in what seemed like inches in front of me. The truck had barely cleared me, and I realized at that moment how close I had come to being killed.

If the trailer had turned over less than a second earlier, I would have been buried under the pile of twisted metal, laying less than a foot in front of me. The truck driver was seriously hurt, and was taken away in an ambulance. It took me a while, but I was able to hitch a ride home, and I continued to have fun raising havoc on campus.

Gator, Box, and Meme all were able to purchase cars, with their refunds from financial aid. I received the same amount as they, and could have purchased an automobile myself, but I elected to purchase clothes instead. I needed them. Hands had a car also, so whenever I needed a ride off campus, one of them would always be available. I walked wherever I needed to go most of the time. I very seldom ventured off campus. Box, Meme, and Gator were all from the Newport area, and started going home more often. They didn't like making the trips alone, so they would always ask me if I would ride with them. I was always happy to receive an invitation to ride home, and more times than not, I accepted.

I often thought about the orange Camaro for sale I used to look at almost daily, on a car lot in Tri City. I would always walk to the lot and check, to see if my dream car was still available. I believed it was meant for me, because no one ever purchased it. It was priced at only five hundred dollars, and I knew Coach had saved more than twice that amount for me to buy a car. My heart would break every time I thought about it, so I tried my best to suppress those types thoughts and emotions.

It was during one of those trips home that I met Ruby. I was riding down 128th street with Mr. Horton. He was our next-door neighbor, and on that particular day I rode with him to the store. I loved Mr. Horton. He was a baseball coach, and he never gave up trying to convince me to let him teach me how to pitch. He truly believed he could make a great major league pitcher out of me. While we were riding, I saw Ruby walking down the street. She was so pretty I demanded that Mr. Horton stopped the car, so I could get out, and meet her.

Ruby was the younger sister of Marty Blue. She had lost so much weight that I didn't recognize her. All I knew for certain was she was beautiful, and it was a top priority of mine, to find out exactly who she was. She was so beautiful, her beauty actually touched me. Her eyes were dark, and her eyelashes were naturally long. Her eyebrows were dark and thick, with a natural arch to them. Her skin was so smooth, and flawless it appeared to be made from some sort of olive cream. She was mixed with black and white just like her sister Marty, so it was difficult to determine what nationality she was from her appearance.

I asked her if I may talk to her. She smiled, and told me she had just gotten off work, and she was very tired. She continued by saying, "If you don't mind talking while we walk, I have no problem with it, but I'm nearly home so you better make it quick." I asked all the necessary questions, and received some of the answers I wanted in the short walk. She told me she had just broken up with her boyfriend, and his name was also Tone. I asked for permission to visit with her later. Her smile was alluring, and I was totally lost in her big brown eyes. Before going inside, she told me she would love to receive me as a quest, if I would allow her enough time to get some rest and freshened up. I agreed, and went directly across the street to my mother's house.

My sisters were looking out the window, and saw me talking to Ruby. As soon as I walked through the door, they rushed to me, and told me everything about her. They told me she used to be obese, but somehow, she had lost an awful lot of weight. She had also just graduated from high school, and was employed at the National Bank. They told me that I would have no problem getting to know her, because she was a sweet person.

I hung out with my brother Albert, and we spent most of the day listening to music and smoking weed. He was impressed by the bass player of a white group named Rare Earth on the Motown label. He thought he was the greatest bass player in the world. Albert had become quite an impressive bass player himself. Jamar lived across the street, next door to Ruby, and he was a very good lead guitar player.

Curtis lived down the street on the same block, and he had become a very good drummer.

The three of them got together and formed a band. They didn't have a name, but they practiced in the basement of Jamar's parent's house. I went with him to their rehearsal to check them out, and I was very impressed. They had a new sound that was a cross between rock and roll, rhythm & Blues and jazz. I hung out with them for most of the day listening to them play, and telling them about other musicians that I had discovered.

Time had passed quickly, and night fell upon us before we even realized it. The windows in the basement were covered with curtains, so when we came up from the basement, we were all shocked to see night had come. I went straight to Ruby's house. I didn't say exactly what time I was coming by, nor did she suggest a time. I would have come sooner, but I believed things had worked out for the best. This way, I wouldn't appear to be desperate.

Ruby's mother answered the door. She was a beautiful white woman with long jet-black hair. I was surprised that she already knew who I was. She had heard about the murder I'd committed, and how I had turned my life around. She told me that she loved black people, and especially black men. She had given birth to four children, and they all had been fathered by her late husband.

She said everyone called her Biggum, but regardless to what happened between me and Ruby, she wanted me to call her Momma. While we were talking Ruby entered the room. By that time, her mother and I were engaged in a deep, non-stop, meaningful conversation. She was excited by the fact that I was seriously interested in Ruby romantically.

She did not like Ruby's boyfriend and she made sure to mention it in front of Ruby. She told Ruby, "I like this one. I think it's a no brainer. You need a boyfriend with a future, and who will treat you like you deserve to be treated. That punk bitch, Tone, never did nor ever will appreciate you."

After we had spent some time talking, she agreed to be my woman. Her mother was happy, but she added, "The real test will be when her old boyfriend shows up trying to beg her back. He's always been able to beg her back. I don't see any reason why this time should be different from the rest... Don't get me wrong, I do hope it is different this time, cause I can't stand that son of a bitch!"

Tone showed up that very night. Momma didn't even want to open the door, after she looked out the window, and realized it was actually him. She mumbled under her breath barely audible enough for us to hear, "Watch this punk beg her to take him back. The only reason he really wants her back is because it's payday." I watched them both very attentively, to see if I could read anything in their body language.

He asked Ruby If he could speak with her in private. I told Ruby the same thing I had told Violet. "You don't have to talk to him if you don't wish to." He was much larger than me, but I had already sized up his heart. I knew I could whip his ass, and I was doing everything I could to provoke him. He must have seen it in my eyes, and in my mannerisms. To my surprise, Ruby said she wanted to talk to him, and they left together. I couldn't believe it, but Momma had warned me of the hold he had on her, even she couldn't understand. Momma just shook her head and said "I ain't never seen nothing like that shit before in my life."

Momma's boyfriend came over with some of his friends, and she introduced me to them as her son. Her boyfriend was a tall older dark-skinned man by the name of Big Willie. We all took seats at the kitchen table, and got acquainted. I rolled some marijuana, while Big Willie and his friends started a game of poker. I was trying to shake the bad feeling of losing Ruby, when she unexpectedly walked through the front door.

Where's Tone?" Momma asked. Ruby smiled and asked "Which Tone? Momma responded by saying, "Your Tone! You know damn well who I'm talking bout." Ruby had a puzzled look on her face that turned into a smirk as she stated, "Now I'm confused. My Tone is sitting right here. I don't know or care where the other Tone went." She walked over to me, sat on my lap, and began kissing me. She placed both of her hands on each side of my face as she stared deeply into my eyes and asked, "You are my Tone, right?" with a huge smile on her face. It was all I wanted to hear. Even Big Willie was happy. He raised his drink and proclaimed, "I'll drink to that."

I spent the entire weekend romancing my new girlfriend. I met her brothers Derik and Leslie. They looked white, but They had black accents as well as black mannerisms. If you closed your eyes, and had a five, minute conversation with them, you would swear they were black, and technically they were. By definition, if you have as little as one drop of black blood in your system, you were considered black. Leslie was married to a black woman by the name of Ivory. She was an elementary school teacher, and they had three beautiful children. Derick had a black girlfriend who had just passed from cancer. It was a great visit, and I almost didn't want to return to school, but I had to.

Things had deteriorated drastically between my parents. My father had another woman, and another household on the other side of town, near his job. What made matters even worse, was that fact that he had stopped providing for our family. The furniture was so old and ragged, my mother didn't allow my sisters or brothers to have company inside the house. There also were days my sisters and brothers had nothing to eat.

My mother was still madly in love with my father. He had gotten so he would only come home on the weekends. He would lay up with my mother only during the weekends, and that was just enough to keep her holding on, and hopeful there would be better days to come. She was hoping to recapture what was now no more than a distant memory. He would take her to the horse races Friday and Saturday afternoons, and he would go play poker every Friday and Saturday night. Sunday afternoons he would get dressed up in his finest clothes, and go to perform at various Baptist churches as a member of a popular gospel singing group.

I always felt guilty leaving my sisters and brothers in those horrid conditions. I lived in a decent place, and ate decent food, but I couldn't concentrate on anything except my family. I felt there was nothing I could do, other than returning to Newport to hustle on the streets, and help to provide for my family. When the fall term concluded, I was informed by mail that I was kicked out due to lack of participation. In other words, I had flunked out. All I had to do was get an appointment to see the president of the school, and I would've been given a second chance. I felt it was best to go home. My family needed me.

The very first thing I did after I had gotten settled in and gotten unpacked, was make a mad dash across the street to see Ruby. When I got there, she was acting strange. She was cold, and distant. Her sister Marty was there. She had moved back to Newport, and was living in a high-rise penthouse, downtown. She wanted to celebrate her return, and was popping the cork on a champagne bottle. She announced that she was going to get too drunk to drive, so she was spending the night. I had some weed, so I took my customary seat at the kitchen table, and began rolling a few joints to smoke.

While I was rolling the weed, someone knocked at the door. Ruby answered the door, and a guy I had never seen before in my entire life walked in. He was of medium height, dark skinned, and he had a huge afro. He took a seat on the love seat in the living room, and Ruby sat on his lap. I was surprised, shocked and angered by Ruby's actions. I didn't appreciate my woman sitting on another man's lap, and the anger began to swell my chest. I called out to Ruby, and requested that she join me in the kitchen.

She got up and came to me. "What's up with the bullshit?" I asked. She looked deeply into my eyes and responded in a tone that displayed nothing but disgust. She never even attempted to conceal her hostility towards me. "Someone very close to you, told me that you said you didn't give a fuck about me." I couldn't remember ever saying anything like that to anyone. It didn't matter anyway. What was most important was the fact that she believed I said it, and as a result of that, she responded by ending our relationship.

Ruby and her new boyfriend excused themselves, retired to her bedroom and closed the door. That left me alone with Marty. No one else was home. They all were out for the night. Marty didn't mind being left alone with me at all. We stayed up all night drinking champagne, smoking weed and getting well acquainted with each other.

She told me all about what it was like to be married to a famous Blues singer, and I told her all about the murder, and the things I had accomplished in my quest to claim control of my life. She knew Ape very well, and he's the one who told her about my encounter with Sleepy. She was interested in knowing details, and I needed someone to talk to.

We soon began flirting with each other. It should have felt awkward to be moving on so quickly after the breakup with her sister, but it didn't. Maybe it was the champagne. To me, she was a dream come true. I felt blessed for things to work out the way they had. I had always had a crush on Marty, so it was a painless breakup. She sat on my lap, and even though my penis could not have been more erect, she sat directly on it.

Al Green's latest album provided the music and the atmosphere, so we danced. We actually were bumping and grinding as we held each other as tightly as we could. I couldn't believe that the woman of my dreams was holding me in her arms as tightly as she could, and grinding up against my erection. She told me that night how happy she was to once again be living in Newport. She told her husband she missed her family, and since he was on the road most of the time, she was left alone in the mansion with his mother. She told me that his mother didn't like her very much, but I had a strong hunch that those feelings were mutual.

Marty assured me her husband would only be in Newport about twice a year, and that left enough time for us to have lots of fun. They rented an apartment in one of the city's finest apartments, The Palace. He also leased a brand new, Cadillac Fleetwood every year for her. Hustlers called all Cadillacs hogs back then, because they hogged all the attention on the road. Hustlers called the Fleetwood model, a Stick of Wood.

She received an allowance of five thousand dollars a month. That was considered an enormous amount of money back then. Factory workers only made about twelve hundred dollars a month, and they were the big money makers in the black communities. We used to ride downtown to Western Union to pick up her money. The money would arrive on a Friday evening like clockwork.

Marty and I used to hang out every day, but she felt I was too young for her to commit to me, and besides, she truly enjoyed her freedom far too much to commit to me, or anybody else. Marty only committed to guys she could control, and would allow her to do whatever she pleased without complaint. The first time she kissed me, I felt my heart stop, then she whispered in my ear "Hang in there, baby. One day we'll be together. I promise." She wanted me to be patient, and to wait for that day to arrive when she would be my woman. She would always say, "Neither one of us is really ready yet Baby."

She convinced me to return to school. "Don't worry." she added. "I'll always be here waiting for you once we're ready. I told her I couldn't return to school knowing my brothers and sisters were struggling to get by day to day. She then suggested that I have a heart to heart with my mother, and let her know how her desire to hold on to her husband, was destroying her children. "She needs to get rid of her, dead beat ass husband, and sign up for welfare. She'll receive a check, every two weeks, and food stamps to buy food. Make her understand that she is setting a bad example for her daughters. She is laying down with this man and allowing him the pleasures of a husband, without fulfilling a husband's obligations. It's not going to be easy to talk to your mother in this fashion, but it is necessary."

I had the conversation with my mother, and to my surprise she was also tired of the situation, but just couldn't think of a way out of the trap she'd found herself in. She was afraid of being lonely, but she realized it wasn't going to get any better, and it was best for her, and her children, to get a divorce.

Then I called the president of the school, and I was amazed at how willing he was to give me a second chance. I hadn't attended any classes during the entire time I had been there, so I had no credits. He was willing to allow me to start all over again as though I were an incoming freshman.

There were quite a few things I missed about school, and now that I knew my siblings were going to be alright, I could leave with a clear conscience. I caught the next Greyhound bus heading to Hudsonville. Marty was thrilled and pleased I had taken her advice on both matters, and she was more than happy to give me a ride to the bus station. I called Gator, and he was happy I was coming back. He immediately offered to give me a ride from the station to campus.

Once we arrived, I was informed by a staff member that I would be sharing a one-bedroom apartment with Paul Mills. It became obvious after a few days, he wasn't going to be spending much time at the apartment. I believed it was because he didn't like the idea of living with me. I grew to resent his absence, and took it personally. I spent most of my nights in Toni's room, but I still resented the cold shoulder I received from my roommate. It was like I lived in the apartment alone.

Whenever I felt like it, I could put out the word that I was giving a party, and everyone would show up. Hands and Flash were no longer attending school, but even without them, I still was able to establish a solid reputation as a party host. People who didn't even attend State would come from as far away as Muskegon and Grand Rapids to attend my parties.

Whenever I needed extra cash, I would wait until Sunday night to rob all the vending machines. It was easy, because there was never more than one campus police officer on patrol. If he was sighted in the dorm area, I would rob the machines in the apartments. If he was spotted around the apartments, I would rob the machines in the dorms. I was guaranteed to get at the very least five hundred dollars in change. I would get a ride to a Bank to get the wraps to put the coins in, then I would ride to another bank and turn the change in for paper money.

I don't know how they knew it, but the county sheriff figured out it was me robbing the vending machines. They were never able to catch me, so they began arresting me on

Fridays, and releasing me every Mondays. It put a real cramp in my lifestyle, so I began alluding capture by staying out of sight until I had stolen, and cashed in the coins.

I still hadn't matured enough to be a responsible student. I was not attending classes, and the women were very attracted to me. It had gotten to the point I had six women on campus. They all knew each other, and they knew they were sharing me. When I threw parties at least a couple of them would stay all night, and we would perform a ménage a trois.

I threw a party one Saturday night, and to my surprise Paul came home for the party. I should have suspected something wasn't right. When the party ended, I instructed Paul not to open the door if the police came. He was to come and get me, and allow me to handle things. The following morning, I was awakened by a knock at the door. Since I was naked in bed with two naked girls, Paul answer the door. I heard him ask, "Who is it?" and then I heard the door open. The next thing I knew, there were deputies from the County Sheriff Department standing over us, demanding that I get up. Paul quickly left the apartment, as I rose from the bed, and began getting dressed.

I thought I was about to be taken to the County Jail, to prevent me from robbing the vending machines that night, but this time was different. They ordered me to pack all my things. I was so angry with Paul. It was now obvious to me, he had been used as part of the plan to sit me up. I was going to use one of my girls to answer the door, if it was the police, and deny I was there. It was my plan to deny them entrance. To make sure that was not the case, Paul was used to give them permission to enter.

I packed all of Paul's best pieces of clothing alone with my own. The police informed me while I was packing I should make sure that I packed everything, because I would not be returning to campus. The county had purchased me a one-way bus ticket to Newport. They took me to the bus station, and waited until I boarded the bus, and watched as the bus pulled off. I was ordered to never return, unless I wanted to risk being sent to prison.

I was back in Newport! I explained to Marty what had happened, and she told me the police had no right to force me to leave. I wanted to leave anyway, so I never pursued the law suit she suggested. I had my fill of dealing with the hassles, and I wanted to be in Newport to help my mother with my siblings.

While I was away she had filed for divorce, and had quit sleeping with my father. She and my Aunt Henrietta had found a nightclub called Sam's, on Joy Road, and they would go out every Friday and Saturday night. My mother was never a drinker before, but now she had started drinking Champale. She still didn't drink much. She would sip on one twelve once bottle, and that was more than enough for her.

I hadn't seen Slim in a very long time, so I decided to look him up. When I caught up with him, he had changed a lot. He was now, spending the majority of his time managing a stable of eight prostitutes. Two of his prostitutes were identical twin sisters! He asked me if I could hang out with him for a few days, so we could catch up. It didn't take much for him to convince me. I missed him a lot, and I had so much to tell him.

We had both heard about Bumpy being convicted of

manslaughter. He had a friend named Wallace who went to a dance being held by a church. Because he was drunk, and below the drinking age, which was twenty-one at that time, he was asked to leave. He became belligerent and extremely hostile, so he had to be physically removed from the premises. He took exception to the physical treatment, and was deeply offended. He caught up with Bumpy, and sought his assistance in terrorizing the dance hall. In the process of terrorizing the people at the dance, Bumpy shot and killed two of the preacher's three sons.

They initially got away, but the church's congregation put together a ten, thousand- dollar, reward, for the arrest and conviction of the gunman. Bumpy's partner turned him in for the reward money, with Wallace's assistance. Peppers then double crossed Wallace, and refused to give him his share of the reward. Bumpy took a plea agreement, and received a ten to fifteen-year sentence. We both agreed that we were going to miss Bumpy, and should we run into Peppers, he will have hell to pay.

Wallace had already been murdered. He was shot to death while sitting in a car near the liquor store on Banger and Warren drinking wine. It happened as soon as I was released from Boys Training School. No one believed me when I denied having anything to do with the murder. It was very fortunate for me that I was living in Tri City during the time of the homicide. Otherwise, I would have been considered a prime suspect.

Slim lived in an apartment located on Woodward Ave. Woodward was considered the main hoe stroll. Pimping was good on Mack Ave., Michigan Ave., Eight Mile Rd., Jefferson St. and Warren Ave., but the fastest track of all was Woodard Ave. There are plenty of broken, lost souls still strolling down Woodward to this very day.

The first night I spent just observing Slim interact with his hoes. I was astonished when they all got on their knees, and recited a prayer to him as he stood before them. In their prayer to him they referred to him as the Mighty Hand. He explained to me later that night he had taken a few verses from the Bible, and changed the wording to fit his purpose. He was actually using the Bible to turn women out into a life of prostitution, and to control his entire stable of prostitutes. It was an amazing couple of days. I was so fascinated that I went back to the neighborhood determine to pull me a hoe.

I hung out with my cousin Otis, even though he was younger than me. Rodger was so addicted to heroin at this point, all he did was get high. He had a job working in a dope house for Brian, but after he got off work, all he ever did was get high.

Otis told me where I could find Sonia, the girl Bumpy used to have when he was trying to pimp. I remembered she couldn't keep her eyes off me. He told me she worked out of a neighborhood bar called Eli's. He allowed her work out of his bar for sexual favors.

When we walked in the bar I could tell that she recognized me by the huge smile she displayed, as she looked in my direction. I walked over to her, and said in a loud enough voice for everyone to hear, "Bitch you better not be a fucking outlaw and think I'm not gonna make yo fine ass mine's!" An outlaw is a prostitute who works without the assistance of a pimp to protect her or to manage her affairs. I heard you were a muthafucken outlaw, and I've been trying to find somebody worth choosing."

I stuck my hand out, and turned my head so I could look over my shoulder at Otis while I waited for her to take my hand. I was smiling because I knew she would take my hand, and I would escort her from the bar. To my surprise, Soni placed a wad of bills in the palm of my hand. I played it off like it was exactly what I expected, and placed the money into my pocket without counting it, or giving it a second glance. I placed my arm around her shoulder, as we walked out of the bar.

We went to my aunt's house, and found Rodger on the couch asleep. I woke him up, and asked him if he wanted some head. Of course, he said yes, so I ordered Sonia to perform oral sex on him. Otis spoke up and added, "I have a hoe too, and she has an identical twin sister!" He told me their names were Madison and Morgan. He called Madison and she agreed to come by the house. She arrived so quickly it was obvious that she lived close by. Sonia had just finished with Rodger when Otis let Madison in. I showed Sonia the bathroom, and handed her a face towel, a tube of tooth paste, a bottle of mouth wash, and a new toothbrush. I instructed her to get herself together, and concluded by letting her know that I would be in the kitchen waiting for her.

I went into the kitchen, and left Rodger snoring on the couch. He was knocked out cold. When I entered the kitchen, Madison was sucking on a large dill pickle. She was demonstrating her technique for performing oral sex. I was imagining how good it would feel to have her performing those oral sexual techniques on me, when Sonia walked through the entrance to the kitchen. She sat on my lap, and joined in as we continued to observe the little girl's demonstration.

After Madison finished, Otis and I were thoroughly turned on. That is when Sonia asked if she could take a turn. She took the pickle from Madison and devoured it. It was as though she were insulted to have been put in the position of competing against an amateur. Not only did she consider herself a professional, but she was confident in her belief that she ranked among the very best.

As soon as she had finished she said, "Fuck a pickle! Let me show ya'll how it's supposed to be done." Her eyes grew with excitement when I agreed to let her perform her technique on me. Before any of us could imagine what would happen next, Sonia had my penis out of my pants, and standing at attention, with her lips wrapped around its' head. She was also stroking the shaft of my penis with her fingers, causing waves of chills to run up and down my back.

I couldn't believe the sensation I felt when she took my penis in her throat, and began stroking my penis with her throat; without gaging. Her throat felt something like a vagina with an amazing twist. The only reason she stopped was to speak to me. She said, "Damn! I'm wanna play with your balls too. You mind pulling your pants down so I can get to em?"

I complied with her request, and she cupped my testicles in the palm of her hand. She then began gently fondling them with her fingers, as she sucked on my penis with her lips clamped down tightly around the shaft. She used her forefinger and thumb on her free hand to stroke my penis while she bobbed her head up and down.

The expression on my face must have exposed the

obvious. I was about to cum, and from the expressions on Otis and Denise faces they also knew I was about to blow my wad in her mouth. I closed my eyes as I began ejaculating, and I wondered to myself if there was anyone else in the world who could do what she had just done to me. She proceeded to suck on my penis until she had swallowed every drop. She flashed her beautiful smile while saying, "You're a freak Daddy!"

Sonia was a very pretty woman. She was the exact color of sweet dark chocolate, with beautiful facial features. Her body was thick, young and tight. She reminded me that she had given me choosing money, and she begged to spend some time alone with me. I agreed. This time when I took her hand, I led her to the bedroom.

After we gotten undressed, and laid across the bed she, suggested that I do everything to her that she did to me. I agreed without realizing we had not established any boundaries. I leaned over to kiss her, and she surprised me by sticking her tongue up inside one of my nostrils and began twirling it. By doing so, she had in fact licked a part of me that had never been licked. It was a strange feeling, but I enjoyed it. I kept my end of the bargain by sticking my tongue into one of her nostrils also. Merlyn taught me a lot about sex that night, and I was a willing student as every discovery was a new world opening up for me.

I had to be near Sonia every single moment. I would watch her back while she worked. The customers were called johns, and at the end of the day we used the rooms that the johns paid for, to sleep. We even tricked every john into believing they had to pay extra to get a room. Sometimes we were able to get up to two hundred dollars extra each day.

Since neither of us did more than smoked a little marijuana and drank wine, we didn't have any expensive drug habits. My bank roll began to swell, and so did our confidence in our ability to not only survive, but to become a successful young powerful couple. No one could have told us our future wasn't bright, but believe it or not, that's when a hustler is most vulnerable.

When things are going great, we get comfortable, and that brings about carelessness. All hustlers are most susceptible to making mistakes when we become distracted, due to some measure of success we may be experiencing. The truth of the matter is, we must always prepare for the worse. Not to do so, is to set yourself up for failure, and that is especially true for street hustlers. There are just too many things to be aware of, like the police, the stickup men, haters, and the curves life has in store for each and every one of us. Life is going to test and challenge every single one of us, and hustlers are no exception to that rule.

Not surprisingly, Sonia's mom was a sporting lady. She was beautiful, and very well known. She had her very own after-hours joint, yet she wasn't an outlaw. She had a pimp that was much younger than her, named Alvin. There was a twenty-dollar cover charge, just to be allowed entrance to their joint, and the place was always jammed pack. They had prostitutes working, while stag movies were being shown. Shocking live sex acts were performed for amusement, while bets were being placed on several different games of chance. Many simply enjoyed the food, the entertainment and drinks.

We were at the Eldorado motel located on Livernois and Ford. It was a big day for us, because Sonia's mother had expressed a desire to meet me. We got dressed and smoked some marijuana, while we waited for three o'clock. It was also very well known that her mother never got up from bed, until three o'clock in the afternoon. We had a couple of hours to kill, so we spent the time smoking, talking, and making love. She sucked my penis for such a long time I can remember thinking she was doing it because she was so nervous about her mom meeting me. Her mom knew me by reputation, and that's all I knew about her. I was excited about meeting her and Alvin. I always enjoyed meeting pimps. I learned something new about the game, with every introduction and encounter.

Suddenly Sonia stopped, and the interruption broke my train of thought. She stared deeply into my eyes in a way that made me realize she wanted my undivided attention. She began by saying "Baby…" I thought she was about to say something profound about the moment. She continued, by asking, "Can I stop now? My jaws are tired." We both broke into laughter, and the laughter broke the nervous vibes.

We decided since it was a nice day we would walk to her mother's house. We never found enough time in a day to talk about all the things that we found interesting. We were so deeply involved in our conversation that before we realized it, we had made it to 128th street. The first thing we noticed was a huge crowd, and the lights on top of the police cars flashing in front of her mother's house. We both took off running towards her mother's house. We both were fearful of what we might discover.

As we got closer, we cautiously approached the crowd. A car from the coroner's office came into view. On the streets, we referred to the coroner's car as the meat wagon. It was always a sign that someone had passed. They were already loading the body on the stretcher, with its face covered, into the back of the car. The next thing we saw, was Sonia's mother being led to a patrol car in hand- cuffs. The buzz from the crowd was Alvin and her mother got into a fight and she shot him to death.

Sonia pretended not to know her mom, as we slipped away from the crowd, and went to my aunt's house. She cried a lot that entire day. It was as though the only thing she was concerned about was her mom, and understandingly so. I couldn't bring myself to make her work under the circumstances. After crying all night, the next morning she woke up, and explained to me exactly why she had to leave. She said her good-byes, and walked out of my life. My heart was broken, but it was just how life is on the streets. She had to move on, and so did I.

I went to see Biggum. I needed to talk to someone, and she always provided a willing ear, with an opened mind. Marty answered the door, and I saw genuine joy to see me, in her eyes. She had missed me. My heart always skipped a beat whenever I saw Marty, and even after all I had been through that day, this time was no exception. Marty was dressed in tight fitting, dark Blue jeans and a red shell halter top. She had on some opened toed shoes and red paint on her fingers and toes. Even though she didn't need a drop of makeup, she always appeared as though she were made up for a cover shoot.

I was crazy about Marty, but I couldn't take her seriously. She would kiss me, and bump and grind with me while dancing in front of everyone, but she wouldn't have sex with me. Every time we arranged it, she would find a way out of it. It was frustrating to say the very least. She was only seven years older than me, but the difference in our ages was a hurdle she found difficult to cross. She kept telling me that one day she would be mine. She always gave me whatever I asked for, and she would drive me wherever I wanted to go. Everybody thought we were lovers, but at that time we weren't. At least not physically, but we made love all the time, in ways others will never understand.

Biggum's boyfriend Willie had moved in with her, and he had an entourage, so the partying became a nonstop affair. Ruby was pregnant by her new boyfriend. That didn't prevent us from becoming great friends, but she still refused to tell me who told her I said I didn't give a fuck about her. She said it was someone very close to me, but that's all she would reveal. I still had no idea who had stabbed me in the back like that.

Marty had a daughter by Johnny Blue by the name of Tab, and I loved her like she was my very own daughter from the first time I saw her. My love for her had nothing to do with my feelings for her mother. She was just so pretty and smart, we connected. She also cursed like a grown woman. Everyone in the house thought it was cute, and she spent the majority of her time there with her mother. She used to listen to Rudy Ray Moore's albums, and she memorized every single word. She was only three years old at the time.

I enjoyed watching her recite all the words to "The signifying Monkey". Rudy Ray Moore was good, but to watch a lovely, charming little girl articulate it in a flawless performance, was hilarious. Something inside me told me it was wrong, but it was so entertaining. I used to tell everybody we were all going to have to face the consequences for enjoying this someday. Everybody agreed, but we all remained her captive audience.

Momma would tell me stories about her late husband. I didn't know if I was a fool for believing the story, but she actually confessed to murdering her husband! It wasn't an exclusive. She told anyone who listen, about how and why she did it. No matter how often I would beg her to never repeat the story to anyone, she continued to do so.

She told me her first husband was so cheap, she couldn't take it anymore. She took an insurance policy out on him, and spied on him because she believed he hid his money in the garage. While peering through the garage window one day, watching his every move, she saw him go to a secret compartment in the floor, hidden under a throw rug and remove a large roll of bills. She watched as he counted out a few hundred dollars, and replaced the remaining bills in the stash spot. She stayed hidden until he left the garage heading back to the house.

There was a shovel standing up against the side of the garage, and she said she retrieved it. She raised the shovel above her head, and as he walked pass, she brought it down on top of his head with all her might. The shovel was embedded in the top of his head as his limp body fell to the ground. She had taken his life so suddenly he never had a chance to utter a sound. She removed the money from his pockets, and the stash spot before going back inside the house.

After waiting a bit, she called the police claiming to have discovered her husband's body in the backyard. She was white, and he was black, so her word was taken at face value. There was no investigation. She collected the money from the insurance company without any complications, and purchased the house on 128th Street.

Tab was a lot smarter than most adults who came in contact with her, gave her credit for. They all figured since she was only three years old, she couldn't comprehend the adult conversations taking place in her presence. She used to act as my eyes, and ears in my absence. She was able to give me the whole story about whatever went on in the house during my absence. We both would laugh at the people in the house. We found humor in their daily activities, and the fact they thought she was clueless about their affairs.

Sometimes she would pretend to be asleep, while she listened to men begging her mother to preform sexual favors. She would tell me all about every single conversation, and she was thrilled to report her mother's ability to embarrass the men who approached her with the offensive propositions. Of course, Marty never did anything in front of Tab. For obvious reasons, I enjoyed listening to the stories, and hearing the outcome.

I could talk to Marty better than I was able to talk to anyone. She kept my secrets, and never judged me. I told her everything about Sonia. She was surprised I had considered pimping, but she understood that a man has to do, what a man has to do, in order to survive.

I spent the entire night sharing my thoughts with Marty, and she as always, gave me her opinion. That night, I realized I didn't want to be a pimp. Marty convinced me that I could do so much better. Besides, pimping isn't for everybody. It takes a certain breed of man to pimp. Polite society will forever frown upon the likes of an individual who considers it a compliment held in high regards, to be addressed as a pimp. However, one must keep in mind, in some circles and cultures, pimping is considered an honorable profession.

The next day I went to the bar that Uncle Lucky was now managing. The huge picture window I had busted out, was now boarded up with plywood, and painted grey. A small rectangular window was in the center of the grey wall. There was a small red neon sign with the word, "BAR" in the center of the small window, which remained lit as long as the bar was open for business. The bar had become known as "The Hole In the Wall" even though there wasn't a sign stating that fact on the outside or inside the establishment. We all called it "The Hole" for an abbreviated version of the popular name.

The area had become quite popular for most of the known pimps, prostitutes, hustlers, and gangsters in the city. Down the street but on the other end of the same block from the Hole was another bar named "The Chanel One". Around the corner from the Chanel One there was another bar named "DD's" and a couple of block east of there was the famous "Bucket of Blood. We all hopped from bar to bar throughout the day and night, networking and executing plays to get paid. The name of the street was Buchanan, and albeit a very popular street, it also was one of the most dangerous. Pimps, hustlers, drug dealers, and gangsters ruled Buchanan.

When I arrived at the Hole, the very first thing I encountered was a breathtaking beauty standing next to the jukebox. She was extremely sexy and flirty, with a confident attitude that was reminisce of Mae West. She had a hint of street hardness about her I had noticed was common among street walking prostitutes. Her body was solid, with nice sized breasts, a very small waist line, wide buttock and very shapely legs and thighs. She had, what we called, a high yellow complexion, and her thick, wavy, jet black hair appeared as though she had just left the beauty salon. Her makeup was flawless, and it was more than obvious that I was quite smitten by her.

I saw Chucky sitting on a barstool at the bar, so I walked over to greet him. I hadn't seen him in quite some time, so we were overjoyed to see one another. Before we could get beyond our initial greeting the girl walked towards us. To my surprise, she kissed me on my cheek, and asked Chucky who I was. Chucky told me that she was his new bride, and introduced us.

They had just gotten married, and had only been married for a week. She smiled at me and said jokingly, "He knew he had to marry me before I saw you. Damn you're a good-looking man!" Just like that, she had me in the palm of her hand. Chucky told her that I was his partner, and he couldn't have run into me at a better time. He then instructed her to give us some privacy, so we could discuss some serious business. She smiled and went back to the jukebox as Harold Melvin & the Blue Notes song, "The Love I Lost" began to play.

Chucky waited until his wife, Norma, was out of hearing range and said, "We are about to hit a lick, but we need one more man. He has to be tested, seasoned, and level headed." He looked around to make sure the bar maid wasn't listening to us, and she wasn't paying us any attention. She was talking to someone on the phone, and was engrossed in the conversation.

He continued by saying, "It's clear that you would

be perfect for the job, if you're looking for some work." He searched my eyes as though he wanted to take a stroll through my mind before revealing more about the job. On more than a few occasions, someone has revealed too much about a job to a potential partner, only to have the guy double cross him, and pull the job off himself.

Satisfied with whatever it was he saw in my eyes, he continued. "It's a dangerous job. We have to be willing to shoot to kill if we run into any resistance. However, we don't want there to be any unnecessary violence. Our whole purpose is to get all the cash and valuables, and get away safely. Hopefully without any complications. There will be about thirty Chrysler workers attending a poker party on their payday, and they've received their cost of living checks too! We're going to hit them."

We knew they had received their Cost of living checks, thanks to a popular disc jockey by the name of The King. He made the announcement on his radio program. That meant there would be, at the very least, fifteen thousand dollars in cash. Chucky informed me there would be five of us doing the job, so I was guaranteed at least three thousand dollars.

"We are going to be impersonating police officers conducting a raid, so I insist that you make the announcement. You have an authoritative tone to your voice, and your pronunciation of words sound very professional, collage boy." He concluded with a chuckle. I used proper English when I spoke. I knew how to cuss like an educated police officer.

I asked Chucky if his wife had any sisters, and was very disappointed to find out she only had a brother. I changed the subject by agreeing to do the job, but I insisted that we all got together no later than the day before the job. He agreed, and I spent the rest of the afternoon dancing with his beautiful new bride.

We got together that Thursday and went over the plan. Everyone was assigned a role to fulfill. That Friday we got together before it was time to go, and meditated on our roles, before we left to actually do the job. Everything went according to plan. There were times I sensed a few people realized we weren't really law enforcement, and a robbery was actually in progress.

I understood that with so many people to watch, we had to be sure to keep complete control. The situation could turn deadly with the slightest mistake. First, we searched everyone individually for their personal valuables and weapons. We were fortunate to confiscate several hand guns that were on the floor. Most were convinced that we were the police, and didn't want to get caught with a pistol in their possession.

I ordered the cook in the kitchen to turn the fire off all the eyes on the stove, and afterwards turn over the proceeds for the evening. She readily complied. Hawk and June Bug hit the tables, and bagged every dollar. Obie, Chucky's older brother, and Chucky searched all the bedrooms and gathered all the furs, cashmeres, and leather coats. We also left with all the jewelry, watches, wallets and purses.

The robbery was so successful, we exceeded all of our expectations. The jewelry was appraised at over twenty thousand dollars by our fence. We eventually agreed to accept eight thousand for it. We got two thousand for the coats, and counting the fifteen thousand in cash we took, we had a total of twenty, five thousand. We thought we would end up with approximately three thousand apiece, and we would have been very pleased, but ending up with five thousand apiece was beyond what we had imagined.

I went straight to my mother's house, and gave her enough money to pay all the bills, and buy some food. I gave all my sisters and brothers some money, and immediately called the Greyhound bus station, to find out what time the next bus was leaving for Tri City. I believed it was the perfect time to get out of the city. Afterwards, I called Joe to get some information on Phillis. I was shocked when he told me she had gotten her own place. I decided to surprise her, by paying her a surprise visit. Spending a couple of weeks out of town, hiding out at her place making love, seemed logical.

Joe picked me up at the station, and drove me directly to Phillis's house. When she opened the door, I could tell by the expression on her face I had surprised her. It was equally as obvious, she perceived it as a very pleasant surprise. She embraced me tightly, and held on to me as though she never wanted to let go. I thanked Joe for the ride, and we made plans to see each other in a couple of days.

Once I told Phillis that my plan was to stay with her, she insisted. She told me she had a roommate that was away at work. "Don't worry about her. She will be fine with you being here. She's real cool, and you'll like her. She's your type."

"What do you mean, she's my type?" I asked. I felt as though she was trying to hook me up with someone else. I couldn't believe what she was saying. Something didn't seem quite right. That's when Phillis told me she had a boyfriend, but he was in prison, and wouldn't be getting out for at least another year. She told me she was in love, and nothing could happen sexually between us. That was the last thing I expected to hear, but I didn't want to change my plans to stay with her, until I had a chance to check out her roommate. Maybe her roommate was sexy enough to help me get over the fact we will be sleeping under the same roof, without sleeping together. It was a blow to my ego, but a blow I was confident of overcoming.

Phillis and I spent the entire day together. She had two Saint Bernard dogs, and they were fully grown. I love big dogs, so we had a ball playing with them a good portion of the day. We never ran out of things to talk about. We shared a nice meal of beef stew that she prepared as I watched. We both called it a night after her roommate came in from work.

Her roommate was a bright yellow woman, with a full figure. She had long, dark, wavy hair, that she wore down on her shoulders. She was lovely, and although I preferred Phillis, I wouldn't consider it a complete letdown, if she were to be my consolation prize.

Before going into her bedroom, Phillis made sure I had everything I needed, in order to be comfortable. She even hooked the couch up with sheets, pillows and a blanket. She gave me a towel, a wash cloth, and a promised to cook a huge breakfast in the morning. Even though her roommate was sexy, and was rolling some marijuana to smoke with me, I still felt a deep sense of disappointment as she closed her bedroom door behind her.

I smoked the marijuana with her roommate, and engaged in a little sexual flirtation. She led me to believe that the night ahead would be full of pleasure. She asked me to wait until she put on something comfortable, and excused herself. It wasn't long before she returned in a sexy, breathtaking, see through, red negligee. She then went into the bathroom, and I could hear the sounds of water running. I also could hear her gargling, as well as brushing her teeth. I assume that she was preparing herself to make love to me. My penis became erect, and began to throb with anticipation.

She entered the room, and sat on the couch beside me. When I tried to touch her, she acted as if I had done something to offend her, and made a loud verbal commotion. I did not understand the embarrassing point she was trying to make. She wanted me to look at her, smell her, desire her, but not to touch her. Her enjoyment wasn't in the fulfillment or fulfilling. She seemed to enjoy teasing me to my brink. I wasn't patient enough to play that game, nor did I find it enjoyable. I wanted a sure thing, and in frustration I thought to myself, "Fuck this bullshit! I'm fucking Phillis tonight"

I apologized as I left her sitting on the couch, with a puzzled look on her face. She acted as if she didn't expect me to leave. I opened the door to Phillis's bedroom, and quietly entered. I didn't want to startle her, or wake her abruptly. To my surprise, I found her sitting in the center of the bed; wide awake. She stared at me as she said, "No Tone. We can't do this."

The light from the moon crept through her window, and danced across her desirable, nude, chocolate frame. The light formed shadows which enhanced her curves, and her loveliness. I was completely aroused, and determine to convince Phillis we both wanted and needed one another. She laid down, and I laid across the bed beside her, and took her in my arms. I enjoyed the feel of her full breast upon my chest. Tears began running down the cheeks of her face, but she offered no resistance. I tried my best to kiss all her tears away, and she eventually began kissing me back. As many times as we had kissed, nothing could compare with the passion we shared at that moment.

She whispered softly, "Look what you're making me do. I can't control myself when you touch me like this." She released herself from my embrace, and rolled on her back. She opened her legs wide, and begged me to penetrate her. She knew how to work the muscles in her vagina so well, it felt as though my penis were being milked. She was tightening and releasing her vagina muscles in rhythm with each of my strokes. It drove me crazy! I was so aroused that we made love for what seemed like hours. The only reason we stopped, was because the muscles in her vagina were too tired to continue squeezing my penis. We collapsed in a lover's embrace, and fell asleep while I was still inside her.

I was the first in the house to awaken that morning. Memories of the night's pleasures flooded my senses. My penis began to rise, throb, and swell with desire as it became obvious I'd become aroused. We spent the entire morning wearing each other out. I was knocked out cold, and later awakened by the smell of nourishments.

I found myself alone in the bed. The sounds of pots and pans were clanking on the stove, and were accompanied by delightful aromas. I got up from the bed, and put my drawers on. before heading for the kitchen. I intended to investigate the source of the sounds and smells, although it didn't take a genius to figure any of it out.

As I passed through the living room I saw her roommate

sitting on the couch. She was still dressed in the red negligee she had on the night before. She sat on one end of the sofa, and the bedding was neatly folded and stacked on the other end. She reached out, and grabbed my arm to stop me as I attempted pass her by. She wanted to make sure she had my undivided attention. "You didn't have to give up so easily. I was going to fuck you." She studied my eyes after saying so, to see how I would respond. She said it loud enough for Phillis to hear it also. Phillis shouted from the kitchen, "You can fuck him tonight. I'm not going to cheat on my man again."

I stayed for a couple of weeks, and every time her roommate and I would try to get together, Phillis would stop it, by demanding to have me for herself. She cried every single time we made love, but that was a complete turn on for me by now. She was crying real tears, because she didn't want to cheat on her boyfriend. She just couldn't find the necessary strength to fight me off, or to control the desirable lustful burning within her loins, which demanded she make love to me. It was because of her sincere desire and lust for me, that I preferred her over her roommate. Phillis also learned that she couldn't stand for any other woman to touch me in her presence.

I went home feeling like a new man. I sought Chucky out to see how things were going, since we robbed the poker party. I found him sitting on the front porch of his parent's home. He was thrilled to see that I was back, and was happy to inform me there were no ill effects following the robbery. He had an idea he'd given some serious thought to, and wanted to run it pass me to get my opinion.

"It's because we've been robbing legitimate businesses

that we've had to worry about the possible repercussions of the law. But, if we robbed dope houses, they can't call the police. We'll only have to concern ourselves with who could be paid to come after us, but If we handle our business correctly, they wouldn't be able to find a nigga they could melt and pour in our direction, let alone pay a muthafucka to fuck with us."

I gave it some serious consideration for a moment, before speaking. I realized that it was an amazing concept. "Hey, that's a hell of an idea Chucky! What they gone do? Call the police, and say somebody robbed my dope house, and took all of my money and my dope?" The thought of it made us both burst into laughter. We talked about the many advantages to robbing dope houses, including the fact that we could get drugs and jewelry to sell, but the most important thing was, we wouldn't have to worry about the law. We immediately began planning to hit our first target, the Beachwood brothers.

The Beachwood brothers had five dope houses in the neighborhood. Chucky and I came up with a plan to rob all five of them in one day, within an hour. It would be easy to do, since none of their dope houses had telephones in them. We could rob them all one at a time, before any of the remaining houses could be tipped off. We got our crew together and put our plans into motion.

Everyone agreed that we had a great idea, and it wasn't long before we were executing the robberies. Every spot we robbed, we left a message for the brothers. If they didn't meet with us, we would continue to rob them until they did. The Beachwood brothers weren't really gangsters. They were just a couple of young brothers with an outstanding connection. They were able to purchase heroin at such a low price, no one was able to compete with them.

The price of heroin had risen tremendously. There wasn't any white heroin to be purchased anywhere. Mexicans had taken over the heroin trade. Their heroin was brown, and was known as Mexican mud, on the streets. It was a lot weaker than the China white, yet it was much more expensive. What used to sell for a dollar was now being sold for ten dollars. There were no penny caps being sold any longer. We decided to get into the business ourselves, and the brothers were the weakest target, since they weren't really gangsters. We knew we could intimidate them. We were willing to kill or be killed, and that gave us a tremendous advantage over them.

The richest drug dealer in our neighborhood was Preston, but he was a seasoned gangster, and so were his close associates. Messing with him would have been a serious mistake. His main man was a Muslim by the name of Kahlid. Kahlid was well known throughout the city. He was considered extremely dangerous, as well as a smooth and clever operator.

There was another drug dealer by the name of Dayton. He was from Ohio, and he took on the role as a mentor for Cat. He made no secret of his fondness for Cat. He treated him like he was his very own son. Cat was a loved, and very valuable member of our crew. We all understood that having such a relationship with a rich mentor, was a great opportunity for him. We didn't want to do anything that would jeopardize their relationship, nor cause him to fall out of his favor. Therefore, the Beachwood brothers became our sole target for intimidation, and a means of getting into the drug trade.

They finally agreed to meet with us after we robbed all their spots every day for a week straight. They insisted that the meeting take place on a busy street, and in broad daylight, so we met on the corner of Warren Ave. beside the African American Museum that day.

They pulled up in a midnight Blue, specially designed, conversion van. It was the very first conversion van I had ever seen. We weren't even aware of anything like it. Cadillac was the trade brand for hustlers in those days. You were considered a success if you owned a Fleetwood Cadillac. The Lincoln Town Cars, and the Mark series, also demanded a lot of respect, but nothing announced to the hood that you had arrived as a hustler like a Cadillac. Here these guys were in a van.

Joe was a young, handsome, light skinned, black man, with a reputation as a lady's man. He got out of the passenger's seat, and as we walked towards the van, he slid the side door open. As the door slid open, the plush dark blue shag carpet that lined the walls, came into view. There was a small white refrigerator up against one of the walls, and two white tables that sat atop one light blue leg, which was bolted to the floor of the van. There were four captain chairs, and a love seat near the rear of the van.

As we entered the van, Joe did all the talking. "What's up brothers?" he asked as we found a seat. We were all in attendance; Chucky, Hawk, Obie, June Bug and myself. Even though we were in a vehicle, the atmosphere was very much like being in a boardroom. It was very easy to visualize this concept becoming the rave of the future. The possibilities for a floor plan would be endless for the creative minds. "This is a hotel room on wheels. What a great idea." I thought out loud.

"That love seat lets out to a queen sized, bed!" Joe added with pride, indicating sexual encounters had accrued as a direct result of having such a convenience. "let's get down to business." June Bug interjected as he grew tired of the small pleasantries.

"Of course," Joe added. "Just what is it ya'll want to happen to keep our spots from being robbed by you guys in the future?"

June Bug proudly announced, "We want to take over all your spots. We'll continue to purchase the product from ya'll, and in exchange we will discontinue robbing your spots. You won't get a percentage of the profits. We'll pay all the bills, and supply all the labor, but like I said, we will always buy all our dope from ya'll."

Joe and his brother broke out into laughter simultaneously. It was obvious how relieved they were. "That's all we've been looking for. We don't want to run any spots. Our goal has always been to find someone who would take on the responsibility of running these spots, and buy all their dope from us. Ya'll didn't have to terrorize our people for that! All you had to do was ask. That began our partnership with the brothers. The meeting was short, but very productive. We purchased four and a half ounces from them, with the money we had taken from them. Afterwards, they accompanied us to each spot, and informed their people that their services would no longer be needed. Just like that, we were in the drug trade.

I missed Toni, and my friends, so I took a trip to

Hudsonville to catch up with them. I didn't give a damn about the warnings the deputy sheriff had given me. I knew they weren't clever enough to discover I had invaded their precious designated space

The County Sheriff's Department started a rumor stating I had cooperated with them, and provided them with the information that led to the recovery of some stolen property. Even though the rumors were proven to be false, my friends used the unfounded rumors to get close to all my girls. I was very hurt and disappointed to discover Gator, Meme, Box, and Day Day had all taken part in spreading the vicious rumors about me a snitch.

Gator was trying his best to get with Panthea. She was my church girl. She used to love to read the Bible to me, but just like Phillis, she couldn't resist me, and I knew it. Believe me when I tell you that I took full advantage of her, even though she was engaged to the pastor's son. She was a breathtaking amazon, and a caramel delight.

Meme had gotten with Faye before I left. She was a scorned woman, so all he had to do was hate on me, to get with her. I didn't mind. As a matter of fact, it was my idea for them to get together. It wasn't even necessary for him to help spread the vicious lie. He already was with Faye. He even wore the diamond ring Faith had given me. She got it back by tricking me into believing she was getting the ring cleaned.

Box was with Karan. Karan had lost an astonishing amount of weight, and gotten in shape while attending State the year before any of us had arrived. We never hooked up, but while I was in Newport, I talked to her on the phone several times, and we agreed to see if we could make a go of it, as a couple. Right after that, Box explained to her why I wasn't ever coming back. It wasn't too much longer before I was no longer the topic of common interest in their conversations, and a romantic bond ensued.

While in Newport I had called, and confided in Box. I told him that Karan was the most beautiful woman on campus to me, and I had a serious crush on her. I told him of my plans to drop everything, and everybody to be with her. I informed him of my plans to get back in school, and try to seriously make a go of things. He knew I had plans, and he admitted to lying to Karan to get her. He told her gangsters wanted to me killed, and if I ever showed my face around Hudsonville again, they would kill me.

Day Day was with Toni now, and they both failed to inform me of that fact, until I was alone with her. I was trying to kiss her, when she broke her silence, and informed me that Day Day was the one who told her about the rumor. As she put it, with tears in her eyes, "He told me you had informed on some gangsters, and they wanted you dead." It was enough to convince her I was never coming back. Now that the truth was out, it seemed not to matter that the rumors were actually viscous lies. The only reason she insisted on seeing me face to face, was to explain how as well as why, she had allowed herself to get involved with a friend of mine. She was in love with Day Day now, and things were never going to be the same.

They all apologized to me for the part they played in the spreading of the rumors. All the pictures of me in the photo albums had snitch written next to them. They scribbled the word snitch from every picture, but I was still very offended. As far as I was concerned, anytime anybody referred to me as a bitch, hoe or snitch, we had serious issues to address. We were so close, I thought we were family. Up until that very moment, I had loved and respected these guys like they were my big brothers.

They threw a party in an honest effort to make it all up to me, but seeing them all coupled and cuddled up with my ex-girlfriends, did very little to inspire forgiveness within me. I was happy to see my ex- girlfriends, and they were happy to see me. I didn't blame any of them for moving on, especially since they were led to believe I was never coming back, by the people closest to me.

I left the party looking for my friend Crystal, who lived in the same building. Crystal was a tall, voluptuous, beautiful blond. I had met her by accident when I knocked on the wrong door one afternoon a year or so ago, looking for someone. I can't even recall right now, who it was I was looking for. Crystal answered the door looking so good wearing a yellow string bikini, that at that very moment, my search for whoever it was I was looking for ended. Looking pass Crystal, I could see there was a room full of white girls, all lounging around the living room. They were wearing an assortment of different styles and colors of bikinis. I thought it was strange, since it was pouring down rain at the time.

Crystal was extremely friendly. She was holding a smoking marijuana pipe in her hand, and offered me a toke. She grabbed my arm, and pulled me inside of the apartment, before I had the opportunity to answer. They all introduced themselves, and motioned for me to join them on the floor, where another marijuana pipe was continuing to be passed around between them.

After smoking for a while, we were all buzzing. Crystal

was sitting beside me, and elected to roll over on her stomach. I sensed it was okay, so I began massaging her shoulders. She responded by moaning and groaning in a throaty voice, displaying her approval, as a broad smile came across her face. I rose up to my knees, and began massaging her entire back. After a long session of gripping every single muscle in her back, causing her waves of pleasure, I went for it and squeezed her round, firm, shapely buttocks with my big, strong hands. She squealed with excitement and pleasure, as the other girls made comments stating how good it looked like it felt. They all began requesting that I do them next. One of them even asked if I had any male friends who might like to come by and party.

"You have to be fucken kidding, right?" I asked. Of course, I knew some dudes who would definitely be thrilled to party with them. "I'll be right back." I stated as I headed for the door. Gator, Meme, Box and Day Day lived right downstairs. This was the perfect setup. I practically ran down the stairs, taking the steps two and three at a time, to tell the fellas the good news.

It was taboo for a black man to have an open relationship with a white girl during those times. If the black women on campus found out a black guy was in a relationship with a white chick, they would blackball him. If the white guys found out a white chick was in a relationship with a black guy, they would disassociate themselves from her. A white guy could be in a relationship with any race, and return to his race without any problems, because the white guys were considered a major catch. A black woman who was in relationship with a white guy is also welcomed back.

The rich, or famous black men, were just about the only

exceptions to this rule. I was a collegiate athlete, and that was another exception to the rule. I knew the fellas wouldn't give a damn about the unwritten rules. Especially once I inform them that the ladies in question were right upstairs. We're talking about seasoned ex-convicts here. We all went upstairs, and the party was on!

Box and Meme enjoyed engaging the ladies in meaningful, stimulating conversations, while smoking the marijuana that we passed between one another. It became obvious that Gator wanted to get with Crystal, but it was as equally obvious that Crystal wanted to get with me. I also wanted her. Day Day coupled up with Grace. Grace was pretty, petite, brunette, and had a striking resemblance to Elizabeth Taylor.

Day Day got her worked up and blew her mind, by explaining his techniques for administering oral sex. Shortly thereafter, they left the crowd, and headed to the bedroom for obvious reasons. Crystal and I were in hot pursuit. One of the girls giggled and yelled, "You guys are so transparent!" and Day Day shouted back, "Everybody's grown up in this camp. Come join us!" We weren't waiting around to see if any of them were going to take him up on his invitation to join us.

There were twin beds in the room. The bedroom had the typical décor for college girls. It seemed like everything was in some shade of pink. There were piles of stuffed animals in different parts of the room, and posters of Led Zeppelin and other heavy metal rock stars I didn't recognize, covered the walls. Day Day and Grace quickly laid across the closest bed, leaving the other bed for me and Crystal.

Crystal and I had barley began kissing, when I noticed

Day Day was already gobbling on Grace's pussy. I asked Crystal if she wanted her pussy ate, and her reply was a resounding "Hell no! I want some cock! she said as she pulled her bikini bottoms to the side, exposing her hairy vagina. White guys eat pussy all the time. I can get that any time. No, I want your big hard black cock." With her fingers pressed firmly upon on her stiff clit, she rubbed it in a circular motion, as she groaned and squirm, putting emphasis on the fact she was ready to impose her will and intentions.

I took my time warming her up. I especially made sure to spend extra time on the nipples of her breast. Her breast were large, firm mounds of natural treasures, and they demanded and deserved every bit of the attention they got from me. The whole time I was warming her up, I was getting myself mentally prepared to pound her pussy like a jack hammer. That's what she needed. There are times you can* sense that a woman wants you to be gentle and make love, but there are other times when she just wants to be fucked into an unconscious state. That's what Crystal wanted, and I was beyond determine to deliver.

I was balls deep, inside Crystal's pussy. My testicles were banging against her crotch with each, and every thrust. The sounds of groans and moans, escaping the throats of the ladies, was a clear indication they were thoroughly enjoying themselves. Crystal whispered in my ear, "May I please call you nigga?" It was an odd request, at a time when my ability to reason was being compromised. It was difficult, to say the least. Her vagina was making slurpy wet sounds, as I continued to bang away. The clapping sounds were a clear indication she was matching me stroke for stroke.

Before I could process and respond to her request, she blurted out, "Fuck this pussy, nigga!" She then arched her back in a feeble attempt to raise her pussy up off the mattress, and thereby offering me better access to her guts! I began thrusting my hard member with all my might, just to see if she could truly take it. "Fuck me nigga!" Crystal screamed. "Fuck me harder with that fucken big black cock of yours', you fucken nigga!"

Day Day and Grace had finished, but elected to remain in the room to watch our performance. He yelled loud enough for everyone to hear him, "That's my nigga! Tear that ass up, Slim!" They both burst into laughter as I made faces before spilling my seed deep inside Crystal's guts.

After Crystal and I were done, we all got dressed and returned to the living room. It seemed like all eyes were on Crystal, and she must have notice, because she felt compelled to announce, "I'm not prejudice, it's just a fantasy I've had, since I've seen that movie, Mandingo."

She continued by adding, "Whenever I masturbate I imagine I have a Mandingo under my control, and I always have the most amazing orgasms ever!" I kissed her, and assured her she needn't imagine any more, or explain. "Whenever you want to role play, it'll be my pleasure!" You could sense we were making the others uncomfortable. Crystal, and I didn't give a fuck how uneasy they were. She and I fed on their uneasiness, and laughed uncontrollably with each nervous smile that they forcibly displayed.

It had been quite a while since I had last seen Crystal. I wasn't even sure if she still lived in the same apartment any longer. I had knocked on her door a many of nights, and each time I received exactly what I needed. This night I felt betrayed. It would take a lot to begin the healing process of my damaged heart, and seriously tattered ego. I was a little nervous. I knew I would have been crushed if Crystal had moved away. I was both thrilled, and relieved when she answered the door and squealing, "My nigga!"

Before she could even close the door, she began kissing me, with her tongue hungrily searching for and finding mine. I pulled away from her embrace, just to close the door. "Are you alone?" I asked as I locked the door. "Yes, I'm alone, and very lonely. Everybody went to spend a week at Grace's parent's cottage up north. They left early this morning, before sunrise." Since we were alone, we decided to make the living room our love nest for the evening.

During the entire week, we made love all over the apartment. We did it everywhere, and in every position. We did it in the kitchen, on the balcony, on the dining room table, on the toilet, on the kitchen sink, and of course in the shower. We did it on the hood of her car at the drive-in movie theater. We did it in the middle of the night, alongside a camp fire we had made in the woods. For a while I forgot all about the loves I had lost. It was one of the most enjoyable weeks I had ever spent in my life, but at the end of that week, I left Hudsonville for the very last time. I said goodbye to no one, except Crystal. She took me to the bus station, and I never saw Crystal again.

I called Chucky that next morning, to inform him I would be home that evening. Obie answered the phone, and expressed an urgency for me to return to Newport immediately. He told me I'd find out everything when I got home, but we shouldn't talk on the phone. I caught the next bus headed home. Something was seriously wrong. I felt deep down in my very gut, something had happened to Chucky.

I stared out of the window the entire trip, during the bus ride home. All the faces of the people around me appeared to be a blur. My mind was consumed with thoughts of what I may discover once I reached my destination. After a while, I gave up trying to imagine, and break down, all the possible scenarios in my mind. I was too jacked up to sleep, so I watched the cars as they were passing by.

The rage which had filled me, as a result of the betrayal by my so-.called friends at school, had return. I dared not to express my thoughts to anyone, because they were far too dark and morbid for most to understand. I'd learned that once you are known to have committed murder, you no longer have the luxury of idle threats, or venting. Every uttered threat of violence is taken very seriously, and understandably so. I thought to myself how unfortunate it was for me to have such a slow bus driver, at a crucial time like this. I had to exhibit calmness and patience, so I meditated as I stared out the window.

The news about Chucky was worse than I could have imagined. Some guys came from another side of town, and set up shop right down the street from one of our spots. It was the ultimate sign of disrespect. Chucky's trigger finger was just as lethal as my own. Most found him quite charming, but beneath that exterior was a cold, blooded killer. Without planning, Chucky promptly went to their humble establishment, and robbed them. They didn't fully cooperate, so there was gun play. He killed one of them, and the man he killed, turned out to be an off-duty police officer. The police arrived so quickly, Chucky never had the opportunity escape capture. Concerned neighbors called the police when they heard the gunshots. It wasn't even discovered to be an off-duty officer that had been killed, until the next day. The post-mortem examination revealed the officer had heroin in his system, and there was no reasonable explanation for the toxic substance to be in his system. He should not have been in that establishment at that time. Anyway, Chucky was in custody, and there was nothing we could do to change that.

Chucky was an extremely valuable member for our crew. We could never replace him, nor did we have any peers equally experienced. JB started hanging with us a lot more, and before we realized it, he had become a valuable member of our crew. He wasn't lacking in the heart department. He wasn't a seasoned stick-up man yet. It was just a matter of continuing to do jobs with us. Eventually he would become a veteran. He also had access to his parent's car just about any time he wanted it. They had a 1973 Buick Electra 225. Hustlers called them a Duce and a Quarters, or simply a Duce.

A few months later, I ran into Chucky's wife in Uncle Lucky's dark, crowded bar. Chucky had taken a plea deal, and pleaded guilty to manslaughter in return for a ten to fifteen-year prison sentence. It was a great relief to know that he wasn't going to spend the rest of his life in prison. This was the first time I had seen Norma, since Chucky had been sentenced.

Norma had become badly addicted to heroin, and although she was still very beautiful, the drugs had robbed her of some of her luster. It broke my heart to see her in such a state. I insisted, and convinced her to accompany me to my mom's house, to get her something to eat, and some needed rest. I didn't want to wake my mom, and break up her sleep at such a late hour, by knocking on the door. It was after three o'clock in the morning. I decided it would be best if I sneaked in the house through the basement window, which I always kept unlocked for such occasions. I took Norma to the front door, and instructed her to remain there until I opened the door for her upon my return. The street light in front of my mom's house exposed the hardness in her eyes, and her struggles with narcotics were much more noticeable. She hadn't lost weight, so she was able to retain her voluptuous figure. I left her standing there, and ran around to the side of the house.

I had sneaked into the house so many times, I had mastered a technique. I was able to open the window, climb through it, and land on my feet, all in a single motion. The basement was so dark I was unable to see. It didn't matter. I knew the basement like the back of my hand. It wasn't necessary for me to use my vision to navigate my way to the basement stairs. I climbed the stairs, and opened the door which led to the kitchen. Something smelled delicious, and I couldn't wait to find out what it was, but first I had to let Norma in.

The house was dark, but not as dark as the basement. The street lights and the illuminated moon light entered the house through the windows, and pierce the darkness. That wasn't possible in the basement, because the windows were painted.

I let Norma in, and held her hand, as I guided her through the house. After leading her to the kitchen, I turned on the lights. "What the hell smells so muthafucken good!"

she asked in a loud enough to wake up the entire house. "You gone wake everybody up!" I protested. "With yo drunk ass!"

I opened the oven door, hoping to discover the source of the aromas. My mouth was salivating. I was disappointed to find what I thought was the remains of a beef roast. It was sure to be pleasing to my palate, but I was hoping to discover something different. I'm not sure what, but the aromas had awakened desires for something different.

I made a plate for Norma and myself. You can't imagine how surprised I was to taste what I thought was the best roast I'd ever tasted. Norma's eyes were as wide in bewilderment as my own. "Are you sure this is a pot roast?" she asked as she devoured her plate. It was quite clear that she was famish. This was the best roast either of us had ever tasted, however, she ate with a gusto that is reserved for starvation mode. We finished our meal, and headed upstairs to one of the bedrooms.

None of my brothers were home. The upstairs had somehow become our personal sanctuary, reserved only for the boys, however, this night none of my brothers were home. Norma and I had it all to ourselves. After we had talked for a while, I noticed that she was shivering like she was cold. She began sniffing, as her nose appeared to noticeably run. I almost went downstairs to get her some tissue, before I remembered my former days as a heroin addict. She was beginning to show signs of going through withdrawal symptoms, right before my eyes.

I took a bag from my one of my socks which contained some dime packages of heroin. It was my personal stash to sell at one of our spots for pocket money. I took a couple of the packages from the bag, and handed them to her. She lowered her head and began weeping. "Is it that noticeable?" she asked, as she hid her face in her hands trying to hide herself like a child. I cupped my fingers, and placed them under her chin. I softly said her name as I gently lifted her head. Once our eyes locked, I began to speak. "The only reason I know what you're going through, is because I used to be strung out." I went on to assure her that although she wasn't keeping herself up like she used to, the average person would think she was coming down with a cold, and nothing more.

She had everything she needed in her purse to inject the drugs, except water. I quickly went downstairs, and returned with a glass of water, and some toilet tissue. I got undressed, and climbed into the bed. I laid there watching Pat injecting the drugs, as I reminisced about my own days of heroin addiction. For a moment, I considered joining her, but then I wondered to myself, why did I suddenly have a desire to self-destruct, by returning to which I came? Though I had been clean for years, the desire remained.

She must have seen it in my eyes, because she to plead with me, "Please don't watch me while I'm doing this." I was puzzled. I had no idea what it was she was talking about, until she mentioned the desire she seen in me. The beast never dies. It lays dormant, and waits for the opportunity to catch you off guard. I understood exactly what it was she was asking. She was begging me not to allow the temptation to get the better of me, while I was observing her. She didn't want to be the one to greet me at the gates of hell. I decided the game I was playing was just too dangerous, and the consequences were too severer to continue, so I rolled over, and fell fast asleep. Once Norma had finished, she removed her garments, and joined me. I was so tired I slept like I had been sleep deprived. The next morning Norma awakened me by stroking my erect penis. My body was responding to her firm grip and stroking. I've been told that the morning erection is a piss hard erection, because the act of urination offers relief, and the erection subsides. However, you may elect to take full advantage of the powerful erection, and have a morning orgasm before racing to the toilet.

I was all in, until I caught myself. "Whoa! You're not Chuck' girlfriend, you're his wife! I won't betray my man like this". Expressions of astonishment, surprise, and amazement swept over her face. "Who would know?" she asked with a wicked smirk on her face. "I would know!" I answered. She appeared disappointed while stating in a matter of fact tone, "Chucky wouldn't give a fuck, if I was your wife! So, you're telling me you don't wanna fuck? Naw, naw, better yet, you're trying to convince me that you don't wanna fuck me?" She began twisting one of her nipples between her thumb and fore finger, while stroking her swollen clit with her other hand. Her eyes slowly closed as she purred, "You know we've always wanted to fuck. I'm so horny right now!

I shook my head as her breathing quickened. She was groaning and pleading, all while her body was gyrating to the rhythm her fingers found on her clit. "I'm going to get off, with or without you." she plainly stated, as she continued masturbating.

I wanted Norma, and what she was saying was true. We had always flirted, and there had been more than one occasion I wished I could have ravished this delectable creature. Maybe this was our opportunity to release the lust we had been suppressing. I don't know. All I knew for sure, was I wasn't comfortable double crossing my friend like that. A lot of our so-called friends would have jumped at the opportunity to experience a sexual encounter with Norma, without giving it a second thought. I knew this to be true, because I'd witnessed every single one of them trying to convince her to treat them to her sexual favors; even before Chucky was transferred upstate from the county jail! Everyone except me and his brother Obie was after that grade -A premium choice ass.

There was a rich drug dealer out of Ohio by the nickname of Dayton. He had made his mark on the west side of the city. He was quite fond of Cat, and we reap a lot of benefits, as a result of the bond they shared over the years. However, he also reaped some benefits. He had access to a very reliable crew of young soldiers, and his choice among the many beautiful young girls that hung out around us.

Norma was his choice, and as far as he was concerned, she could do absolutely nothing wrong. She would take his Cadillac, and disappear for days at a time. He wouldn't care, because he owned several Cadillacs. She stole large amounts of drugs and money from him, but he would always forgive her transgressions, and beg her to come back. He also fed her an unlimited supply of heroin, and it was slowly, but surely, dragging her down. All the money and drugs he gave her, wasn't quite the blessing she believed it would be. It turned out to be the proverbial anchor around her neck, and her struggles to remain afloat became obvious to all who knew and loved her.

I felt horrible because no one knew better than I, the degradation and humiliation young female drug addicts endured trying to survive, and to help others survive on the streets. Many were under-aged children are some of history's unsung heroes. Many of them sacrificed themselves by agreeing to have sex with pedophiles, who had their own homes, and were willing to allow a group of us kids to crash in their place, if she did so. There were many of us who would have died from hypothermia had these young girls not bartered their bodies, for our sake. I too am included in the number of children saved from hypothermia, by these heroes.

Their dignity, value systems, and self-esteem are slowly compromised. It erodes, and eventually is stripped completely away. Eventually, they will walk the streets aimlessly, like zombies, in search of another hit. Their shamelessness will sometimes be marketed, as though it was a commodity. If I hadn't learned anything while overcoming a serious drug addiction as young homeless drug addict myself, I've learned, only the addicted can emancipate themselves from dependency. My heart offers prayers for those young sisters every night, who struggled to help others in spite of their own shortcomings. My prayers are offered for those young girls from the past, the present, and the future, who've sacrifice themselves for the sake others.

Chapter 7

Our new business venture was going quite well. June Bug brought a slightly used Ford Thunderbird, and although our business was doing well, the proceeds for the purchase its self were under scrutiny. It all began after a conversation Cat and I had with Dayton, while we sat in his Cadillac convertible on a corner of Buchannan. He was impressed by the organizational skills we had displayed in our daily operations. He wanted in badly, but we already had too many paid partners on the payroll. In order to be a part of our plans, Dayton agreed to sell heroin to us at a much cheaper price than we were receiving from the Beachwood brothers. I was extremely excited. It was a tremendous opportunity. As a direct result of this deal, our profit margin would more than double. Hawk and I agreed to inform the rest of the fellas about the tentative agreement that very evening, with Dayton present. That way we could work out all the details.

That evening I waited at Uncle Lucky's bar for Dayton. When I first arrived at the bar, it was packed. It was a Friday night, and the entire hustling crowd was hoping to get lucky, laid, or both. I found Cat setting at the end of the bar near the pool table nursing a rum and Coke. He had a look of disappointment on his face as he gripped a pool stick in one hand, and the drink in the other. His hopes of getting another shot were dashed, when his opponent sunk the eight ball in the side pocket.

When he noticed me, he suddenly got in a big hurry to leave. The bar was directly across the street from an apartment building where His girlfriend Mary lived. Mary had been complaining about him not spending time with her. He wanted to spend some time with her, but he couldn't wait for Dayton's arrival, and be with her at the same time. I assured him that I would wait for Dayton to arrive. He made sure I understood he would be having sexual intercourse with Mary, and I could find him there, once Dayton arrived. I watched as he headed towards the door, and noticed a beautiful dark-skinned sister sporting a huge perfectly shaped afro, and shinning shapely legs, sitting all alone at one of the tables up against the wall. I decided to kill some time waiting for Dayton by getting to know the sister.

There was a storage room at the rear of the structure that also doubled as an office for Uncle Lucky. Only certain people were allowed in the office. Uncle Lucky had gotten involved in drugs, and in addition to his operations in Newport, he had interest in Saginaw, Cleveland, and Canada. You were allowed to enter the room for the purpose of business only, and since I wasn't conducting any business, I wasn't allowed to join the crowd of the privileged few.

The young woman's name was Bernice. She wore silver hot pants, and a white satin halter top that displayed an amazing cleavage, with proud perky nipples. Her shapely legs were shinning, because she had taken the time to oil them. She was truly into me. She seemed to be mesmerized by my every word, and clung to each and every syllable and phrase. Suddenly a conversation with threatening tones could be heard over the loud music and noise of the large crowd of drunkards. This undoubtedly, was the first of many warning signs that should have alerted everyone in attendance of the possible imminent danger.

Uncle Lucky came out of his office to see what all the commotion was about. He suddenly became visibly upset, while talking to a young, gentlemen, and promptly removed his .357 magnum from its' holster. The buzz of the crowd became screams, and shouts of terror when someone shouted out, "He's got a gun!" Everyone was ducking, diving on the floor, or racing towards the establishment's only exit. Everyone except me that is. I remained seated, and continued to enjoy this gangster's demonstration of how to check an individual, and at the same time terrorize an entire crowd.

He had the fella jacked up by his collar, while he was striking him upside his head over and over again, with the butt of the pistol. It was my first time witnessing a pistol whipping, and I was thoroughly enjoying his technique. The guy's face became covered with blood, as the blood poured from the wounds on his head. It was a ghastly sight, and the crowd responded by becoming even more frightful.

Uncle Lucky added a little twist to his pistol, whipping technique. Squeezing off a shot, while simultaneously striking his victim upside his head, was ingenious. It was an amazing display of creativity, and my jaws dropped with astonishment. People who had ducked or dove to the floor, immediately returned to their feet, and in a panic, they were all racing towards the now crowded, and jammed up exit. The poor guy thought he had been shot, and collapsed in a heap upon the filthy floor. To be truthful about it, there was so much blood even I thought he may have actually been shot, but he wasn't.

After calmness had been restored, the patrons began to file back inside of the bar, as others picked themselves up off the floor, from which they had sought refuge just moments ago. The majority of the conversations, were about the pistol whipping technique used, but others found amusement in my calmness during the altercation. I didn't think it was such a big deal, but quite a few did. There was a moment during the altercation that the so-called fight was practically upon me, yet I remained seated, as though I were totally unfazed.

No one realized I was frozen by the beauty of the creativity displayed during the pistol whipping. My dark side had found amusement in the response the violence had generated. It was like viewing a master piece for the first time. The respect, love, attention and admiration that was bestowed upon Uncle Lucky afterwards, did not go unnoticed by me either. I made a promise to myself, I would one day be the conductor of a crowd controlled by fear.

I was so focused on the pistol whipping, I didn't notice Bernice had departed, however, finding her now was a priority. After I had thoroughly searched the bar unsuccessfully, I decided to check outside. It was the only place left. If she wasn't out there, I'd just have to wait until another time to continue our conversation. I was a little disappointed when she was nowhere to be found. Just as I was about to give up my search, and return inside, Dayton pulled up in a red convertible Cadillac, with the top down. The white leather interior was so clean it appeared to illuminate the night with a light of its own.

"Where's Cat?" he asked. I could detect a slight sense of urgency in his voice. I mistook the urgency for excitement. Why wouldn't I? We were about to embark upon a business venture which had unlimited earning potential. I thought to myself, "This must be it." We were about to get more product than we've ever handled, which in return meant we were about to generate more revenue than was possible to estimate.

"He's at his girl's crib waiting on you." I answered. He asked me to show him which apartment was Mary's apartment, which led me to believe Cat had to have said something to him. Otherwise, how would he even know Mary's name? I felt a sense of accomplishment as I led Dayton directly to Mary's door. Something huge was about to go down, and I was about to be one of the founding partners, just by being present for the negotiations.

After I knocked on the door, Mary's voice could be heard on the other side of the door. "Who is it?" she asked. I notice Dayton exhale in relief and then he smiled. I quickly answered "It's me…Tone. Is Cat here?" There was the sound of rustling, and whispering. Eventually, after a moment of silence, there was movement and the sound of metal clanging upon metal as the locks were released.

Dayton positioned himself. so he could enter the apartment ahead of me. I had no issues with his maneuvers. Guys who possess the type of money he had, always display an attitude laced with the air of entitlement.

As the door swung open, he rushed past me, and entered the apartment. I entered slightly behind him, and what I observed nearly sent me into a state of shock. There were furs, leathers, and cashmere coats piled on the couch. The coffee table was completely covered with jewelry accentuated with diamonds, which caused an eruption of brilliant colored lights throughout the entire living room. The sight was simply astounding! I had never witnessed, nor even imagined viewing anything like it. There were large stacks of money on both end tables, and bricks of heroin in the recliner.

Slim, June Bug, Cat and JB were all standing in the living room, and I was able to gather from their verbal exchange they had robbed Dayton's sister. The very last person they expected to see was him. Their eyes were as big as saucers. They were stone cold busted. We all knew this situation could turn very ugly, but both parties were able to come to an agreeable compromise, because neither side would be able to prosper during a war. Contrary to what most think about drug dealers, most street hustlers preferred to avoid violence when at all possible. It's bad for business. It's as simple as that. Dayton received all off his sister's jewelry and coats. In exchange, my friends kept all the drugs and cash. The matter was squashed.

He left with his sister's property in tow, and it was now time to discuss the betrayal. I was extremely upset, and rightfully so. I had just walked in on my partners right after they had pulled off a robbery, and the score was more than ten times the amount of any robbery we had ever executed, and I had been omitted. There were plenty of awkward vibes in the room as they all tried to explain to me why I wasn't included. It was obvious the bond I shared with them wouldn't be severed, but things between us would never be the same. These were the closest friends I had in the world, and they had betrayed me. All of their explanations fell on my death ears. I was hurt and numb. I could see their lips moving, but to this very day I couldn't repeat verbatim what was said. Some tried to feed me the bullshit about them believing I would look at it as compromising my morals, principles, and standards to rob someone I did business with for no reason, and I wouldn't agree to doing the job. I had taken part in robbing the Beachwood brothers in order to gain control of their operation, so their explanation made absolutely no sense at all to me.

The others tried to explain that it was a spur of the moment thing, and they had to go with the people who were available. J.B. had the means of transportation, so he was included in my place. They weren't certain what type of money the score would bring, therefore, they wanted to make sure it was no more than a four-way split. Being opposed to a five way split, but agreeable to a four-way split, didn't add up either. I played it off like I whole heartedly accepted their explanations. We had always had the type of bond, whereas, even though it was never verbally expressed, it was understood and implied in our actions and deeds, we had each other's backs until the caskets dropped. This was an out and out betrayal spearheaded by greed, and it was as simple as that. As karma would have it, the robbery and the betrayal were both exposed, and I was the one to bring Dayton to the premises. How ironic was that?

A couple of days later June Bug showed up on the set driving a late model Ford Thunderbird. The word of June Bug driving a new car spread like a wild fire throughout the entire neighborhood. There was dissension among those who took part in the robbery. The rumors were, they suspected June Bug of stashing some of the money for himself during the robbery. The problem was, no one could prove it. Everyone had taken off all of their clothes, and their garments were thoroughly search by one another. He had to be like Houdini to pull off such a feat, yet it was more than obvious he had done exactly that. There was a lot of grumbling behind his back, but none dared to approach him with their assumptions. I could have been wrong, but in my heart, I believed the apprehension was due to the fear of there being a reprisal accompanied by his wrath. He and I became damn near inseparable after that, and because of that.

Dayton was no longer interested in doing business with us after the robbery incident, so we continued our business arrangement with the Beachwood brothers. It wasn't as lucrative as it would have been, had Dayton honored the agreement we had made with him before the robbery. However, it was still a lucrative business, and it was all ours.

After a quick inventory, it became obvious that one of our dealers had taken advantage of our preoccupation with the riff between JB, Cat, and June Bug. He worked at our newest location on Ohio and Grand River. After picking up his daily supply from each one of us, even though he was supposed to get his daily supply from only one of us, he promptly disappeared. To make matters even worse, he was an addict. We mistakenly believed the fear we were able to instill in those we dealt with, was far stronger than any drug addiction. Tyler, the missing drug addict, mistakenly believed he and his brother in-law could play on our intelligence, and keep our money. Both mistakes proved to be disastrous. The miscalculations brought about devastating results which nearly proved to have lethal consequences for Tyler.

We were young, and hadn't yet learned the benefits of not mixing business with pleasure. As a matter of fact, we actually sought out ways to make money while partying. We had to take care of the missing runner, so we decided to make an evening of it by picking up a few of our female fans. We were treated like celebrities everywhere we went now. Rounding up a whole crew of girls willing to do anything sexual that we wanted done, was a far cry from being a problem for us. They were always available and willing. We had two apartments in the same building the missing runner lived in with his wife and children, so we gathered some ladies, a few bottles of alcohol, and headed to our apartment. We had business to attend to, as well as a party to give. Since we were giving the party, eager, beautiful, young ladies, excited about the opportunity to display their skills, as well as their eagerness to please, would be in attendance.

After we had gotten everyone settled in, it was difficult for me to pull myself away. I had Myrtle in my arms, and her tongue down my throat. Myrtle was an amazon of a woman, as well as a beautiful young tender that truly drove me crazy. Everything about her felt right. She had strikingly beautiful features, and smooth dark chocolate skin. Her body was as full as any grown woman's. Her cleavage was deep and inviting. Her hips were voluptuous. Her entire aura was intoxicating to me, and I found that thick frame of hers extremely enticing. I wanted her so badly my knees were buckling, and I could have sworn the beat of my heart, accompanied by the throbbing of my erect penis, had become one and the same.

Now, on the other hand, I found June's voice to be quite irritating. He was insisting we take care of the business at hand, before we became too comfortable. He was right, but as far as I was concerned, it was already too late for all that. Myrtle and I had to be literally torn apart, which did nothing to improve my disposition. As we headed down the stairs, it was as though I were a wounded bear. I was hell bent on making someone pay for this intrusive interruption, by extracting a fair share of flesh, as payment.

After knocking on Tyler's door, the door opened quickly. A skinny, straggly, dark complexioned woman of medium height, opened the door. she took a position in the entrance of the door, as though she were trying to block it. This was an alert for me. What was she trying to hide, I asked myself. The fact she actually was trying to get rid of us without inviting us in, did not set well with me, nor was it undetected by the others.

My gut told me that fool was hiding in the apartment, and they thought she could tell us anything because we were young. I noticed a small group of children huddled up on a dirty, bare, wooden, unkempt floor, in front of a television set. For a moment I attributed the woman's attempt to block our entrance to her paternal instincts. That is until we all heard the dull thump sound coming from the back of the apartment, right after she had informed us there was no one there, except her and the children.

From that point forward, there was no need to be pleasant. The silent rage had been released from within us, and we now sought out our victim. It was time to unleash our version of a reign of terror. J.B. practically knocked the hag off her feet as he forced his way through the entrance.

The slight nudge she received from Cat as he passed, completed the job, even though her arms were flaring in a feeble attempt to catch her balance. She landed on her backside, with her legs sprawled, exposing the nastiest pair of panties I had ever seen in my entire life. We all rushed pass her, heading towards the direction of the unexplained noise.

The apartment smelled of urine, and soiled diapers, mingled with the aromas of food cooking coming out of the kitchen. Even though the apartment was void of furniture, it felt quite toasty and had a cozy atmosphere. I stopped for a moment and stared at the innocent children as they enjoyed their television program. They were totally oblivious to the imminent danger they all were in. Bugs Bunny had their undivided attention.

The nostalgic moment was interrupted by the sounds of Tyler's pleads for mercy as J.B. and Cat drug him by his arms across the floor. "Where's our shit bitch" I growled as soon as we made eye contact. "Not in front of the kids, man." Cat pleaded. "Let's take him upstairs. The kids don't need to see this." We were known for a lot of things, but abusing children was not one of them. Tyler was a horrible father, but we still understood the devastating effects it would have had on the children to watch us work over their father in an attempt to extract the necessary information. It could get quite ugly, and no child deserves to witness the father they love, receive such a severe beating. We were all in agreement, so we left the apartment, and went to an empty apartment we were renting next door to our main apartment. The empty apartment served as a stash spot, and where we cut and packed the drugs. We also kept weapons and extra ammunition there.

Once inside the apartment we commenced to delivering a beating unlike any before. Tyler collapse in a heap on the floor, offering no resistance whatsoever. The more submissive and docile he responded, the angrier I became. The mayhem increased with each and every cry for mercy. It was as though the flames of my anger fed off his cries for mercy like fuel accelerant. I began jumping as high as the ceiling would allow, and coming down on his head with the heels of my boots as hard as I possibly could. I even did a twist upon each landing for an even more devastating effect. JB and Cat had to intervene to prevent me from literally stomping him to death.

"How you expect to get our shit back if you kill the nigga Tone? I know you're mad, but we have to think nigga. Killing everybody is not the answer all the time." I thought about what he was saying, and he was correct. I had to get a hold of myself if there was truly going to be any chance of us recovering our merchandise. June Bug wanted to make certain that I understood, and agreed with the point he was trying to make. He waited until we made eye contact, and he received a slight nod from me to reassure him.

He then turned his attention to Tyler. "Where is our dope" he asked. With bewildered eyes, the accused made eye contact with each and every one of us seeking out a friendly face, or a face of compassion. There was no solace to be found in the eyes that reflected the souls of this group. There was nothing but disdain. He could sense death knocking at his door, so his entire demeanor changed.

"Okay, okay!" he managed to say as he seriously

attempted to catch his breath. "My brother in-law convinced me that he could sell the shit in his neighborhood, and I could catch my regulars over here, and that way we could make a come up, and never look back by selling twice as much shit every day." On the surface, it seemed like a pretty good plan. "What went wrong?" June Bug asked.

"You guys figured the shit out quicker than we thought ya'll would. We won't be finished for at least another hour." That didn't seem like a bad plan at all, if indeed it worked out the way they had planned it. We stepped to the side, out of his hearing range, and had a private discussion. We all agreed to give him another hour. It may be unnecessary for us to unleash the savages we become whenever we moved in unison to bring about destruction.

June Bug placed his arm around his shoulder, and walked him to the door. All the while they were walking, he was explaining in a fluid conversation exactly what would happen in the likelihood he should decide to take a permanent hiatus. I distinctly recall the mentioning of his wife and children in a hostile, unflattering manner. Johnny said all the right things as he headed for the door, just like he was a politician.

I would have placed bets at that time he was not going to return. Suddenly it dawned on me that Myrtle and I would have a whole hour to kick it. I really was looking forward to killing an hour making out with her. She absolutely enjoyed sucking on my tongue, and stroking my penis. I knew she would get me so worked up that by the time all the Johnny mess was cleared up, we could go straight to the bedroom and make love.

Unfortunately, things did not work out the way we had

hoped. Shockingly, Tyler did return, but not with the desired results. His brother in-law had run off with the portion of heroin he had vowed to sell, and now he was nowhere to be found. He said that he still had his half, and he hoped that we would allow him to work off the remaining balance.

We had a serious decision to make. We could not afford to become known as guys you could run off on, without there being serious consideration given to the possibilities of very severe consequences. "Let's see how much shit he's got left before we decide." I suggested. "It's very possible he could be bull shitten trying to stall." Cat suggested we take the lame to his apartment, and get whatever he had left, and then "…fuck his bitch ass up." We actually had no choice. There was no way we could possibly afford to let the word get out on the streets that we had allowed such an outrageous transgression, without there being sever consequences. At that moment, I decided whatever happened, I would make sure Tyler met with a fatal, untimely demise. I knew no one would agree with my plan, but I'd always found pride in my ability to make these types of difficult and unpopular decisions.

This was a necessary evil that was sure to usher in the respect we needed. In order to continue conducting business, using our method of operation with untrustworthy people, fear would have to be used like a reliable tool. There are no consequences more severe than the death penalty, and that's the memo I wanted to release. We would issue and execute the death penalty for those who dared to cross the clear and precise boundaries we had established.

We decided if Tyler had close to half of the product left we hoped he had, we would just beat the hell out of him, and then allow him to continue working until the remaining balance was taken care of. It was also established that if he returned with nothing, it would be my call to do whatever I deemed necessary. I was the enforcer. That is a position that isn't assigned. In the process of putting in work on the streets, those with talents for certain types of jobs will surface. Each and every individual processes a skill. Some in different areas than others. I had a talent at a very young age of being able extract redemption from where there seemed to be no hope for justice.

I'd become much more than an equalizer. Sometimes there are things that are considered justice in white society, but sometimes those very same things are considered a miscarriage of justice, or travesty of justice to the black masses on the streets. It had gotten to the point that people who didn't trust white law enforcement, would call me instead! When someone had cause to see me, it is usually for me to turn out the lights on that party.

Something deep within me relished the opportunities to straighten out issues that had a high probability for random, senseless acts of violence. I didn't realize it at the time, but I was extremely impulsive. Both are excellent attributes for the making of a great enforcer. An enforcer must be an uncontrollable loose cannon, ready to explode at any given moment. I was everything that an enforcer should be, and to say I excelled in the position without a title, would be a gross understatement. The fear we generated was completely justified and, second to none. Almost every single random act of violence was spearheaded by my famous temper, and or my impulsive behavior. I had indeed established myself as the enforcer.

We all gathered, and made the trip to Tyler's apartment. He played it off to the very end. He gave the performance of a lifetime, then again, his life did literally depend on it. He continuously thanked us for the opportunity to make some real money, so he could better provide for his family. He was so confident in his mannerism, and his demeanor, that I began to second guess myself, and question my judgement.

It wasn't very long after we had arrived, before it became obvious we were being taken. He pretended to be in a state of panic. He claimed the kids had gotten into the drugs, and threw them in the toilet. We looked into each other's eyes in total disbelief. From that point on, his pleads for mercy fell on death ears. I did take a peek into the toilet just to be fair, and the sight was hilarious. Floating on top of the water were two empty packs with our insignia stamped on the cellophane envelopes, and in the corners of each pack there was residue. That wasn't enough evidence to sway my opinion in his favor. As a matter of fact, I believed it collaborated, and reinforced our beliefs that he was using smoke screens and mirrors to stall. What he was stalling for is still a mystery to me, but I made the call. Time had run out.

"Get that bitch back upstairs" I barked while still trying my very best to contain myself in front of the children. We had done so many jobs together over the years that we knew what the other was thinking without uttering a single word. JB knew I was trying to contain myself and why, so he unplugged the television over the objections and cries of the hag, and the children. Without a word being said Cat immediately assisted JB as they removed the television from the apartment. That was their way of saying to me, "Fuck these kids!" I hated to see the hurt and disappointment on their faces, but they were right. That floor model television set would help in offsetting some of the loses.

As soon as we reentered the apartment the previous beat down resumed. I joined in, but I had grown weary of this game. The more we beat him, the more I realized we weren't going to get our money back. At that moment, I remembered there was a concrete paved parking lot outside the window. We were on the seventh floor, and a fall to the parking lot from that height would almost certainly cause his death. I solicited Cat's assistance in attempting to toss him out of the window. I opened the window all the way up, and grabbed Johnny by his arm, and leg. Hawk did the same, and we carried him screaming to the window.

Tyler was a frail shell of a man. The heroin addiction had robbed him of his muscle mass years ago. I don't believe he was taller than five foot seven, and he most certainly didn't weigh more than one hundred and thirty pounds, fully clothed and soaking wet. No matter how hard he struggled, I found ease in getting his foot out the window, but each and every attempt to toss him, was met with resistance. It was because every time we tried to toss him, the heel of his shoe on the foot Cat was holding would find the window's ledge, and Gator onto it. I looked in Cat's eyes, and I saw something I never thought I'd see. He had reservations about committing cold blooded murder. I knew JB wasn't a cold blooded killer, and now I knew the same of Cat. They were both killers, but not cold blooded killers. Up until that moment, I had counted Cat among those of us who were cold blooded. I never revealed to anyone what happened at the window that night. That was between me and Cat.

I believed it was each man's right to decide if he wanted to go before his maker with the blood of his brother on his hands or not. It doesn't make you any more gangster, or less gangster. A killer will kill, when and if it is absolutely necessary. That's all that really matters.

Cat didn't feel it was a necessary killing, but I knew he wouldn't. I knew that none of them would feel the urgency I felt. If runners started running off, we wouldn't be in business for very long. It would also make my job extremely difficult. I had to convince everyone to take him to the area that had abandoned houses near the projects, fuck him up, and leave him there to be found and taken to the hospital. I knew by mentioning the hospital they would go for it, because it suggested that I intended to leave him alive. Only I knew that at the very first opportunity I got, I would turn the lights out on this party. I was sure there would be hard feelings and objections, but not one of them would process the power to reverse the assassination. Once he was dead and found, they all would see the benefits of a deadly reputation.

It wasn't difficult at all to convince everyone that the only thing we were accomplishing by continuing to beat him there, was drawing attention with the noise we were making. "Those abandoned houses near Trumbull would be the best place to take care of this type of business. We're already near Trumbull, so it would be just a simple trip down the street." I suggested after interrupting them. They all were full of rage, frustrated, and they were releasing it on Tyler's ass.

We agreed to leave JB behind with the girls, and for him to watch over the fort until we came back. We gathered the necessary tools for the job, and headed to the exit at the rear of the building. The elevator was always in constant use, but hardly anyone ever utilized the stairwell. I was carrying a sawed off, 12 gage shot gun, and it was extremely difficult to conceal, so we took the stairs to avoid coming in contact with anyone entering or leaving the building.

Once we reached the bottom of the stairs next to the rear exit, Tyler spoke. "Please check with my wife one last time." he urged. "Something may have happened since we last talked to her. She's still trying to catch up with her brother through her mother."

There was nothing to lose by checking one last time. June Bug and Cat left to go check it out while I was left to guard the prisoner. I was far too weary of this game, and I wanted to shake things up. "Listen…" I told Tyler. "I'm high and tired. I ain't playing no fucking games with you." I then instructed him to sit on the bottom step. Before the barrel of the shot gun was laid to rest upon the top his head, I warned him "I'm taking the safety off, and I'm so fucked up that I know I'm going to nod off sleep. If I feel any sudden movements, I'm pulling the trigger while I'm waking up. If I have a fucked-up dream, I'm going to wake up pulling the trigger. Nigga, I don't like yo bitch ass, and any reason I get to blow yo punk ass away, will be straight with me. Now move muthafucka! Please… I want you to."

I was startled awake by the eventual return of Cat and June. Just as I had anticipated, I nodded off a couple of times, but fortunately for Tyler, when I was awakened, I didn't wake up pulling the trigger as I'd promised I would. "Let's go handle our business." June's tone of voice gave every indication that he too had grown weary of this game.

He was frustrated now, and just as irritated as I was. It was time to bring this ordeal to a conclusion, one way or another.

I escorted him from the building to the rear of June's car. As the door closed behind us, we realized we didn't have the key to the back door. Even though we were locked out the rear, we could reenter through the front of the building, so there was still no need to be concerned. We were going to be gone for a while anyway, and it wasn't like we were locked out the building.

June opened the trunk of his car, and ordered Tyler to get in. Tyler turned to plead his case to June Bug about why he could be trusted to ride inside the interior of the car. I have no tolerance for our instructions not being followed. Instantly, my instincts made me crack him upside the back of his head with the barrel of my shot gun. The blow landed near the base of his head, where the spine begins. The force of the blow turned the lights out for him. He crumbled into a heap upon the floor in the trunk. After rearranging his body, I closed the lid with absolutely no hesitation.

Just as I closed the lid, we noticed some head lights heading in our direction up the alley. During those days, the Newport police used a model of car which made it easy to tell it was them by the park lights on the vehicle. Unfortunately, we used to use Obie's car to rob people, while impersonating the police. Obie drove the same model car as the police, but it was far too dark to see if it was Obie's car or not. Since we weren't sure, we threw our weapons under the car. We couldn't reenter the building, so we began putting as much distance between us and the car as we possibly could, before being overtaken by the approaching vehicle.

Once we heard the loud crackling sound of the police

radio piercing the silence of the night, we knew it wasn't Obie, and we were treading on dangerous grounds. We were three black men alone in a dark alley, being accosted by armed, white, aggressive, and possibly racist police officers. There were two undercover officers sitting on the front seat, and it was easy to tell that they were vice. As they passed under a rare street light, the light shined directly on the two of them, confirming our suspicions.

"Where are you boys headed?" the officer under the wheel asked as he shinned his flash light in our faces. He was reading our facial expressions, searching for signs of panic, nervousness, our anything that seemed out of sorts. We had been stopped by the police often enough to know this, so we were very careful to act as normal as possible. You can't look too calm, or otherwise they'll sense they're being conned. It is a delicate balancing act to learn, but one that must be mastered in order to survive on the streets.

Leaving out the fact that we had some weapons hidden under the car, and a badly beaten man in the trunk of the same car, I did my best to explain our dilemma to the police. We simply had gotten locked out of the building accidently, while taking out the trash. My delivery was without hesitation, and sure. I also included the simple solution to our situation. We merely had to walk around to the front the building to get buzzed in.

Satisfied with the explanation I gave him, and with what he was able to read in our facial expressions and mannerism, he lowered the beam of the flashlight away from our faces, and to the ground near our feet.

Right after he had uttered the words, "You boys have a nice evening, and try not to get locked out of the building anymore." The beam of light from the flashlight happened upon a live, green, 20 gage shot shell not far from my feet. I was horrified by the sight of it, because I knew the conclusions that would be drawn by the vice officers in an alley, late at night, with three young, black, male suspects. Once that live shotgun shell was spotted, we became suspects, and that was before any crime was even detected. It was easy to detect the officer's attitude and demeanor had changed by the way he asked me about the shell. My reply was truthful, but sure to fall on death ears. "I don't know sir." I stammered. There was no longer a need to keep up the charade. The masquerade was over without a doubt, and we would be thoroughly searched, as well as the entire alley.

CHAPTER 8

The activity increased, with the arrival of each set of officers. Some cars were as many as four officers deep, per car. The first thing they discovered were the weapons we hid underneath the car. "We have some hand guns and a shotgun under this Ford. Check them for Ford keys." One of the officers shouted, after about 20 minutes of searching. "I'm betting one of those bastards is driving this fucken car."

They found the keys in June's pocket. I was standing right beside him, when one of the officers actually pulled the keys from his front pocket. To my surprise, June denied knowing who the Ford keys belonged to. He and the officer were going back and forth with each other about where the keys were actually found. The loud noise, and the sounds from all the activity, must have awaken Tyler because he began screaming for help at the top of his lungs.

"We have a kidnapping in progress!" one of the officers yelled, as they all pulled their weapons from their holsters, and trained them on us. We were all swiftly handcuffed, and placed in the backseat of a marked squad car. Before I was situated in the backseat, Tyler was being assisted getting out of the trunk. He and I made eye contact, and I tried to give him the most threating facial expression I could muster.

Cat and June were already seated in the backseat, when Tyler suddenly began insisting that we were not the guys that placed him in the trunk.

"You heard him!" I said, as I twisted my body, so the handcuffs would be facing the officer who had been assisting me. But instead of removing the handcuffs, he growled "Shut the fuck up!" and kicked me in my buttocks so violently that I fell across the laps of both June and Cat. It was a struggled to help me get upright, but we were successful.

Cat immediately began speaking in a language we called Pig Latin. Pig Latin was just another form of broken English with certain prefixes and suffixes before or after each word. The white officers hated Pig Latin, and would order us to shut up, because they knew we were communicating in a language they didn't understand. He basically was telling us we were going to be given a choice between making a statement against ourselves, remaining silent, or demanding a lawyer. He put emphasis on choosing to remain silent, and expressing the desire for the representation of an attorney. June and I already knew all of those things, but it was our very first and only time getting flagged together, while putting in work. Cat was looking out for himself, by looking out for us. At that very moment you couldn't find a better example of why wanting for your brother, what you want for yourself, is so beneficial. That was the creed we lived by, operated by, and functioned under. We always looked out for one another. That would prove to be our greatest, most valuable, asset as the years passed.

We were taken to the 16th precinct, finger printed, photographed for mug shots, and placed in separate cells. We were officially charged with Assault with Intent to

Commit Murder, Possession of Firearms, and Kidnapping, at the arraignment the next morning in 136th district court. We were ordered to be remanded to the County Jail until the date of the Preliminary Examination.

It was amazing to me how there were hundreds of prisoners jammed into several large bull pins, and we knew no one there, other than one another. The same was true for several prisoners. You could tell who knew each other by the way they responded upon seeing one another. All the reunions weren't pleasant. There were fights braking out everywhere. I learned a long time ago that jail is a very violent existence, and the more you appear to love violence, and the more violent you are, the more loved and respected you will be.

I promise you, every time you whip somebody's ass in jail, there will be cheers from an enthused audience, and you will gain some endearing fans. I also promise you, if you get your ass whipped in jail there will also be cheers from an enthused crowd, and depending on how well you fight will be the determining factor if someone else wants to try you or not. You don't have to win, just prove that you were not a soft target. A lot of guy spend their entire sentence, searching for easy victories.

We were given draws, socks, shower shoes, and dressed in green uniforms before being issued what was called a bed roll. We had to sign a paper saying we had received the things from the itemized list. The bed roll consisted of what looked and felt like a horse blanket. There were also two sheets, a wash cloth, a bath towel and a pillowcase included in the bed roll. We placed the clothes we had on, when we were arrested, on hangers, and placed our shoes in a shoe bag. We later were taken upstairs, each to different floors, to await the preliminary examination.

I was taken to a floor with separate cell blocks. There were long cell blocks that had almost twice the number of cells as the short cell blocks, on the other side of floor from them. I was taken to a short cell block, and told to find an empty cell as they slammed the heavy steel bared door behind me. While looking for an empty cell, I saw an old classmate from Jr. High named Antonio. He had a grey patch of hair in the front of his head, and was the sharpest dresser in the entire school, besides me and Chance of course.

I was as excited to see him as he was to see me. He helped me to find the best empty cell, and afterwards showed me how to tie knots in the sheets to make them into fitted sheets. That made the bed more comfortable. We ended up talking for hours about our days in Jr. High, and the dances every Sunday at the Party Room, on Maine Ave. There were a lot of classmates I hadn't kept up with for a while, and he filled me in on how and what they were up to. I realized at that moment that I had begun spending all my time exclusively on the west side. I had completely lost touch with my friends on the east side. The east side was more gang orientated, and I wasn't looking to bang over territory. I was seeking ways to get organized, but instead of fighting, the activities would be centered around ways to create revenue. The west side was so different from the east side. It was as if they were two different cities.

We were interrupted by the sounds of the evening meal being passed out. "Come on man." Antonio insisted. "They're not going to wait on you here. If you're not in line when the last meal is passed out, they will leave. Then you'll have to wait until they feed the entire floor, and hope they are not too tired, or that nobody has pissed them off. They're all assholes, but you have to hope the asshole is kind enough to come back."

"So, they do come back?" I asked, as we were leaving my cell. "Yeah, they do come back, sometimes…, but most of the time they don't give a fuck if you eat or not. That's just the way it is homeboy." It was believable. The majority of the deputies, were young white guys. They were basically glorified babysitters, because all they really did was watch us all day. Nearly none of them lived in the city. Mostly all of them lived in the suburbs.

While we were in line, a brother approached me and asked if he could talk to me after I had finished eating. I told him that would be cool, but I was curious about what he could possibly want. I had never seen this dude before in my life. "What's it about?" I asked. He had a strange smirking expression on his face when he answered, "Your homeboy." and walked away without even looking back.

After we had finished eating, the guy who had approached me while I was in line came to my cell. He looked directly at Antonio, and snarled, "Let me holla at you." I didn't like his attitude or the tone of his voice. I was shocked by Antonio's response. He jumped up and left the cell immediately. It wasn't my business, but I had a strong desire to whup that guy's ass.

I sat in my cell reflecting on the kidnapping charges, and the events that led up to the actual incident, but before I was able get lost deeply in my thoughts, I was abruptly interrupted by the same guy. "I'm sorry to keep disturbing you like this brother man, but there are some things about your homeboy that you should know." His approach was so respectful that I felt compelled to give him an attentive audience.

"First of all, do you fuck with boys?" Some guys on the street would have been offended by the question, but I had been raised in an institutional system, and I was very aware of the culture. It was once believed in this culture that if you participated in homosexual activities while incarcerated, it didn't mean you were gay. He was asking me if I fucked boys, or allowed boys to suck on my penis. I wasn't offended at all by the question, but I did not partake in homosexuality in any form. I made sure he understood that.

"What's this all about?" I eventually asked. I was beginning to become more and more irritated, and I'm sure he could sense the tension that was building between us. "Listen I have no problem with you, but follow me. I can show you better than I can tell you."

He led me to a cell down the corridor, and I literally walked in on Antonio giving a blowjob to a guy sitting on a bunk. I was shocked, but not surprised. The way he allowed this guy to address him was suspect. I never spoke to Antonio again. Not because he was gay, but because he was gay, and belonged to someone. The best way to avoid jail house, homosexual drama, is to leave absolutely no room for misunderstandings to be had. By not speaking to him, his boyfriend knew there was no doubt that I had no interest in him at all. It would have been nice to have someone I could look back at the past nostalgically with, the time pass by. However, I survived on awful food, and without talking to Antonio. Before I realized it, it was time to return to court.

I couldn't wait to see June Bug and Cat. I was concerned about them. Not because I believed they couldn't survive, but the opposite was my concern. I believed they could easily get in serious trouble defending themselves or trying to get the things they needed. We were never victims. We produced victims, but we were never victims ourselves.

Early the next morning, before the Sun had risen, a deputy woke me up and told me to "Shit, shower and shave. You'll be leaving this floor, and will be taken down stairs. Down there they will get you dressed for court. They will be here to get you in about an hour."

After I had gotten showered, the gate to the cell block opened up. I thought I was running late, but a deputy placed a huge steel coffee pot in both the big block, and the short block. What a convenient weapon, I thought to myself. The coffee was so hot you could seriously scald a person with it. The steel coffee pot also had a handle on it, so you could use the pot as a weapon to beat someone to death after you scald them. I made a mental note. If I ever had a problem, I was going to help someone start their day in this fashion. I also made a mental note to never sleep through the deliverance of the hot coffee.

After a while, I began to wonder where the transporting officers were. I was becoming a little uneasy, and they still didn't arrive for another thirty minutes. When they did arrive, they were running late, and they were in a big hurry. We were ushered to the bull pins that were normally used for visiting, directly across from the elevators. We were left in these bullpens for hours. I didn't know anyone, so I did a lot of ear hustling. The bull pins were full of black men, and stories. It would amaze the average person to hear some of these amazing stories. The level of stupidity was astounding, yet there I was among them, so I was not any different. I was definitely in no position to sit in judgement of anyone.

I learned that although I had been thinking that it was called a cell block, the prisoners called it a rock. I sat and listened to story after story of fights on the different rocks, and of Goon Squad horrors. The Goon Squad was an emergency response team that consisted of deputies called in on situations where there was a potential for violence getting out of control. They were big, cruel, rude white men, armed with mace, and clubs. They wore helmets, uniforms with padding in certain areas, and carried a huge fiberglass shield that was wide, and long enough for them to hide behind it.

After what seemed like hours the elevator doors suddenly opened, and a sergeant got off accompanied by several deputies. He carried a stack of cards about the same size as index cards. "Listen up fellas." he said as he held the cards in the air and waited for all conversations to cease. "Listen up for your name. When you've heard your name called, respond by saying, 'Here', then line up against this wall. There will be absolutely no talking allowed gentlemen. Are there any questions?" he asked in conclusion.

There were no questions, so he proceeded to read off the names on the pink and Blue cards. As he read off the names and we lined up, there were deputies waiting to handcuff us to handcuffs that were connected to a long chain. There was a handcuff on each side of the chain, which allowed us to be chained by twos simply by cuffing on hand. We were then loaded onto the elevator, and ordered to face the rear, before heading down.

When we got off the elevator, we were marched through

what seemed like a maze of corridors and stairwells, before coming to the booking area. The area seemed to be in a chaotic state, but there was a system in place, and it was working. It just didn't appear to be. We were lead to a bull pin, and handed a breakfast before entering the bull pin. The breakfast consisted of a pack of powered donuts, a small orange juice, and a small carton of milk. There were about fifty prisoners in this particular bull pin, and I found it amazing that I didn't know anyone. Quite a few of them seemed to know each other, but you could tell from the conversations that most seemed to know each other from previous jail terms served together.

Over all the noise, I heard June's voice talking shit about the breakfast that was being passed out. He stepped into the bullpen, and appeared to be his jovial self. His eyes lit up every time he has ever seen me, and this time was no difference. He greeted me with a hug, then he filled me in on the latest information. He had received letters, and visits from his women. He was a true ladies man.

There was a crew out looking for Tyler and his wife, but there were no signs of them anywhere. It was believed they were being held up somewhere by the authorities, so they could be cleaned up, and then testify against us. The names he gave me of the brothers who were out looking for Tyler, was quite impressive. If they couldn't find them it was quite possible our fears had been realized. Obie was in charge of calling all the shots, and making all the decisions in our absence. J.B. proved to be a tremendous help. He made sure all the girls made it home safely. He personally contacted all our families, and informed them of the situation. He even lined up people whom he thought may be of some assistance in raising bond money, in case a bond was set.

While June was filling me in on everything, Cat walked up. He too was complaining about the breakfast, but he was joking. With a stone cold, serious facial expression, he asked, "How you gonna serve a retired pimp this shit? Damnit! And where the fuck my hoes at wit my bond?" When everybody looked at him, they all burst into laughter. It was quite obvious he was only joking, but it served as an excellent icebreaker. The conversations went up an octave or two, as the nervousness gave way to entertainment. We had to be warned to keep the noise down several times. Eventually we were threatened, and even that didn't deter anyone.

We were herded like cattle from one bullpen to the next, and with each stop there was a task that was to be completed. Eventually, once all the systematic movement was completed, we found ourselves, fed, changed from jail clothes to street clothes, chained up, and lead through a series of tunnels between the County Jail and The Halls of Justice, where most of the court rooms were located.

This court appearance was the Preliminary Examination part of our due process. The prosecutor merely had to prove that a crime had been committed, and it was probable to believe we had committed the crime. We were lead to an elevator which took us directly to the floor the courtroom we were assigned to was located. We found ourselves in a fortified area re-enforced with steel doors, and solid concrete walls. Everything was painted beige. There were two bullpens, and they were directly across from one another.

Every courtroom's bullpen has its share of what's known

as jailhouse lawyers. Most of them had been through the system so many times they could actually predict the outcome of certain cases. They could even predict what prosecutors would be willing to offer in order to obtain a conviction. I had overheard one of them explaining about the possibility of getting your case thrown out at this stage. It was made very clear that if a witness appeared in court, and testified against you, there was no doubt about it, you would be bonded over to stand trial. The opposite was also true if no witnesses showed up. They were required to drop the charges, and release you immediately. It doesn't happen too often, however, it does happen. I began hoping the couple all this fuss was about, had skipped town.

Here we were waiting again. I was beginning to notice a pattern. Everything was hurry up and wait. We would be rushed from one location to the next, only to find ourselves waiting for long periods of time. Sometimes we were moved from one side of the room to the next, only to find ourselves waiting for long periods of time before the next movement.

The tension and the nervousness were mounting at a feverish pitch. Mercifully our wait ended, and our names were called. As we entered the courtroom, the sight of such a huge crowd of familiar faces out to show support for us, was reassuring. I found the support quite comforting, until I scanned the crowd. What I found, astounded, shocked, and filled me with both confusion and horror. We all had to control our reactions to finding J.B. sitting in the courtroom, waving at us.

"Is this nigga some new kinda crazy or what!" Cat whispered in a tone that made you realize he would be yelling to the top of his lungs if it weren't for the circumstances we were in. To say we all were full of rage, would have been a gross understatement. It was difficult to contain my anger as we were being seated at the defendants table. One of the deputies warned us that we would be removed from the courtroom if we looked back and communicated with anyone in the courtroom. It was hard not to look back, but as it had been explained to us by the jailhouse lawyers, there would be some extremely important testimony during this portion of the proceedings. I was determined not to miss anything that may prove to be helpful.

A lot of preliminary procedures took place before they finally called their first witness. I was the first to recognize the witness as Tyler's wife. I would have never recognized her, if we saw each other in passing. She had gained weight, and had an amazing body. She wore a dress presentable enough to wear to church for Sunday service. The way she carried herself, you would have had a difficult time convincing anyone that this beautiful woman was indeed a heroin addict.

Her testimony was very truthful. She even explained how she and her husband were convinced, by her brother, to get as much drugs as they could, because they could sell it on the eastside, and make twice as much money. Her brother had refused to bring any of the money to save her husband. According to her testimony, the experience was so traumatic she was able to kick a ten-year heroin habit. She actually teared up when she recalled the hurt and disappointment in her children eyes when we left with their television set. There was an outbreak of moans and groans from those in attendance, showing their disapproval of our behavior. I wasn't ashamed. The whole television incident was necessary. I kept up my brave face, to show a sign of solidarity. There must never be a chink in our armor, and I've always vowed to never ever be the weakest link in any chain.

Tyler was next to take the stand, and he also showed signs of living the good life. He had an off the rack suit on, but an off the rack suit doesn't look so cheap when you're as skinny as a rail. After establishing himself as being the kidnapped victim, his answer to the routine question, "Do you see the men who kidnapped you here in the courtroom?" sent the case into a different direction.

"I see all four of them here." He boldly stated. Most of the courtroom staff was puzzled and confused, but there were a few of us who knew exactly what he was saying. The prosecutor asked, "What do you mean you see all four of them? There are only three defendants sitting at the table." The courtroom became a buzz as several hushed conversations erupted.

"Yeah, the other one is sitting in the back, over there." He said as he rose to his feet and pointed to the back of the courtroom, in JB's direction. The courtroom erupted into pure chaos, women were screaming, and the judge was beating on the gavel with his mallet demanding that everyone return to order. He eventually realized that order wasn't about to be easily restored, so he ordered the bailiff to remove us from the courtroom, and the prosecutor ordered JB's arrest.

We were in the bullpen talking among each other about what had just happened. There were quite a few bored prisoners in the bullpen who had already been to court. They became an attentive audience, holding on to every word. Suddenly the steel door to the bullpen across hall was opened up, and through the small rectangle shaped window on the door, we were able to see JB handcuffed, with his head down. He was being placed in the bullpen with the handcuffs left on. The officers turned their attention to us as they opened the door to the bullpen we were in.

"Okay listen up gentlemen, when you hear your name called, step into the bullpen across the hall." He then proceeded to call out all three of our names, just as we had expected. JB was smiling so hard, you could see every tooth in his head! He was genuinely excited to be reunited with us. I must admit, other than being upset, not understanding why he brought his crazy ass to court, I was happy to see him. I was wondering why they left the handcuffs on him. Something didn't add up.

JB immediately filled us in on all the things that had been done to find Tyler and his wife. They couldn't be found anywhere. He also put us up on the names of the people who joined in on the search. It was a pretty impressive list that included Uncle Lucky, John T, Bumpy Taylor, JC, Big Bean, and several other brothers very well known for taking care of this type of business.

After filling us in, even he had to admit that he saw the stupidity in his current situation. He truly believed that since they couldn't find them, the couple had gotten out of town. In his mind, he thought we would be getting released after the case was dismiss, due to the lack of witnesses.

The conversation then shifted to our court appointed lawyers. I was the only one happy with the attorney assigned to my case. The only time I saw him was when it was time to go to court, but there was something about him that filled me with a sense of confidence. I believed in him. When he took charged, he always seemed to know something none of the rest of us knew. We all were content in allowing him to take the lead in the team of lawyers. He presented and defended our case by arguing our points of law, without the need of encouragement to do so. He was that rare court appointed attorney that truly gave a damn, and was willing to bring his A-game for the sake leveling the playing field. Money had nothing to do with this.

The door swung opened after we heard some keys jingling. We all thought we were going back to the county jail, but we were informed by the deputy we were going back to police headquarters to be rebooked. "Thank your buddy!" one of the officers added. "He's the only reason we all have to stay here until y'all are recharged, rebooked, and arraigned! This is going to take hours!" he whined.

"I'd rather be down here than in my cell!" Cat injected into the conversation in an attempt to throw shade on the officer's assumption that we shared in some sort of solidarity. "You muthafucken right Cat." June Bug added. The opinion was unanimous among us. We could all just relax, and do everything in slow motion as far as we were concerned. We were in no hurry to be locked back up.

Once again, we were handcuffed to a chain, and led to an elevator. The elevator released us to a yellow brick tunnel with a maze of corridors. I can't remember exactly how many different halls we were led down before we reached a garage with the doors opened, and the sunlight shining through.

My heart leaped with excitement at the thought of being able to walk down a city sidewalk, albeit, in handcuffs.

It doesn't take long after you've lost what you've always believe to be your freedom, before you begin appreciating any semblance of the many things you had once taken for granted. Such as enjoying the outside air, with the warmth of the Sun on your face, as you stroll leisurely down the street. We were going across the street to Police Headquarters, and I was not about to take this opportunity for granted.

As we approached the opened garage doors, I imagined how lovely it would have been, to have a crew of youngsters waiting, armed and ready, like George Jackson's younger brother Jonathan P. Jackson was, in his attempt to forcibly free his brother. Jonathan was only 17 years old at the time of his demise, but he'll forever be remembered as a hero in the black community, among those of us who remember his unwritten story. Most only remember Angela Davis, but it was Jonathan who put the work in on that day. The only things waiting for me on this journey was outside air, the warmth of the Sun, and maybe a glimpse or two of some beautiful women. The scent of a woman's perfume would have exceeded any and all expectations.

Once we made it to the entrance, we were ordered to stop. We were than given instructions on what we could and couldn't do. Mainly, we were not to make any attempts to communicate with anyone while we were in route. The Sun was shining through the opened doors, and a bright warm beam fell upon my face. I threw my head back, closed my eyes, and allowed myself to bask in the warmth of my old friend. All I could hear from that point forward from the officer giving us instructions was, "Blah, blah, blah..." It had been nearly two weeks since I had last been outside, and I had no idea when I would be able to enjoy such a wonderful simple pleasure again. I didn't come out of the trance until we were actually on the move.

We may have made it approximately one hundred feet from the court house, before the sweet intoxicating aromas, from a passing lady's perfume, filled the evening air. She walked ahead of us, so we were in the perfect position to continuously smell her perfume, and enjoy watching the rhythm of her rear end as she walked. She was a tall white woman with not much ass at all, yet as small as her ass was, it still swayed from side to side underneath the clinging summer dress she wore.

We reached our destination before she did. As we climb the steps of the building, still watching her, Cat said, "Damn! I better not see her naked when I get my check!" It broke the silence, and we all laughed. Even the officers, who also were watching the young lady walk down the street, had to laugh.

They tried to prevent us from coming into contact with any civilians. It was difficult, but we were successfully led to the counter. Once there, the whining officer began to whine again about having to stay throughout the entire process. "And that would be necessary because?" a young officer standing behind the desk asked.

It was obvious he was suggesting their task had been completed, and they could in fact go home. He continued by explaining that it would take quite a while just to complete the booking process. All they would need, was the paperwork to take us to the arraignment. The other tasks were done by them. Before anyone could wink an eye, they had given the paperwork to the officers in booking, and made their unapologetic exits.

After a few moments, I knew from the conversations I'd overheard between the officers in booking, that there were some discrepancies between the original warrant, and the new one. The new warrant added JB as a codefendant, but the only charge was Conspiracy to Commit Murder in the Frist Degree. It wasn't clear if the prosecutor wanted to omit the other charges, or add the charges to the new warrant.

Every attempt they made to contact the prosecutor, was met with failure. They were eventually informed that the prosecutor assigned to the case was in the middle of closing arguments in an armed robbery trial. It was getting close to time for the courts to close, so they had to make the call. No one could figure out what to do, so they decided to go by the letter of the new warrant, and omit the original charges. Not long after that, I learned the confusion had caused them to make the serious error by charging us solely with Conspiracy to Commit Murder. I wasn't very well versed in the law, so I wasn't aware of the potential break we had just received. I only felt a sense of hopelessness.

After the officers completed the task of booking us, we were taken before the Honorable Judge Rio to answer on the warrant. We were arraigned and officially charged with Conspiracy to Commit Murder in the First Degree. A Charge which carried a maximum of up to life in prison. We were very fortunate to have a bond sat at twenty-five thousand dollars, cash, but we weren't wise enough to have put any money away, just in case we had such an emergency. At that very moment, I vowed to never be caught slipping like that again. I thought to myself, should I find my way out of this hot mess, I vowed to always put money away at every given opportunity, for unexpected expensi like bond money!

We were returned to the county jail, and placed in one of the many bullpens. It was late, so the majority of the prisoners who had court appearances that day, were already dressed in green jail house garb, and taken upstairs to their respective floors.

Once our charges were read aloud, the fellas left in the bull pen began giving us space. We had missed dinner, so for a rarity we were granted the opportunity to break bread together once they issued our meals. The meal was horrible and forgettable, but we relished in the opportunity to encourage one another, and make it known that the love we shared, was real. I also warned JB, and explained to him why he should not tell the doctor he was depressed. If he did so, he would have been stripped butt naked, and locked in a cell on the mental ward.

We were once again dressed in greens, and was separated. We knew we would be seeing each other again soon. My lawyer informed us that according to the law, we were entitled to due process, which meant there had to be a preliminary examination within twelve days.

CHAPTER 9

I was moved to another rock. This particular rock had a television and a radio. While ear hustling, I overheard a conversation about Gator, Day Day, Meme, and Box! I let the guys talking known that I knew the guys they were speaking of, with so much respect and fondness. Of course, they gave me the third degree. Jails are full of fake ass people. All jails are notoriously known for having fake ass people, all pretending to be more than they ever were, or will be. Name dropping is a tactic used by fake ass people, who are unable to find a comfort zone in simply being themselves. It's fear that drives them. Detected fear often leads to an unnecessary physical confrontation. It could be fear of physical harm, or ridicule. The wise learn quickly, you are much better at being yourself, than any fictional character you may be able conjure up. Of course, I was able to answer all of their questions with earnest, and provide them conformation about the rumors they had heard. Only someone who truly knew these guys would have the information I was providing them with. I knew their whereabouts, current situations and the conditions.

For the next few days we exchanged war stories. I told them stories about college campus life. All the stories I told them were about the fellas they knew, and how they were having a ball among the squares and lames. They told me war stories about the fellas I knew in the penitentiary. I have to admit, every time we finished talking, I wondered could I survive under the brutal dehumanizing conditions that existed in the penitentiary. In my heart, I knew there was the distinct possibility I would be finding out, sooner than I'd hoped.

They also knew Bumpy! He had picked up a pot gut, and along with it, the nick name of 'Pot Gut'. He was in Marquette, a disciplinary prison for dangerous and difficult to manage convicts. He had gotten into a knife fight with another convict, after being there for a year. A guard tried to intervene, and Bumpy stabbed him in the neck. He didn't kill the screw, but the attempt was there. He could have been charged with attempted murder, but instead he was transferred to a higher level of security as discipline.

The other guys I asked about hadn't faired so well. Most of the guys who were my age, had been raped and turned out to an existence within the circles of homosexuals. I was schooled by the stories they told me of how certain techniques were used to bring about confrontations, which ultimately led to a target's demise.

In one scenario, there would be cigarettes and candy left on your bunk. When you ask about them, no one will respond, because no one except the person or people trying to target you for a confrontation knows, where the items originated. However, once you've smoked the cigarettes and ate the candy, here comes the drama. He will explain that in a mix up the items were mistakenly placed on your bunk, but the problem could easily be rectified by returning the items.

The unsuspecting inmate, being unable to return the used items, now becomes the sole source for the convict's rage. A ridiculous amount of interest is placed upon the items used, and a deadline is set for the debt to be paid. This would eventually bring about the type of confrontation the convict desired.

I became curious about there never being any cigarettes or candy left upon my bunk. I inquired as to why. "What would you have done?" Hit asked. Hit was a friend of Gators. They had grown up together. "I would have eaten the candy, and smoked the muthafucken cigarettes." I answered. I also added, "As soon as anybody stepped to me with that bitch shit, I would have taken off on his punk ass with a flurry of combinations to his fucken head. No negotiations or compromise, no questions asked."

Everybody burst into laughter, and a brother whose complexion was so dark his nick name was Blue added, "That's why nobody tried you." The jails and prisons are filled with soft targets, and easy victories for the individual who chooses his battles wisely. I was not a very wise choice by any means or stretch of the imagination. There were a lot of prisoners who were a lot softer than me to mess with, and test. The path with the least resistance has proven to be the wisest, and the likeliest path chosen. However, there are exceptions to every rule.

Time was flying by. Every morning I would get up before it was time for the coffee to be placed inside the rock. That was approximately five, forty-five, and breakfast was served about six. After breakfast was served, most would eat breakfast, and return to bed. Not me. I would wait for the cleaning supplies. After the rock was dusted and mopped, the guards would pass out the daily newspapers, and turn the power on for the radio and television. I would read the paper, and watched the news every morning. I was hoping there would be nothing about our case in the news. I was concerned about becoming the focus of the prosecutor's office due to bad publicity.

There were several cases that warranted the attention of the public, and there was a public outcry for justice because most of the cases were horrific. There was a case which involved the kidnapping and murder of a young child. The parents gave the police the money for the ransom, but the police elected to give the kidnapers cut up newspaper instead. In another case, a crew of young guys were attending the funerals of the rich, and robbing everyone in attendance of their valuables. One of them made the crucial mistake of raping a nun. There also was a serial rapist terrorizing all the prostitutes working on Woodward Avenue. In yet another case, a suspected hit man was taking insurance policies out on young unsuspecting girls-friends he sat up in luxury apartments, then he would allegedly murder the women and collect the insurance money. There was more than enough going on in the news to keep us out of the lime light's proverbial fifteen minutes of fame.

After everything I had been through, fate finally decided it was time to smile upon me. The smile came in the form of an attorney visit. My attorney wasn't a young man, but he wasn't an old man stuck in his ways either. He was a black man, and if he was a wealthy man, there was no way you could tell by looking at his attire. He wore

Moe Love

glasses, and carried himself like a brainiac. He was super intelligent, hung his hat on his knowledge of the law, and to my amazement he was extremely optimistic! That's unheard of among court appointed lawyers working pro bono.

We had gotten caught with a severely beaten man in the trunk of a car, and my lawyer sat before me with the task of convincing me, first of all, that according to the letter of the law, we had a better than seventy percent chance of beating the case.

He began his task by asking me a simple question "Can you trust your partners to keep their mouths shut?" I was almost insulted by the question. He was insinuating that it may be possible for my comrades to flip the script, and become rats. After explaining to him, the history I shared with my partners was real, and we were truly more like brothers, he then explained to me how valuable that was and would be.

"Do you know what confidentiality means?" he asked. "It means that anything we talk about, between you and me, is protected by law. By law, I must keep all of your secrets. No one can order me to reveal them. Do you understand this?" He asked. I knew all of these things already, but when you are fighting for your life, it feels very reassuring to be reassured. He had an attentive audience in me, and that was for sure.

"The one and only charge that you and your brothers have is Conspiracy to Commit Murder. Now tell me what happened?"

After I had finished giving him my recollection of the events, he clapped his hands, pushed his chair from the table, and stood up. All while smiling broadly, he began

284

pacing the small interview room as he spoke. "Wow, Its' just as I thought. You guys didn't plan any of this. The only way you can get convicted is if the prosecutor can convince you or one of your partners to get on the stand and lie. He would have to lie and say you guys planned this whole thing, and according to you, there's not a chance of that happening."

"Now for the tricky part. You'll have to go with a bench trial instead of a jury." I quickly interrupted his presentation with my dissent. "All my life I've been taught twelve is better than one. My mother, who has never been arrested in her entire life, taught me it's harder to convince twelve, than it is to convince one. Even she knows better than that!"

It was my lawyer's turn for his rebuttal, and he knocked it out of the ballpark with his views and arguments, based upon his opinions. "If a jury of layman citizens were to hear the facts of this case, which involves drugs, violent beatings, kidnaping, and guns, I believe it would be too difficult for them to follow the letter of the law, after hearing the sequence of events. They'll be horrified, and all they will see when they look at the defendants table will be monsters. Whereas, if a judge were to be the sitting judge, and heard the facts, he would be compelled to follow the letter of the law, and make his rulings based upon the merits of the case, or lack thereof."

"All the activities that occurred during this altercation were done spontaneously. There is no evidence, or proof beyond any reasonable doubt, that anything was done in an attempt to fulfill an agreed upon plot to commit a murder. We're not going to defend anything that happened. There was a severe beating. There was a kidnaping. There were illegal firearms, but none of it was a part of a conspiracy."

It was as if he had suddenly become my savior. I instantly appreciated this man's time, knowledge of the law, and fruitful efforts. Before the interview ended, he recommended we wave the preliminary examination. His thoughts on the subject were, since our strategy was to force the State to prove its case, we should make them do everything with one unprepared shot, during a bench trail.

He explained to me what a motion for Discovery was, for which he had already written a brief, and petitioned the court. He promised to send me a copy of the Discovery package as soon as he received it, and advised me to study it daily, once I received it, until I'd memorized its entire contents. That way, you'll be able to assist me, should I need you.

I could hardly contain myself. I had received what was necessary in order to see the light at the end of the tunnel. I too now understood why there was a seventy-five percent chance I would be found not guilty. It seemed too good to be true! Over the next few months, I enjoyed the facial expressions of the guys who just couldn't understand how it was even possible to get caught with someone in the trunk of a car, and walk away scott free. They all warned me not to get my hopes up too high, but it was too late. I believed with all my heart, all I had to do was find ways to keep myself occupied, until it was time to go to trial, and then I would be released.

Once I received the Discovery package from my attorney, I had something positive to do, to occupy my time. I read it religiously! I was instructed to do so by my attorney, and I was determined to comply. He was the smart one, and he was concerned our defense wouldn't be as prepared as needed, unless at least one of us had studied the evidence. It was my understanding that since I wasn't trained to recognize what might be of importance, I was to concentrate on anything I didn't agree with, or anything I questioned, and report it directly to him by mail.

Since we waved our rights to a preliminary exam, we weren't able to see one another and discuss our case for months. My attorney kept me abreast of any, and all new developments, or anything else pertaining to the case, which included offers from the prosecutor's office to any of my co-defendants.

The first one they approached was J.B. Not so much because they figured him to be the weak link, but more so because he had an armed robbery case pending, and was out on bond. That made him the most vulnerable among us. Armed robbery caries up to life in prison, so they offered to drop the conspiracy charge, and give him six months in jail for the armed robbery. Since he already had served three months, he would only have serve another three months to be released as a free man.

My lawyer informed me that JB became so agitated, the officials had to threaten him with new charges in order to get him to settle down. They had to restrain him until he cooled down. Needless to say, my attorney was thoroughly impressed by the true test of loyalty that was on display. JB had just been insulted by an offer from the prosecutor's office of ninety days in the county jail, even though he was facing two life sentences. It was the fact they were asking him to betray his brothers, and become a rat to save his own hide, that he found so terribly upsetting and repulsive.

June Bug was the next logical choice. Cat and I were

considered seasoned veterans. An offer was never made to either one of us. The opposition was very aware of the fact their case was too flimsy to obtain a conviction. JB's response had already shocked them. They were almost certain he would've folded with a case pending. If none of us folded, we all were almost certain to walk.

They offered June ninety days. He didn't go ballistic like JB did. It wasn't his style. He has always been considered Mr. Smooth. It is very difficult to get him upset, but once he is riled there are no holds barred. As far as he is concerned, once he's in a fight, his entire repertoire is considered fair game. In this particular case, he simply rejected the offer.

The county jail was a place that things happened every day. Guys were getting raped, robbed, extorted, and beaten daily. The idled minds were busy, and functioning on a level I'd never imagined existed. Negotiations with certain members of the staff allowed us to arrange to have drugs smuggled in. Most of the time I stayed to myself. I found the Discovery file as entertaining as it was informative. I was young, so I certainly took part in my fair share of mischief and foolishness, however, for the most part, I studied the law and my file.

CHAPTER 10

The day I went to court was quite eventful. I was going to trial that afternoon, so I wasn't with the first group. I sat on the metal table connected to the bars, and bolted to the cement floor, like I did every morning, before the coffee arrived. After the coffee was delivered, an inmate tip toed out of his cell. He put a finger to his perked lips, as sign langue to shush me, as he continued towards the coffee. It was obvious he was up to something sinister, so I never took my eyes off his movements.

He quickly, but carefully, picked up the huge steel coffee pot, which was filled to the brim with the boiling hot liquid. My heart began to race when I remembered he had gotten into a verbal confrontation with a fella the night before. Now here he was slowly inching up to the fella's cell, as the fella lay asleep, totally oblivious.

I thought to myself, that was exactly why I was up every morning. I wasn't about to get caught slipping like that! As far as I was concerned, everyone who was asleep at that moment, had been caught slipping. It could have very easily been any one of them. Having never seen a guy get scald before, prompt me to move and situate myself, to be assure of a better view. Once that scalding hot coffee hit his skin, I wished I could've unseen what I had just seen.

As the boiling hot liquid made contact with his skin, it peeled away the top layer, leaving a glistening, bright pink flesh in its wake. The skin that didn't peel away with the liquid, bubbled and steam swirled from his body as he rose from the bed to an excruciating awakening. His contorted facial features expressed the agonizing pain. The scream was stuck in his throat. Before he was able to gather himself, his attacker swung the steel coffee pot, with what appeared to be all of his might. The pot caught the careless inmate, while still in his twisted rising motion, square across his face. He was knocked unconscious, before he could utter a sound.

The attacker hurriedly replaced the empty pot in its normal position, and quickly ducked back into his cell. I decided that it would be wise if I did the same. I laid on my bunk, and waited for the sure to come chaotic fallout.

It all began with a blood curdling scream. I braced myself for what I knew was next to come. "Got dammit!" the floor commanding officer barked. "Everybody get the fuck out your muthufucken cells right got damn now, and line up at the muthufucken gate! I'm not playing with you muthufuckas today! Damn! First thing in the fucking morning? It's going to be a long day."

Of course, no one said anything. We were about to be split up, and we knew it. There was just a bit too much solidarity shown among us, for the staff's comfort. They had all the guns, all the ammunition, all the keys, and the best of technologies at their disposal, but on many occasions, we still were able to gain the upper hand.

Prisoners understand why the staff fears solidary.

Solidarity spews with a tenacity to emancipate its self. It also inspires creativity. Convicts have created more ways to use a paper clip, than George Washington Carver created ways to use a peanut. We relished the rare opportunity when the watchful eyes blinked, and something as simple as a paper clip could make the difference.

We stood totally nude in the hall for a long time. It was obvious the staff had decided to play some sort of psychological game with.us. The results rendered were no better than the previous attempts. We were thoroughbreds, and now we were in full throttle. There was no turning back for us now. We only had one question. We wondered if they would be willing to put our entire rock in segregation, as a form of punishment.

The sergeant made the usual empty threats, and we in return gave him the usual blank stares. Nobody gave a damn about the sergeant, or his limited powers. We weren't convicted, and even if we were, we wouldn't be doing our time in the county jail. We were hard core felons, so we knew eventually they had to release us, even if it were into the custody of the State's Department of Corrections to begin a sentence.

I truly paid him no mind. I was about to go to trial, and face the possibility of being convicted. A conviction would surely be accompanied by a life sentence, but that wasn't the reason I couldn't care less about any of the morning activities. I didn't care because I knew I was about to be found not guilty. There was not a doubt in my mind. All this extra drama, would play its self out without me.

We finally were given permission to put our clothes back on, and were lead to a holding cell near the elevators. This particular floor housed both men and women, on opposite sides of the floor. Because of our living arrangements, every now and then we'd see a female inmate, and offer up some seriously raunchy cat calls. Whenever a female prisoner was escorted pass us, we would sound off without hesitation.

Except in photographs or on television, I hadn't seen a woman in months! I participated in the cat calls, and enjoyed the view. It didn't matter that I was about to be released at all. I was beyond thirsty, and just about any drink would have quenched my thirst at that point. The female prisoners loved all the attention they received, and flirted back while exposing their breasts, or other more private parts. Over all the ruckus, I heard my name being called out. That was the announcement I had been waiting for. That announcement rendered all the jailhouse fun I was having, an obsolete distraction. It was time to get intensely focused for my trial.

As we approached the bullpens, which were filled to capacity. I heard JB's voice over the loud noise. He believed we would be found not guilty, and he was sharing his opinion with everyone within hearing range. Because of the disturbance that had occurred on my floor, I was late enough to have cause them concern. I received my breakfast, and joined my comrades.

As I made my way through the crowd, I could hear conversations buzzing about what was believed to have happened, on the rock the prisoner was assaulted. What was most amazing to me, was the fact that none of them were present during the assault, yet their recount of the assault was extremely accurate. The only part missing from the story was the fact that I was a witness to the entire offense.

Cat was the first to walk up to me. He greeted me with a warm hug, and a firm handshake. Everybody else followed suite, as we search for a section of the bullpen we could claim as our own. We showed no respect for the boundaries put into effect by lames. All we did was politely ask that they find themselves somewhere else to sit, and allow us the privacy necessary to discuss our case. After the lames had scattered, we established new boundaries designed to guarantee our privacy.

Once I was sure no one was listening to us, I gave them an eye witness account of the morning's activities. It was yet another woeful, gut-wrenching tale of the deplorable ways we attack one another, with deep seeded malice. I call that deep seeded malice, the Willie Lynch syndrome. We were taught to hate ourselves, as well as one another. The self-hatred as well as the self-destructive culture we've embraced, surfaces in our lack of mercy and compassion for one another. I had witnessed just how cruel, barbaric, and inhumane we can be to one another, during those few months I had spent in the County Jail.

At last we changed the subject, and began briefing one another about our case. We were confident we would be found not guilty, so we spent most of the time sharing stories about the doubters who continued to predict we would be found guilty. There were plenty who loved us, but had to be honest when asked about our chances.

"They offered me six months for my armed robbery case, and to grant me immunity on this case, if I turned state evidence." JB informed us. We all had already heard about the offer, and about him going ballistic. Cat shouted at the top of his lungs "What about they offered June Bug ninety days!" Neither Cat nor I had received an offer from the prosecutor's office, but we didn't mind being slighted.

He continued talking to everyone in the bullpen who was still listening, and they all were. "Y'all better take note! We some young niggas on the rise. Make sure when you leave here, ya'll tell everybody that you were in the presence of some young thoroughbreds! We gonna show all you lame ass niggas how shit spose to go down. We kept our muthafucken mouths shut, and now we gonna go up in that courtroom, and whup that prosecutor's ass!" We burst into gut bursting laughter, but it was obvious we were laughing alone.

Most in the bullpen hadn't kept their mouths shut, and everything they were warned would be used against them in a court of law, was now being used to send them up state to the penitentiary. Some didn't believe it was possible to beat the white man at his game, so they took plea agreements. The rest were just haters in search of someone to share in their misery.

I was so nervous I felt like there were literally butterflies fluttering around in my stomach. While I was changing out of my jail clothes, I felt a breeze, and it brought about a chill I couldn't shake. The chill made me tremble noticeably. I had to concentrate in order to control the trembling. I refused to let any man see anything in me that could be interrupted as fear or weakness, and trembling could be the sign of one or the other, if not both! The level of concentration it took to control my trembling, was enough to take my mind off the uneasiness I felt from the nervousness in my stomach.

All of our lawyers came to the back of the courtroom to visit us in the prisoners holding tank. They were in agreement, and expressed a belief that the prosecutor's case was so weak, he would more than likely be requesting a continuance. It was my lawyer's opinion that if the prosecutor tried to play that particular game in front of the Honorable George Jr, he would be able to present a convincing enough descending argument, to get the continuance denied. That was the desired ruling. My co-defendants and I were beginning to feel a little bit claustrophobic from sitting in the county jail.

It had been a few months since we had last actually appeared in a courtroom. The prosecutors kept getting the dates pushed back in hopes of finding the proverbial smoking gun, during the eleventh hour. The many familiar faces, the smells of leather, wood, ink, cologne, and of course the perfumes of the ladies, filled my nostrils with the confirmation I needed. We were indeed in a courtroom, and this nightmarish of an ordeal would soon be ending. It had proven thus far to be an extremely exhausting and trying experience for us all.

The proceedings began with the prosecutor's motion, asking the court to grant a continuance based upon the merits in the brief he had submitted to the court. "A motion for a continuous will be our first order of business for today." The Honorable Judge George began, after slamming his gavel a couple of times, and announcing that court was officially in session. He then turned the floor over to the prosecutor.

He began his opening argument by stating, "There has been a huge miscarriage of justice. Because of the heavy case load, and the serious understaffing due to the recent budget cuts, there was no one in the office available to represent the people of the state during the arraignment. We were obliged to make some provisions to accommodate the situation. The adding of an additional codefendant, which was totally unforeseen by us, could not be handled by an experienced staff member. It was because of that, some of the charges have been omitted mistakenly. The continuation would allow the people the amount of time necessary, to straighten out the situation, and resolve the issues at hand.

The prosecutor's argument sent chills down my spine. My heart began racing, and it became even more difficult to control my trembling. Even I was convinced it would have been fair, if the judge had granted the motion for a continuous, in an attempt to protect the rights of the people of the state.

My lawyer's rebuttal was equally as brilliant. "The people were aware of this situation months ago, your honor, and yet they elected to move forward, believing a conviction was still possible. Now here we are in the eleventh hour, and the people want a continuous based upon the error in judgement. They've shown no due diligence in correcting said error. As a matter of fact, it was their office which began making plea offers by their own volition. That is a pretty good indication of their plans to move forward. Had there been any attempts to correct the error, it would have been on record. I'll tell you the reason you won't find anything on record. They were depending on the defendants to provide them with self-incriminating evidence, and now they've realized it is quite obvious there will be no such forthcoming evidence. Now, the people's office want to sight the error. The people have had a reasonable amount of time to prepare and present their case. The people's motion for a continuous should be denied, based upon their failure to show due diligence in correcting said error."

I looked into the faces of my co-defendants to see if they were as confused as I was, and they appeared to be just as confused. Our confidence had wavered. You could tell we weren't as certain of the outcome, by the nervous glances we shared amongst one another, but my attorney was like an anchor. I began feeding off his confident energy, and found a comfort zone.

The judge ruled against the People's motion for a continuous based solely on my lawyer's persistent focus on the prosecutor's failure to show due diligence. That is when the prosecuting attorney interrupted the proceedings as well as our brief celebration. "Excuse me your honor, I had hoped I wouldn't have resort to such tactics, but your ruling leaves me no other alternative."

He sighted a law that basically and clearly states if a judge is familiar with the transcripts from the preliminary examination, he may only sit during a jury trial. His point was simple. Significant portions of the transcripts from the first preliminary examination were raised in the motion. Since the judge had ruled on the motion, he was thus eliminated, because he had to read a portion of the transcript, in order to make a ruling.

He had been outfoxed, and out maneuvered by the prosecutor, and he didn't appreciate it one bit. The way things stood, we either had to have a jury trial in front of judge George, which we all knew would be akin to committing suicide, or postpone the trial until another judge had an opening on their docket. You could almost see steam spurring from the judge's ears, and his eyes were blazing with rage. We watched as the prosecution team, celebrated. They were shaking each other's hands, and patting each other on their backs.

The judge ordered a ten-minute recess, and hurriedly left the bench. None of us had a clue where he was headed, or why he left in such a rush. We had no time to ponder over the judge. What could possibly occur, was enough to rock the very foundation of our world. If the prosecutor was able to get a continuation, he could manipulate the system, and get rulings in front of judges he knew would rule favorably. Eventually he may even get the trial in front of one of his good ole buddies.

We were just about to contemplate exactly what our next move should be, when the judge re-entered the courtroom, and ordered the bailiff to announce recess had ended, and court was now back in session. There were no longer any signs of the judge ever being upset. There was now laughter in his eyes, and his lips were twisted into a smirk. It seemed he knew something the rest of us didn't know, and some of us present weren't going to like the announcement he was about to make.

What an ideal situation to be in, and it couldn't happen at a better time for us. We were caught in the middle of a power struggle, between the prosecutor's office, and the judge. Judge George Jr. was a living icon in the city of Newport, because of his involvement in the civil rights movement! His participation inspired and motivated many of us, because he rolled up his sleeves, and got down in the trenches with the rest of us, and fought with all he had for the rights of our people to be treated like human beings. He was an extremely close friend of the Rev. Dr. Martin

L. King, and marched at protest gatherings, right by his side. The prosecutor's office feeble attempt to show him up appeared to have been a done deal. They really didn't know what the man was made of. He had rightfully earned the reputation of being a fearless, relentless and strong, willed fighter whenever he is challenged.

During the recess, he had gone to the courtroom next to his own, and had a talk with his longtime buddy, Judge Samuels, and secured his assistance. He got the okay from the presiding chief judge, to move forth with a bench trial in front of Judge Samuels, and he amazingly arranged for the trial to be held at that very moment.

He instructed us to pack all our belongings, and move to the courtroom next door. The prosecutor was stun and furious. He attacked his perfectly organized table, and suddenly threw it into shambles. There was no way for him to stop this train which the judge had set into motion, and it was crushing all the opposition in its wake. It was a three hundred sixty degree turn around for both sides.

We didn't celebrate at all. We didn't trust the system enough to believe it would remain intact long enough for us to benefit from it. Although things looked promising, we all can remember being disappointed at least a couple of times by the broken promises of the so-called blind justice system. It's as though she is really peeping. For a white person to receive justice, it was the norm and expected. but it is always a game of chance, for black people.

It wasn't as though we were innocent of the horrible acts. We were trying to beat the white man at his own game, by forcing him to play by his own rules. There were a lot of black people in our community who were more than certain that we had lost our minds, and the penitentiary was our only true destination. They dared not to imagine the type of boldness we would display, if we were allowed to walk away from these charges on a technicality, after getting caught with a man beaten nearly to death. We proceeded with guarded enthusiasm, but we knew once they had riled Judge George, it was a done deal. We were about to accomplish the unthinkable, and walk away from a potential life sentence without spending a single cent.

The events that followed were exactly as my lawyer had predicted. The judge couldn't have looked, or been more uninterested. All the testimony was the same as in the first preliminary examination. At one point, he actually placed his feet on the bench, and closed his eyes. I thought he had fallen asleep, until his ruling against the prosecutor's objection proved beyond any doubt that not only was he paying close attention to the testimonies, he also was able to anticipate objections and rule as soon as they were risen according to the point of law.

The testimonies were still quite compelling, and the audience responded in a way that surly would have influenced a jury. At one point my mother tapped me on my shoulder, and asked, "Do you still believe you're gonna come home today?" Before I could answer she searched my eyes for the answer, like mothers seem to always do. My mother always told me "You know your child." She has always been able to tell if I'm lying or not. I did my best not to let her know she was right one hundred percent of the times she has told me flat out, "You're lying." Most of the times I was able to prove I could have possibly been telling the truth, but the truth was, she was always right.

I looked into her eyes, and saw how confused she was. She and I both knew we had once again stumbled upon one of those rare moments in life in which I understood what was going on, better than she. Her reaction to the testimonies confirmed how a jury would have reacted. My mother found it difficult to understand how you could commit such horrible acts, and the justice system still had to let you go. I looked deep into her eyes, and once again she looked deep into mine. As I spoke, I watched as a calmness swept over her. She found my voice as reassuring as my words of conviction. My answer had to be swift, because we weren't supposed to communicate with anyone in the audience.

"Yeah ma!" I answered under my breath. She exhaled, sat back in her seat, and relaxed. She has always known, when I say something with confidence, you could put money on it. I wasn't as sure as I wanted to be, but in a court of law, nothing is guaranteed.

After their final witness had completed his testimony, the prosecution rested their case, and so did we. Both sides offered their closing arguments, and waited for the final ruling. Most of the time the judge retires to his chambers to go over the evidence, but he announced that it wouldn't be necessary. "In light of the evidence presented to the court, I'm prepared to make a ruling right now. The defendants are guilty of Kidnapping. The defendants are guilty of assault with intent to commit great bodily harm, no less than murder. The defendants are guilty of possession of illegal firearms, but they are charged with Conspiracy to commit murder, and I've failed to see the conspiracy. Not guilty!" He immediately slammed his gavel, and left the bench.

The judge had said we were guilty of so many offences, that many were confused as to rather we were guilty or not. My lawyer and I saw the humor in the situation, and shared a warmed hearted laugh, before he explained everything. It was as though he were making an announcement, so quite a few people paid close attention. After he had finished, the many well -wishers and supporters we had in attendance, erupted into an explosion of festive celebration. Since the judge had already left the court room, the celebration was allowed to continue uninterrupted. What a triumph we were sharing. We had dared to have faith in one another, and it paid off.,

We had to return to the county jail, but only long enough to make sure there were no other warrants, or hold on us. It was just a formality for prevention. I had left some things in my cell. I was asked if I wanted to wait until they were retrieved. What a joke!

While we were in the bullpen they told JB his bond for the armed robbery had been revoked in view of his proven recent activities. He would have to remain in the county jail until his next court appearance, which was a week away. I hated leaving him behind like that, especially considering how strong he had held up. He and June Bug were the main reasons we were able to defeat the system.

CHAPTER 11

My brother, Albert, gave us all a ride home from court in his Duce and a Quarter. My mother rode with us, and she seemed to stare at me the entire ride. I could sense she was concerned about my path. I had become a hardcore gangster, and she knew it. I tried to lighten the mood by singing along with the Dramatics on the radio. They were singing their latest hit single "Door to Your Heart." Everyone joined in, as the car hit the ramp to the freeway. We were on our way home, and that was incredible enough in its self. We shared stories about the experience, and relaxed as the effects of the hard times and loneliness, seemed to just fade into nonexistence.

Albert made a serious observation. "Ya'll sound like ya'll was having fun in there." We all had to stop and reflect on that. After some discussion, we came to the conclusion that although there were plenty of hilarious moments, there is no way any of it was truly fun. It's more like laughing in the face of pain, and refusing to allow depression to rule. When you put on the brave face, and not allow your enemies to witness your suffering, sayings such as "This all ya got?", "If it ain't tight it ain't right!" and of course the most popular of them all "This ain't shit!" derived from such bravado.

That night the Hole was lit up like a Christmas tree. I had never seen it so crowded, or so festive! As far as everyone was concerned, we were heroes. In the hood, whenever someone or a group gets busted for a crime that carries an enormous amount of time as a maximum penalty, people who haven't had a thing to say in years seem to come out of the woodworks with their opinions and predictions of doom. "They ain't gone never get out." They're through!" "They'll be old men by the time they get out!" "You can stick a fork in them, cause they're done." All of these were phrases used to describe our predicament.

They all looked us in our eyes, and swore they had predicted we would be found not guilty. We received phony expressions of endearment throughout the entire night. They pat us on our backs and smiled in your faces. The song "Smiling Faces" tells it like it really is. A smile very well could be just a frown turned upside down, but tonight we overlooked the obvious back stabbing and hating. I was too engrossed in a gleeful victory celebration over the establishment, to allow the obvious to ruin it. Not tonight.

There were some who were genuinely filled with joy to have us back, and were indeed truly impressed by the entire affair. A young brother that everybody called Boogaloo was one of these people. His honesty was deeply appreciated. He approached me with a broad smile, and his hand extended. I excepted them both as he confessed to telling everybody that he didn't see any way for us to come from under the predicament we were in. He was overwhelmed with joy to be wrong.

"Listen… You won't believe who wants to meet you!" he added. Before I could give the thought much consideration he answered. "Unck!" I never imagined he would say Unck! As a matter of fact, I was already thinking some girl wanted to meet me. The name sent my heart racing. I had heard of Unck. Who hadn't? He was the most connected man in the city. I don't know how it was possible, but he knew every hustler who was getting big money, nearly every hustler who was trying to get big money, and every hustler who was about to get big money. He had summoned for me to come to a party he was attending. The party was given in our honor, to celebrate our victory over the system. Boogaloo told me he promised he would do his best to get me to at least drop by.

"When can we leave?" I asked. "He told me to call first to make sure he was there, and if he is, he wants us to catch a cab there. He's going to pay for it." Boogaloo then made his way through the loud, festive crowd, headed towards the payphone.

The ladies were all over me. They were buying me drinks, and dragging me to the dance floor to dance. I had a reputation as a great dancer. They all knew we could either go to the floor to enjoy the dance, and to make each other look good, or to compete. Most of my dance partners never try to dance with me in a way to show me up, however, there have been times that I've been called out on the dance floor, and showed up. We called that getting "Burned". I was in the process of getting burned by Dot when Boogaloo got my attention. Getting burned by Dot was nothing to be ashamed of. She burned everyone who dared to dance with her. He waved in a manner that indicated he wanted to me to follow him towards the exit. I was very happy to comply. Dot was doing the robot, and she was in rare form.

By the time I made it to the door, Boogaloo was already climbing into the back seat of a City cab. He was instructing the driver on the best route to take to get to Dexter and Joy Rd. while I was climbing into the back seat beside him. Cab drivers were also hustlers. They will take you the longest route you will allow them to take. The longer the route the more money they make. They test you to see just how much you know about the city. That's the standard they use to determine the routes they will take to reach each destination.

As soon as we reached the so-called party, I was ready to return to the Hole. There was practically no one there! I was glad there was no one there once I was introduced to Unck and Auntie. Unck was a short older man in his forties, with a big pot belly, a huge silver afro, and silver goatee. Of course, he was immaculately dressed in the latest fashion. The light beige alpaca sweater he wore underneath his double breasted, leather jacket, matched the light beige alligator shoes he wore. He wore a diamond studded antique Longine watch, with the eagle on the face, and the classic alligator skin watchband. Even though the diamond ring he wore on his baby finger was capable of lighting up an entire room, it was no match for his pearly white smile.

Auntie was a natural beauty. Her hair was worn in a huge afro. It wasn't a crown, but it appeared as such. Her skin was flawless, and her smooth cheek bones sat so high, it made you want to kiss them. She was covered in a long, flowing, flower print summer dress, that was hemmed at her ankles. She too had a mouth full of pearly white teeth to flash, but hers were much brighter than Unck's, because she had a special glow about her. It seemed to come from deep within her bosom.

She looked at me with such love and admiration in her eyes that I instantly fell in love with her. No one had ever looked at me that way before. She hadn't yet verbally claimed me as her son, but somehow, I knew this woman was to be like a mother to me. She told Unck, "Ain't no doubt about it Unck! That's our child! He's just like Henry.

I talked to them for what seemed like hours, and I enjoyed every single moment of it. I learned that Henry was Unck's father, and he was a mean as a rattle snake. Unck's mother, who was called Granny by everyone, was a strict Jehovah's Witnesses whom they said couldn't wait to meet me. Henry had just passed. He was in his seventies and was out on bond, and facing a second-degree murder charge. It was amazing the vast differences there was between Unck's parents. Henry was also a stone cold blooded street hustler, so there were many things he did which she just did not approve of. Neither Unck nor Auntie said anything to indicate how Unck's parents interacted with one another. I was curious about the relationship, but I felt like if I were to press the issue at that moment, I would have been intruding. Besides, I had a feeling all of my questions were going to be answered soon enough. I had become Unck's latest prodigy.

To be continued

SUMMATION

Once in a great while, there comes from among us, an author who has the skills to tell our story. Most of the time the writer has the skills to tell a story, but they've never really lived the life, or the writer has actually experienced the life, but does not possess the skills necessary to tell the story. Moe Love happens to be one of those rare writers who possesses the skills necessary to write fiction that allows us to glimpse into life on the street.

The Inner City Concrete Jungle is the first Book from the series, Trying to Fly With One Wing. This book delivers the gut-wrenching experiences that molded and shaped the attitude and mind set of a young boy. He was trying to survive, and find the proper path to follow, in an adult world laced with predators of all types and kinds. He was raised and nurtured in an atmosphere designed to foster bad decision making, based upon self-hatred, as well as self-destruction. These things were disguised as success, in the form of pimps and drug kingpins. He became a ruthless, cold blooded drug lord after being exposed to the life. This is the beginning of his story. May his mistakes enlighten, as well as brighten your journey.

Printed in the United States
By Bookmasters